Making Hispanics

Making Hispanics

How Activists, Bureaucrats, and Media
Constructed a New American

G. CRISTINA MORA

The University of Chicago Press   Chicago and London

G. CRISTINA MORA is assistant professor of sociology at the
University of California, Berkeley.

The University of Chicago Press, Chicago 60637
The University of Chicago Press, Ltd., London
© 2014 by The University of Chicago
All rights reserved. Published 2014.
Printed in the United States of America

23 22 21 20 19 18 17 16 15 14   1 2 3 4 5

ISBN-13: 978–0-226–03366–2 (cloth)
ISBN-13: 978–0-226–03383–9 (paper)
ISBN-13: 978–0-226–03397–6 (e-book)
DOI: 10.7208/chicago/9780226033976.001.0001

Library of Congress Cataloging-in-Publication Data

Mora, G. Cristina, 1980– author.
  Making Hispanics : how activists, bureaucrats, and media constructed
a new American / G. Cristina Mora.
      pages cm
  Includes bibliographical references and index.
  ISBN 978-0-226-03366-2 (cloth : alkaline paper) —
ISBN 978-0-226-03383-9 (paperback : alkaline paper) —
ISBN 978-0-226-03397-6 (e-book)   1. Hispanic Americans—Politics and
government. 2. Hispanic Americans—Ethnic identity—Political aspects.
I. Title.
  E184.S75M663 2014
  323.1168'073—dc23

                                                    2013019929

♾ This paper meets the requirements of ANSI/NISO Z39.48–1992
(Permanence of Paper).

Para Alexis y Adela
y
Crescencio y Maria

Contents

Illustrations

Preface

Why does a relatively well-off, third-generation Cuban American fall into the same category as a working-class immigrant from Mexico? Why is a Mexican American who does not speak Spanish categorized similarly to an island-born Puerto Rican who does not speak English? And why do Central American, Dominican, and even Spanish immigrants belong to a broader Hispanic category in the United States?

Today the Hispanic category is invoked widely and loudly: politicians speak about winning a larger share of the Hispanic vote, census officials report on the growing Hispanic population, corporations strategize about how to break into the Hispanic market, and Hispanic media are growing at an exponential rate. Yet for all the discourse surrounding Hispanics, few can explain what the category means or why it encompasses such a diverse mix of people. Hispanics in the United States represent different national origins, skin colors, socioeconomic classes, regions, generational statuses, and even languages. So why does one single category contain so much variety?

I thought about these questions often during my time in graduate school as I delved into the research on racial and ethnic classification. Much of the literature in this area focuses on the state, contending that racial and ethnic categories such as white, black, and Hispanic encompass so much diversity because these broad categories help government officials to simplify and make sense of the complex set of peoples that they oversee. It is easier, so the argument goes, for census officials to create broad categories and compare

"Hispanics" to blacks and whites than it is to develop scores of more narrow classifications and compare demographic trends among Mexican Americans, Puerto Ricans, Irish Americans, and African Americans. Moreover, these broad categories allow state officials to create laws or programs that cover entire sets of people, thereby streamlining policy making. Again, creating a government agency or social program to help "Hispanics" is simply more feasible than creating separate programs for each of the Latin American origin groups.

Far from settling the "category" issue for me, however, the existing research raised more questions than it answered. I began to wonder about the politics of categorization, about who or what determined to which category, however broad, a person belonged. I became especially interested in the question of how state officials had developed the Hispanic category in the first place. Why, for example, did the category seem to cover non-Spanish-speaking Mexicans but not Spanish-speaking Haitians? Finding few answers, I realized that this story had not been told in empirical detail, even though the subject appeared to have far-reaching implications.

I began digging through archives and discovered that a profound shift occurred in American history between 1960 and 1990. During this period, federal agencies developed a separate Hispanic category that effectively lumped together all Latin American communities. At the same time, large Mexican American activist organizations began courting Puerto Rican and Cuban American constituencies in an effort to develop the nation's first panethnic, Hispanic political advocacy groups. Additionally, media executives began connecting Spanish-language television stations across the country to one another, forging a national "Hispanic" network that reached Mexican American, Puerto Rican, and Cuban American audiences alike. These findings fascinated me, in part because they suggested that government bureaucrats might not have been the only ones trying to construct and promote a new Hispanic, panethnic category. Something broader had happened, but what exactly? And what could the history of the Hispanic category teach us about the process of racial and ethnic categorization?

To answer these questions, I identified and researched the major national organizations that had pioneered the development of the Hispanic category. I focused on two federal agencies—the Cabinet Committee on Opportunities for Spanish Speaking People (CCOSSP) and the Census Bureau—as well as on a major social movement, the National Council of La Raza, and media organization, Univision Communications Corporation.

As my research unfolded, I was taken aback by two developments. First, the move toward panethnicity turned out to involve collaboration across fields. For example, I found that the same people who had helped develop federal agencies and policies for the "Spanish-Speaking/Hispanic" population later went on to help Mexican American activists build and develop national, panethnic, Hispanic activist groups. I also found that the Census Bureau had nurtured close working relationships with the newly emerging set of Hispanic organizations, even asking activists and media executives to help them convince individuals to identify as Hispanic on census forms. Over time, state, social movement, and media organizations became so integrated that by 1990, media executives would routinely ask activists or census officials to appear on news segments and public affairs programs about Hispanic panethnicity.

The second surprising aspect revealed through my research concerned the meaning of Hispanic panethnicity. I found that activists, bureaucrats, and media executives never fully defined who Hispanics were or what united them. Narrow definitions arguing that Hispanics were united because they all spoke Spanish were occasionally used, but more often, organizations employed vague arguments about the common values and cultural habits that united Mexicans, Puerto Ricans, Cubans, and others. Far from hindering the new category, this strategic use of ambiguity, I will show, proved crucial for the rise of panethnicity.

Ultimately, this book argues that the Hispanic category became institutionalized as bureaucrats, activists, and media executives forged networks and worked together to build panethnic organizations that popularized the notion of a Hispanic identity. Therefore, each empirical chapter focuses on a different organization and demonstrates how its adoption of panethnicity was predicated on the assistance and resources that it received from other organizations in different fields. Readers looking to examine the particular histories of certain state or civic organizations can thus profitably read each chapter as an individualized case study. Taken together, however, the chapters tell a much more powerful story about the web of networks, strategies, and resources that helped to institutionalize the Hispanic category in the United States.

As such, readers will find that this book deals more with how organizational stakeholders promoted Hispanic panethnicity in America than it does with how local-level groups and individuals interpret or make sense of panethnicity. Indeed, several community studies show that churches, schools, and neighborhood associations provide Latin American immigrants with spaces for panethnic expression. These stories are important, but they depart from the larger question of how the Hispanic category became nationally institutionalized in America. Similarly, studies on individual identity pay less attention to the institutional mechanisms that helped to create and reify the Hispanic category and more to issues of self-identification and solidarity. To be sure, the organizational actors that I examine did study and try to predict who would identify panethnically, but they also recognized that the category had to be developed and promoted before individuals would identify with the concept.

This book depicts the main actors as neither villains nor heroes. The activists, bureaucrats, and media executives whom I study were certainly motivated by strategic interests and the desire to secure more resources, and the Hispanic category that they developed did mask crucial differences among Latin American subgroups. When activists claimed, for example, that Hispanics across the country faced similar socioeconomic disadvantages, they were obscuring the fact that the Cuban American community in Miami was quite upwardly mobile. And yet the story of Hispanic panethnicity is also about a critical fight for recognition within the American political landscape. Indeed, several social movement and media organizations would likely not have survived, nor procured as many resources for Latin American immigrant barrios, had they not developed the notion of a national, Hispanic community (problematic as it was). The panethnicity narrative is about the frustrations, struggles, and compromises that ultimately placed the nation's Latin American diaspora at the center of America's discourse on race and ethnicity.

Before I conclude, let me speak a bit about labels. Here in the Southwest, I am often asked why I have entitled this book *Making Hispanics*. Having been born to Mexican immigrants and raised in Los Angeles, I understand the deeper sentiment behind the question. For many in the community, the term *Hispanic* seems more conservative than *Latino* because the former seems to emphasize a cultural connection to Spain. Growing up, I for one cringed when someone referred to me as Hispanic. I preferred to be called Latina because to me the term conveyed an alternative vision of panethnicity based less on a cultural link to Spain and more on how the legacies of colonization have united persons south of the US-Mexico border.

So why, then, did I title this book *Making Hispanics* and not *Making Latinos*? Simply put, because this is a book about history, and I felt it necessary to use the labels that the actors and institutions in question favored. Other categorizing labels—*Raza, Spanish Surname, Spanish, Latino*, and *Spanish-Speaking*—were also employed by these actors from time to time, but none was as popular as *Hispanic* was between 1960 and 1990.

Whatever the label, *Hispanic* or *Latino*, the category is by design ambiguous. The pages that follow reveal how this ambiguity became a critical strategy used by activists, media executives, and bureaucrats to promote the rise of Hispanic panethnicity and shift the politics of race and ethnicity in America for decades to come.

Acknowledgments

This book would have been impossible to write without the help of the various individuals and institutions that believed in me and in this project even when I doubted. The project began during my time at Princeton University, where Paul DiMaggio, Miguel Centeno, Robert Wuthnow, and King-To Yeung patiently guided me through several early drafts and revisions. Paul and Miguel were especially generous with their advice and mentorship, and I have benefitted greatly from our continuing friendship. I simply can't thank them enough for their support.

In addition, I was fortunate to have two other important mentors at Princeton, Marta Tienda and Patricia Fernandez-Kelly. These women seemed to always keep their door open and provided an encouraging space for me to discuss just about anything, whether of the mind or heart.

I received a Provost Postdoctoral Fellowship at the University of Chicago after I completed my graduate work at Princeton. I was welcomed there by a dynamic set of colleagues who took time to read sections of this book, discuss my ideas, and guide me through several revisions. In Sociology, John Levi-Martin, Cheol-Sung Lee, Elizabeth Armstrong, and Kristen Schilt pushed me to clarify the book's contribution to the field and made the department an exciting place to come to work every day. I am also extremely grateful to Mario Small for taking the time to encourage my ideas and for being an overall excellent mentor—gracias, Mario. Outside of sociology, I'd also like to thank Ramon Gutierrez, Cathy Cohen, and Kenneth Warren for their incisive comments and faith in my project. Nell Gambian, Salome Skivirsky,

Claudia Sandoval, and the members of the Center for the Study of Race, Politics, and Culture also helped to make the University of Chicago an exhilarating place in which to think and write.

I joined the sociology faculty at UC Berkeley in the fall of 2011. I simply could not have asked for a more supportive environment. Claude Fisher, Neil Fligstein, Dylan Riley, and Michael Burawoy read entire drafts of the manuscript and provided critical insight that greatly improved the final product. Cybelle Fox, Irene Bloemraad, Raka Ray, Ann Swidler, Heather Haveman, and Laura Lopez-Sanders all read portions of the manuscript. Raka and Ann deserve special thanks for having mentored me since my time as a young Berkeley undergrad—your support has instilled in me a sense that I have something important to say. Outside of the department, Alex Zaragosa and David Montejano also read the manuscript in its entirety, while Michael Omi and Ian Haney-Lopez both sat down with me over lunch or coffee to discuss the project at length.

Huggy Rao, Suzanne Oboler, and Mara Loveman sat alongside David Montejano, Neil Fligstein, and Dylan Riley in an all-day manuscript miniconference for this book in the spring of 2012. The event was one of the most intellectually inspiring experiences of my career, leaving me with a notebook full of extraordinarily incisive comments and a deep sense of gratitude. To those who participated in the event, your generosity means more to me than you know.

I've also been fortunate enough to have received critical feedback and encouragement from scholars outside of Berkeley. Edward Telles, Alejandro Portes, John Skrentny, Mario Garcia, Leisy Abrego, Woody Powell, Arlene Davila, Shannon Gleeson, and Pablo Boczkowski either read the manuscript in its entirety or spoke at length with me about how to push the project forward. Margo Anderson was also incredibly helpful and steered me toward important data sources early on. I'd also like to thank Doug Mitchell and Tim McGovern at the University of Chicago Press for their assistance in ushering this project to book form. Doug deserves special praise for believing (and helping me to believe) that this book would see the light of day even as I trudged through difficult times.

Of course, I'd also like to thank the men and women who took time out of their busy schedules to be interviewed. They are mentioned by name in the following chapters. As they jogged their memory to answer my questions, many interviewees were kind enough to dig up important documents from their personal collections, to steer me toward other data sources, or to follow up with me when they recalled events. I only hope that the story conveyed within these pages can bring to light the important ways that these people helped shape American history.

The project also benefitted from the assistance of various librarians across the country, including those at the National Archives, the Ford and Nixon presidential libraries, the Special Collections unit at Stanford and the University of Illinois, Urbana-Champaign, and the Federal Communications Commission Records Division. Aaron Benavides and Fernando Sanchez, both bright academic stars in their own right, provided critical research assistance at various stages throughout this project. Rebecca Frazier and Matthew Seidel also provided superb editorial support.

This work would have also not been possible without the financial assistance from the Center for Human Values (Princeton University), the Mauricio Gaston Institute (University of Massachusetts, Boston), the University of Chicago's Office of the Provost, the National Science Foundation, the Ford Foundation, the Hellman Faculty Fund (UC Berkeley), and the Institute for International Studies (UC Berkeley).

My friends and family served as lifelines as I have tried to figure out how to forge a life in the academy. They reminded me of the bigger picture when I agonized over the smallest details of the revision process. For their friendship and encouragement, I'd like to thank Shannon Gleeson, Sofya Aptekar, Leslie Hinkson, Hana Shepherd, Yael Berda, Amada Armenta, Cybelle Fox, Kristen Schilt, Eleonore Lepinard, Pierre Kremp, Laura Lopez-Sanders, and Gregoire Mallard. Thank you for reminding me that book-writing pain is nothing that a hilarious anecdote or an overdue phone call or visit can't fix!

My family has not always been too clear about what sociology is, but they have nevertheless always supported my efforts, maintaining an unwavering faith in my ability to bring this book to fruition. Albert and Priscilla Mora, my adorable nephews, and my amazing niece serve as constant sources of support and warmth. Jesus Mora was always there to listen to my frustrations with love and patience. Maria Chacon and her family; my grandmother, Maria Ascencio; and my aunts, Gina, Julie, and Blanca, sent notes, lit candles, and reminded me that I had an extensive fan base back home. And my parents, Maria and Crescencio Mora, always believed. Though my father did not make it past grammar school and my mother never finished high school, they had no doubt that I would make it through Princeton and end up on solid ground. Their constant love, support, and prayers strengthened me from within and made this book possible.

This book is dedicated to my parents, as well as to my partner, Alexis Torres, and our daughter, Adela Torres. Alexis, thank you for seeing strength in me and for listening to virtually every research idea that has ever crossed my mind. I would not be where I am today without your love and your insistence on laughing and dancing together on a daily basis. And Adelita, thank you so much for waiting patiently as I put the finishing touches on this book. You were born days after I completed the revisions on this manuscript, and your father and I so very much look forward to witnessing your first precious smile, steps, and laughs. For all this, I am truly grateful.

Organizations

AGIF   American GI Forum
CCOSSP   Cabinet Committee on Opportunities for Spanish Speaking People
FNHO   Forum of National Hispanic Organizations
HACER   Hispanic Association for Corporate Responsibility
IMAA   Inter-Agency Committee on Mexican American Affairs
LULAC   League of United Latin American Citizens
MALDEF   Mexican American Legal Defense and Education Fund
NCLR   National Council of La Raza
NHQC   National Hispanic Quincentennial Commission
SICC   Spanish International Communications Corporation
SIN   Spanish International Network
SOAC   Spanish Origin Advisory Commission (later renamed Census Advisory Committee on the Spanish Origin Population)
SWCLR   Southwest Council of La Raza

Making Hispanics: Classification and the Politics of Ambiguity

"We have the numbers! We Latinos can now decide who will win and who will lose this election year."[1] The summer and fall of 2012 were abuzz with talk about the dramatic growth of America's Hispanic community. The US Census Bureau had announced that there had been a stunning 40 percent surge in the Hispanic population since 2000 and concluded that Hispanic children would soon make America a majority-minority country.[2] Activists and community leaders quickly capitalized on the bureau's announcements by appearing on Spanish-language media to discuss the political implications of the Hispanic census figures. "This means that there could be as many as 22 million [Hispanic] voters this November . . . a 25 percent increase since the 2008 election!" the director of a prominent Hispanic advocacy group declared.[3] Univision, the nation's largest Spanish-language television network, also joined the chorus. In the months leading up to the election, the network broadcast a series of news segments and special programs designed to showcase the size and scope of the Hispanic vote and to mobilize political participation among viewers. "Hispanics . . . could decide who will guide the future of this country," announced a network journalist as she outlined the steps viewers should take to register to vote.[4]

Once the 2012 election results had been tabulated, the discussions about Hispanics reached fever pitch. Hispanics had voted in record numbers,[5] and media networks across the country reported on the critical new role that Hispanics now played in American politics.[6] The message was clear: Hispanics had become one of America's most sought-after electoral groups, and the nation's foremost political institutions could no longer afford to ignore them.

Yet while the fanfare about Hispanics continued to grow throughout 2012, ignored was the more complicated question of just who "Hispanics" were. The media buzz depicted Hispanics as a close-knit community united by clear political goals and unique cultural bonds. A review of American history, however, suggests otherwise. Looking back just a few decades reveals a much different picture.

During the 1960s, Mexican Americans, Cuban Americans, and Puerto Ricans made up the overwhelming majority of the Latin American diaspora, but they lived in separate worlds in separate parts of the country.[7] Mexican Americans were the largest group, more than twice the size of Puerto Ricans, and they were clustered mainly in the Southwest, where their political organizations tackled issues like farmworkers' rights and bilingual education. Puerto Ricans were primarily living about two thousand miles away in the Northeast, where they established civic groups in cities such as New York and Philadelphia that organized around issues like urban poverty and Puerto Rican independence. The small but growing Cuban American community, centered in Miami, established organizations that remained intensely focused on the developments of Castro's Cuban Revolution.

The political and geographic differences among these communities were so great that early efforts to promote panethnic coalitions often disintegrated amid "shouting matches" and "floor fights."[8] Puerto Ricans in the early 1970s worried that Mexican Americans would try to impose their political agenda on them and divert coalition resources to southwestern areas. Mexican American leaders argued that they should first unite and tend to their own community's needs before aligning with Puerto Ricans. And both groups were skeptical that they would be able to find anything in common with the seemingly more skilled and economically well-off cluster of Cuban Americans in Florida.[9] In fact, the infighting among these groups was so prevalent that high-ranking political leaders doubted whether the groups could ever come together to establish a united political front.[10]

Even bureaucrats, especially those in the Census Bureau, seemed hesitant to classify Mexican Americans, Puerto Ricans, and Cuban Americans under the same category. Although they surmised that these groups might feel a linguistic connection to one another, they tabulated these populations separately. The 1960 decennial census, for example, did not include a question or a category that offered persons of Latin American descent the opportunity to identify as a national panethnic community. For census officials, this omission reflected a consistent empirical finding: Mexican Americans, Puerto Ricans, and Cuban Americans overwhelmingly considered themselves to be separate groups. They "didn't really identify" with one another, and they "didn't really know what Hispanic meant!"[11]

Media organizations appeared to share this attitude. In the 1960s, there were no television networks or media firms connecting Mexican American, Puerto Rican, and Cuban American audiences across the country. Instead, Mexican American television entrepreneurs in cities like San Antonio and Los Angeles purchased programming from Mexico and broadcast it to audiences in the Southwest. At the same time, media entrepreneurs in New York traveled to San Juan to buy Puerto Rican variety shows for New York's Puerto Rican audiences. And because Cuban Americans could not return to Havana to purchase Cuban programming, they rented production studios in Miami and created their own news shows. These preferences for coethnic media were so entrenched that early attempts to connect communities—for example, by providing Mexican programming to Cuban American audiences—were met with resistance. "Cubans complained . . . [about] Mexican programming . . . and the Mexicans would raise hell if we substituted their soap operas with anything else," recalled one former media executive.[12]

The political and media environments of the late 1960s, however, stand in sharp contrast to the current ones. Terms like *the Hispanic/Latino community*, *the Latino vote*, and *Hispanic culture* are common today, and it is difficult to find a government report, media story, or political statement that does not describe persons of Latin American descent simply as "Hispanics" or "Latinos." Additionally, there are now several panethnic Hispanic organizations in the United States that claim to represent the political, cultural, and social needs of Puerto Ricans, Mexican Americans, and Cuban Americans, not to mention Central and South Americans and Dominicans.

This historical shift toward panethnicity began in the 1970s. Over the course of that decade, Congress and the Executive Office of the President began experimenting with different ways of providing resources for the Latin American diaspora and of securing their vote. Concurrently, activists established some of the first national political coalitions, which eventually evolved into powerful, national Hispanic civil rights lobbying firms. During that period, census officials also began testing a panethnic

Hispanic census category for the 1980 decennial census form. Further-more, throughout the late 1970s and into the 1980s, Spanish-language media networks like Univision developed panethnic Hispanic news and variety programming, hoping to connect Mexican American, Cuban American, and Puerto Rican audiences across the country.

The national rise of Hispanic panethnicity, however, was far from in-evitable. *It did not have to happen.* Mexican Americans, Cuban Americans, and Puerto Ricans could very well have remained distinct, separate groups with distinct, separate organizations. While some have argued that an increase in Cuban, Mexican, and Puerto Rican immigration led to more diverse, panethnic Hispanic communities in America,[13] for the most part these groups lived in distinct areas of the country throughout the 1970s and 1980s[14]—precisely during the period when government officials and ethnic leaders were busy forging panethnic organizations. Moreover, while Central and South American (as well as Dominican) migration did eventually diversify ethnic enclaves in cities like New York and Miami, leading to the rise of panethnic, Hispanic churches, neighborhood asso-ciations, and local-level Hispanic cultural and political movements, this process occurred mainly in the late 1980s and 1990s—well *after* the rise of a Hispanic census category and after the emergence of national Hispanic political and media organizations.

In fact, throughout the 1970s and even into the 1980s, Latin American subgroups were still tightly clustered and separated from one another by thousands of miles. Their political agendas were also distinct. Immigra-tion reform, for example, became an important Mexican American policy goal but was of little interest to Puerto Ricans, who were citizens by birth, and to Cuban Americans, who gained citizenship through their refugee status. Puerto Ricans in New York focused on issues of Puerto Rican inde-pendence, but this cause fell on deaf ears in Mexican American and Cu-ban American communities. And while there were certainly some issues that these groups shared, such as bilingual education and discrimination, many of the joint, panethnic mobilization efforts addressing these topics were either highly local or short-lived.[15]

Perhaps more critical, the acceptance of Hispanic panethnicity could have been impeded by the different historical understandings of race re-tained by Mexican Americans, Cuban Americans, and Puerto Ricans. The first wave of Cuban immigrants identified as white, and many believed that they had biological ties to Spain.[16] As a result, Cuban Americans dis-tanced themselves from minority group labels such as "persons of color." This view clashed with the ideology of some of the faster-growing Mexi-can American movements in the Southwest, whose members rejected "white" labels and assimilationist paradigms. Chicano youth activists of the 1970s, for example, proclaimed themselves part of a "brown" racial mix of indigenous and European bloodlines, arguing that they were a subjugated minority in the United States.[17] Young Puerto Rican nationalist groups, such as the highly visible Young Lords Party, acknowledged and honored Puerto Rico's African heritage and pointed to their political and cultural similarities with African American nationalist groups.[18] Indeed, Mexican Americans, Puerto Ricans, and Cuban Americans were so distinct in terms of geography, political agenda, and cultural understanding of race that coming together to identify and organize under a common category could very likely have remained unthinkable.

This book examines the rise of Hispanic panethnicity in the United States by focusing on how activists, government officials, and media executives, institutionalized the Hispanic category and developed a national movement to popularize the Hispanic identity. Two critical factors enabled the development of panethnicity in the 1970s and 1980s. The first was the establishment of a series of networks between state and nonstate actors. Productive links were forged as instances of conflict and co-optation between federal bureaucrats in the executive office, Census Bureau officials, activists, and media executives gave way to negotiations and collaborative relationships. Indeed, by the late 1970s, these stakeholders were working together to define and popularize the idea of Hispanic panethnicity. A typical Spanish-language television viewer could thus turn on her television set in 1980 and see activists and census officials featured together on news programs about Hispanic panethnicity. One broadcast program even filmed activists, media personalities, and census officials standing together "holding up the 1980 census form, [which had a] big circle around the new 'Hispanic' [census] question . . . and introducing the category to viewers," recalls one former Univision executive.[19]

The second critical factor was the category's ambiguity. Government officials, activists, and media executives never precisely defined who Hispanics actually were. Instead, they made broad, ambiguous references to the group's unifying culture and contended that Hispanics were Hispanic because they were all hardworking, religious, and family focused, characteristics that could have been applied to any group. Ambiguity was important because it allowed stakeholders to bend the definition of Hispanic panethnicity and use the notion instrumentally—as a means to an end. Activists thus described Hispanics as a disadvantaged and underrepresented minority group that stretched from coast to coast, a wide framing that best allowed them to procure grants from public and private institutions. Media executives, in turn, framed Hispanics as an up-and-coming national consumer market in order to increase advertising revenue. Last, government officials, particularly those in the Census Bureau, framed Hispanics as a group displaying certain educational, income, and fertility patterns significantly different from those of blacks and whites.

Over time, the state-activist-media networks and the strategic use of ambiguity they employed reinforced the notion of Hispanic panethnicity more broadly. Activists used Hispanic census data to support grant applications and develop Hispanic policy reports, while media executives incorporated the census data into their Hispanic marketing manuals. Census officials, in turn, relied on media and activist groups to help popularize and promote the Hispanic category, even holding workshops that taught activists and media executives how to analyze Hispanic data. Moreover, media executives and activists forged their own links with each other. Spanish-language television networks eventually hired activists to appear on public affairs programs as their in-house "Hispanic political analysts." Alternatively, Hispanic activist groups hired Hispanic media executives as image and project consultants. These diverse stakeholders could work together because while they framed Hispanic panethnicity differently, they also referred to a common, albeit ambiguous, narrative about Hispanic cultural values and they became reliant on one another for expertise, data, and resources.

In short, the period between the late 1960s and the early 1990s saw an unprecedented rise of new, intertwined networks connecting government officials, activists, and media executives. While sometimes contentious, these links led to important acts of cooperation as stakeholders set aside many of their differences to help one another advance the notion of an American, Hispanic community.

What Makes Hispanics Hispanic?

This book focuses on the historical developments of the late twentieth century that led to the institutionalization of Hispanic panethnicity.[20] To be sure, the idea of panethnicity had already existed for some time before then, but it was in this period that stakeholders formed the country's first national Hispanic civic and media organizations and developed an official government category.

Indeed, the idea that persons of Latin American descent share some commonality has deep historical roots. In the nineteenth century, political figures tied panethnicity to Latin American independence movements, arguing that the nations south of the US border shared a common struggle to break free of Spanish colonial rule.[21] Ironically, Spanish politicians later contended that the communities of Latin America shared a similar cultural and historical bond with Spain.[22] In the mid-twentieth century, as Latin American immigrants began to pour into the United States, mainstream media and native groups used terms like *Spanish* to refer to Mexican Americans and Puerto Ricans alike.[23] In response, Mexican Americans in states such as New Mexico referred to themselves as "Spanish American," often because it signaled class mobility and sounded less foreign than the alternatives.[24]

Despite these historical instances, research has shown that important socioeconomic and cultural factors have historically divided people of Mexican, Puerto Rican, and Cuban (not to mention Central and South American) origin who live in the United States.[25] For the most part, Puerto Ricans and Mexican Americans have historically been less well-off than Cuban Americans and some South American immigrants.[26] Cuban Americans have primarily identified as Republican, whereas Mexican Americans and Puerto Ricans have primarily voted Democratic.[27] Some political issues, such as America's foreign policy toward Cuba, have been important considerations for Cuban Americans but not necessarily for Mexican Americans or Puerto Ricans.[28]

Other cultural and historical issues challenge the most basic assumptions of panethnicity. For example, although some would argue that the Spanish language unites the Latin American diaspora, a significant number of those persons born in the United States speak only English.[29] Furthermore, not all persons of Latin American descent have a Spanish surname, not simply because people marry outside of their ethnic group but also because Latin America has long been a destination for Asian and Western European migration.[30] We do not normally think of names like *Fox* and *Fujimori*, the surnames of recent Mexican and Peruvian presidents, respectively, as typically Hispanic. And although some argue that all persons of Latin American descent are united by a shared Catholic faith, this contention is difficult to support when we consider that Latin Americans have historically practiced strikingly different forms of popular religion and that the twentieth century has witnessed an uneven rise in Protestantism throughout Latin America.[31]

Moreover, available attitudinal data reveal that persons of Latin American descent are quite ambivalent about panethnicity. On the one hand, when researchers ask individuals to list the labels that best describe their identity, survey respondents overwhelmingly state a preference for national, rather than panethnic, labels. Persons of Latin American descent are much more likely to answer that they are Peruvian or Puerto Rican, for example, not Hispanic or Latino. This pattern holds true for Mexican Americans, Puerto Ricans, and Cuban Americans, as well as for Central Americans, Dominicans, and all other Latin American origin groups. The preference also holds regardless of whether the respondents immigrated to the United States, were born in the United States to immigrant parents, or belong to the lower, middle, or upper class.[32] One study on immigrant identity summed up the importance of national identity succinctly by pointing to a bumper sticker that was widely circulated in Miami during the 1990s. It read: "Don't Call Me Hispanic, I'm Cuban!"[33]

But the preference for national identity is only one part of the story. Cross-national research also shows that Hispanic panethnicity has become an important, although complex, form of secondary identification. Mexican Americans, for example, are apt to tell survey researchers that they are "Mexican" first, but that they are "Hispanic/Latino" second. The proportion of Latin American origin respondents who express this form of secondary identification has doubled from about 40 percent in 1990 to over 80 percent in 2012.[34] While significant, these findings are complicated by the fact that the respondents have been hard-pressed to state what exactly constitutes Hispanic panethnicity. Surveys reveal weak support for statements such as "Hispanics/Latinos share a common culture,"[35] and qualitative research shows that persons of Latin American descent are often unsure about which political and cultural issues unite them.[36] Hispanic panethnicity is thus an increasingly popular yet largely undefined form of secondary collective identification.

Prevailing Accounts of Hispanic Panethnicity

The historical divisions among Mexican Americans, Puerto Ricans, Cuban Americans, and others, as well as the general ambivalence displayed toward panethnicity, raise the question of how the Hispanic category became so popular in America. At one point in time, these groups had virtually no organizations bringing them together at a national level; they even expressed antagonism toward one another. How, then, did panethnicity become the basis of a new set of Hispanic civic organizations, government categories, and media networks?

Researchers have tried to answer this question by appealing to the broader literature on ethnic and racial categories, a main strand of which emphasizes the symbolic role of the state. Thus, much work on the Hispanic category centers on the US Census Bureau and the Office of Management and Budget, arguing that federal officials somehow imposed a panethnic category onto Mexican Americans, Puerto Ricans, Cuban Americans, and others so that they could better track their ever-increasing numbers.[37] The research suggests that once this government category was in place, other civic and market organizations merely followed suit.

Although there is no question that government agencies wield immense symbolic power, focusing exclusively on the state's workings leaves several questions unanswered. For example, such an account provides scant information about why the Hispanic census category was ultimately deemed an ethnic and not a racial classification, and it offers few insights into how census officials were able to convince individuals to identify as Hispanics on government forms. For example, the only research that systematically examines US Census Bureau records reveals that census officials were reluctant to create a Hispanic panethnic category, in part because they judged that persons of Latin American descent were quite diverse and would eventually assimilate and identify as white. It turns out in fact that Mexican American activists played an important role in pressuring hesitant state and census officials to institutionalize the Hispanic census category.[38]

Other research on Hispanic panethnicity draws on the racial and ethnic classification literature emphasizing the role of political entrepreneurs. Specifically, this work explains the rise of panethnicity by focusing on the civic sector, shifting attention from the federal government to social movement organizations and advocacy groups. These studies contend that Hispanic panethnicity emerged as Mexican American and Puerto Rican activists in the 1970s joined to pool their money, numbers, and other resources.[39] This consolidation ultimately allowed activists to form louder, larger, and more powerful organizations that could lobby for common goals, such as alleviating urban poverty in Hispanic communities.

While important, this research does not take into account Cuban Americans, whose numbers were smaller and whose focus was not on poverty and underrepresentation, the primary concerns of Mexican Americans and Puerto Ricans in the early 1970s. In fact, Cuban Americans spent most of their organizing efforts trying to influence US foreign policy toward their island nation.[40] A strict political mobilization interpretation would thus adequately explain the rise of Mexican American and Puerto Rican multiethnic coalitions, but not necessarily the establishment of more general, panethnic coalitions that included Cuban Americans.

A third scholarly approach to Hispanic panethnicity focuses on market organizations and considers how Spanish-language media convey messages about panethnicity. Studies of this type reveal how news producers and journalists broaden their reach by creating programs that piece together stories from different Latin American countries and touch on different immigrant groups.[41] A typical news hour on Univision, for example, might include a story about Cuba, another about Mexican American community groups, and yet another about Puerto Rican politics. In addition, this research details how marketers create advertisements that emphasize differences between Hispanics (or Latinos) and whites while deemphasizing differences among Latin American ethnic groups.[42] Although this marketing strategy is employed primarily for economic reasons, it is argued to nonetheless foster a sense of panethnic identity.

While these scholarly approaches have helped to identify the multiple arenas in which Hispanic panethnicity has emerged, what has developed is the suggestion that the Hispanic category emerged from three separate, or at best loosely linked, processes. This interpretation not only leaves several issues unresolved but also obscures the inherently relational and interdependent aspects of history. For example, as soon as the US census director decided to include a permanent Hispanic category for the 1980 decennial census, he arranged two sets of meetings. In one set, he met with Mexican American, Puerto Rican, and Cuban American political leaders and asked them to hold town hall meetings across the country to teach people how to identify as Hispanics on census forms. In another set, he met with Spanish-language media executives to ask them to create commercials publicizing the Hispanic category on their networks. In other words, state officials relied heavily on assistance from activists and media executives; without their help the Hispanic category would not have been successfully recognized and adopted.

What is needed, then, is a more interactive account that considers the Hispanic category as a result of the relationships that arose between state and nonstate actors. This book provides such an account by highlighting how stakeholder conflict, negotiation, and collaboration led to the rise of Hispanic panethnicity. In doing so, it presents a more accurate historical account of the Hispanic case and provides a more dynamic framework for understanding how contemporary racial and ethnic categories become institutionalized.

Classification Struggles within Fields

Sociologist Pierre Bourdieu's notion of a "classification struggle" provides a useful analytic tool for assessing the Hispanic case and for understanding more generally how categories emerge.[43] Bourdieu argues that organizational actors, be they state officials, community leaders, or market executives, assume stances on determining group boundaries that reflect their relationships with their fellow actors. Categories emerge not from one particular source but rather from the interactive relationships between sets of actors. These relationships play out in what Bourdieu calls a "field," a crowded social landscape wherein stakeholders contest and refine different definitions and understandings of group categories.[44]

This book describes the emergence of just such a field as activists, bureaucrats, and media executives sought to define and categorize persons of Latin American descent in the United States. The relationships among these actors were antagonistic and riddled with conflict, especially early on. Activists and even media executives initially clashed with government officials when the state insisted that Mexican Americans and Puerto Ricans were simply white Americans who were destined to assimilate. Activists argued that there were thousands of third- and fourth-plus-generation Mexican immigrants who faced discrimination and still did not identify with Anglo Americans. Media executives also argued that unlike European immigrants, Latin American groups in the United States held on to their language and immigrant culture well beyond the second generation.

Over time, however, these relationships became more cooperative. After much criticism, census officials became more solicitous, inviting select activists and media leaders to sit on census advisory councils and help devise a new way of categorizing persons of Latin American descent. Collaborative relationships also formed between media executives, who wanted to increase their market share, and activists, who wanted to broadcast their political messages to national audiences.

While Bourdieu's notion of a classification struggle emphasizes conflict, his concept can be expanded to suggest that there are different moments, or types of relationships, that emerge within fields over time. Struggle and conflict are certainly important characteristics of a field, but negotiation and cooperation, even if arising in response to antagonism, can be equally significant.[45] Drawing on the Hispanic case, this book details three moments that help define the relationships forged through classification struggles more generally. I label the first moment *co-optation through state classification*. Co-optation occurs as government officials respond to the criticism and demands of ethnic political leaders by changing the classification of a certain racial or ethnic group. To accomplish this, officials first devise a new category, then proceed to respond to the aggrieved leaders' claims from within that new category. Next, officials provide resources to the organizations that agree to adopt the state's category. Even if the state's response is not ideal, ethnic leaders soon come to understand that there are important material resources to be gained by accepting the state's new categorization of their group. For example, in the late 1960s, congressional leaders responded to Mexican American and Puerto Rican protests about discrimination and inequality by establishing a committee that would address the needs of "the Spanish Speaking." State officials then devised a list of the general needs of "the Spanish Speaking" and proceeded to funnel resources to the social movement organizations that seemed willing to address those state-defined needs. In effect, congressional leaders combined the two aggrieved parties, Mexican Americans and Puerto Ricans, into this new "Spanish Speaking" category, thus redefining not only the ethnonational boundaries of these groups but also their demands. As a result, nationalist Chicano and Puerto Rican claims were sidelined as leaders focused on developing more inclusive, and moderate, claims on behalf of the "Spanish Speaking."

The second moment concerns *negotiations over data*. While co-optation can help bring some ethnic leaders in line, it cannot fully institutionalize a new category because political groups can still clash with the state over how to measure and define a new category. At this point, ethnic leaders can demand to take part in Census Bureau decision making. During these moments, census officials must reconcile scientific tenets, such as categorical validity and reliability, with the political visions that ethnic leaders hold about who belongs within their group. Throughout the negotiating process, both parties attempt to preserve their negotiating power by appealing to their networks and by developing narratives about the nature of ethnicity. For example, in the late 1960s, Mexican American and Puerto Rican activists turned their attention to the Census Bureau and began protesting that the agency categorized both groups as predominantly white. Facing a legitimacy crisis, census officials and other federal leaders invited activists to join federal advisory boards and participate in public meetings to discuss a new categorization strategy for these communities. Whereas Census Bureau officials worried about retaining proper statistical procedures, activists in these meetings pushed the agency to adopt a more inclusive measurement of their community. What ultimately emerged was a broad, panethnic Hispanic census category that addressed most of the concerns of officials and activists alike.

The third moment concerns the *collaborative marketing of new categories*. Once state officials and ethnic leaders agree on a new category, they embark on cooperative projects to help legitimate and advance that new category. Media executives play an important role in this process because they use their organizations to broadcast new categories to mass audiences. This book argues that Spanish-language media advanced the notion of Hispanic panethnicity in two ways. First, news programming offered platforms from which census officials and ethnic leaders could promote the Hispanic census category. Second, entertainment programming linked the Hispanic category to images and cultural messages about panethnicity. Throughout the 1980s, Univision developed a series of talk shows, variety programs, and news shows that depicted Cubans, Mexicans, and Puerto Ricans as part of a unified Hispanic community.

Taken together, these three moments describe more generally how state, civic, and market organizational actors forge a new field and institutionalize a new category. In this field, stakeholders learn to monitor and respond to one another, and eventually develop a shared interest in sustaining a new category. As state and nonstate actors learn to set aside their differences, they share resources and frames that allow them to further institutionalize a new category within their respective arenas. Government officials thus provide ethnic leaders with data and resources for the category, while ethnic leaders create cultural narratives, panethnic images, and arguments that historicize and legitimate the government's new classification.

These cooperative efforts, however, can only be carried out because stakeholders learn to talk about new categories ambiguously. Strictly defined categories are often too rigid to accommodate stakeholders' divergent interests. We can imagine, for example, that a narrow definition of Hispanics as Spanish speakers would have been too restrictive for activists, both because many did not speak Spanish fluently themselves and because such a definition would have decreased the size of the activists' constituency. Ambiguity, then, allows stakeholders to capitalize on a category's flexibility so as to better pursue their organizational interests. Thus, media executives, activists, and government officials developed a broader narrative about some sort of vague Hispanic common culture. This narrative not only made Hispanic panethnicity seem expansive but also accommodated the stakeholders' more strategic interests about consumption, minority disadvantage, and statistical correlation.

Ultimately, what sociologist Peter Berger calls a plausibility structure develops as networks between state and nonstate actors become reified over time.[46] That is, a group of categorical experts emerges, authorities who use the same symbols and narratives to reinforce one another's efforts and legitimate a new category. In the Hispanic case, activists became Hispanic political analysts, census officials became Hispanic data analysts, and media executives became Hispanic marketers. These experts all came to know and help one another, and they created images, symbols, and frames about what the Hispanic identity meant. And the more they worked together, the louder their messages about panethnicity became.

Overview of the Book

This book comprises four empirical chapters that, taken together, reveal how activists, government officials, and media executives developed national Hispanic organizations and institutionalized the Hispanic category. Rather than examining select historical time frames, each chapter focuses on a single flagship organization and then traces how that organization adopted the idea of panethnicity. This approach allows for a detailed, meso-level analysis of how the classification struggle over panethnicity evolved and the various pressures that motivated state and nonstate organizations, such as the Census Bureau and Univision, to adopt the notion of panethnicity. Moreover, this approach better tracks the way that organizational actors developed relationships across social arenas to form a new, broad field centered around Hispanic panethnicity.

The chapters are ordered in loose chronological fashion, but they do cover overlapping time periods, providing a window into how the adoption of panethnicity affected different arenas simultaneously. It is important to note, however, that panethnicity was not adopted uniformly: some organizations adopted the notion of panethnicity in certain areas of practice but not in others; others used panethnic labels even though they functioned more like multiethnic umbrella organizations; still others adopted the notion of panethnicity early on only to discard it later—and then adopt it yet again. In other words, the path to panethnicity was far from smooth. Guesswork and wrong turns delayed progress before sustained coordination and collaboration eventually led to the category's institutionalization.

Chapter 1 examines how the federal government responded to the early demands of Mexican American and Puerto Rican activists within the political context of the 1960s. By that time, the African American civil rights movement had created a political opening that sensitized elected officials to the demands of racial or ethnic minority groups. Specifically, the chapter traces how Congress and the Lyndon Johnson and Richard Nixon administrations addressed the panethnic question by establishing the Inter-Agency Committee on Mexican American Affairs (IMAA) and its successor, the Cabinet Committee on Opportunities for Spanish Speaking People (CCOSSP). I argue that federal officials used the panethnic "Spanish Speaking" classification to co-opt and defuse potential threats from nationalist Puerto Rican and Mexican American activist groups. I also show how East Coast elected officials pressured CCOSSP to become representative of all "Spanish Speakers," including Cuban Americans, in order to win votes from this broader constituency. In response, CCOSSP developed a national, panethnic agenda, and by the early 1970s it served as the official government platform for discussing the issues of Mexican American, Puerto Rican, and Cuban American communities alike.

Chapter 2 looks at how activists responded to federal efforts by exploring the evolution of the National Council of La Raza (NCLR), the nation's oldest and most prominent national Hispanic political advocacy organization. This chapter argues that NCLR, which began as the Southwest Council of La Raza (SWCLR), transitioned from a Mexican American to a Hispanic organization so that it could obtain more grants and resources. As NCLR competed with African American organizations for government resources in the 1970s, it quickly learned that embracing Hispanic panethnicity would best help the organization gain support from CCOSSP and other state grant-making agencies. Moreover, the notion of panethnicity allowed NCLR leaders to claim to private foundations that its constituency was as large as, and thus as worthy of grants as, the African American constituency. Over time, NCLR used its resources to attract Puerto Rican and, later, Cuban constituencies, and became America's foremost panethnic advocacy organization by 1980.

Chapter 3 examines the negotiations undertaken by census officials to develop a Hispanic category for the 1980 enumeration. It shows that the bureau faced a legitimacy crisis following the 1970 census when CCOSSP bureaucrats and activist groups disputed the bureau's estimates for the Mexican American and Puerto Rican populations. Activists also questioned the bureau's classification practices and demanded that it stop lumping data on Mexican Americans and Puerto Ricans in with data on Anglo Americans. The bureau responded to these demands by forming advisory councils staffed with Mexican American, Puerto Rican, and Cuban community leaders, some of whom had ties to NCLR. After several rounds of negotiation, the Census Bureau and the advisory council eventually adopted the panethnic "Hispanic" category. Throughout the process, the bureau shifted its perception of racial and ethnic categories and came to understand that categories were fluid and ambiguous rather than static and objective.

In chapter 4, I examine the role that the media played in promoting the 1980 Hispanic census category and in institutionalizing the notion of panethnicity more generally. I trace the evolution of Univision from a regional Mexican network into a national Hispanic one. Specifically, the chapter recounts how the network became heavily involved in census promotional activities in the late 1970s as media executives discovered they could use census data to create Hispanic marketing manuals. Hispanic census data also allowed media executives to prove to advertisers and corporate firms that their audience was sizable and national in scope. As media executives became increasingly reliant on census data, they began to change their programming formulas. By the mid-1980s, media executives had established a series of studios in Miami that produced Hispanic, panethnic entertainment and news programs geared toward Mexican American, Cuban American, and Puerto Rican audiences alike.

The concluding chapter reemphasizes how the tight web of media, state, and activist networks has upheld the notion of Hispanic panethnicity to this day. It contemplates what effects the growing acceptance of the Hispanic category has had on American politics and the broader discourse on race in America. It argues that despite the political gains that the category has delivered for Mexican Americans, Cuban Americans, Puerto Ricans, and others, the wide application of the category has also masked important differences that should make Hispanic leaders proceed with caution. Taken together, the chapters that follow reveal a story about state power and political and economic interests, as well as a narrative about a critical fight for recognition in postwar America.

ONE

Civil Rights, Brown Power, and the "Spanish-Speaking" Vote: The Development of the Cabinet Committee on Opportunities for Spanish Speaking People

The late 1960s were rife with protests and demands from Mexican and Puerto Rican civic leaders. In the Southwest, Mexican Americans took to the streets to forge grassroots organizations whose goal was to bring national attention to the discrimination that they endured and to the appalling conditions suffered by migrant farmworkers. Thousands of miles away in the Northeast, Puerto Rican activists created organizations that mobilized their communities around concerns related to urban poverty and the ever-present issue of Puerto Rican sovereignty. And in Washington, the Johnson and Nixon administrations grappled with how to manage the unrest. While the protests were not as loud or as well organized as those staged by African Americans, Johnson's and Nixon's advisers feared that they eventually could be. With potential electoral votes on the line, both administrations sought ways to turn Mexican American and Puerto Rican protests into political opportunities.

This chapter sheds light on that era by focusing on the establishment of Johnson's Inter-Agency Committee on Mexican American Affairs (IMAA) and tracing how it evolved into Nixon's Cabinet Committee on Opportunities for Spanish Speaking People (CCOSSP). It argues that the IMAA and CCOSSP reframed activists' claims by developing an administrative category for the "Spanish Speaking" population, which lumped together demands from Mexican American and Puerto Rican communities. As part of this effort, bureaucrats penned reports that defined the needs of Spanish speakers, they lobbied for the collection of data on the Spanish speaking, and they helped elected officials create campaign strategies for securing the Spanish-speaking vote. This process of co-optation through classification developed as federal officials took measures to disarm and discredit the nascent, but growing, Chicano and Puerto Rican nationalist projects and as they sought to institutionalize the idea that Latin American subgroups were part of a national, panethnic constituency.

The story begins, however, in the mid-1960s, with the tense struggles of the African American civil rights movement.

The Civil Rights Context

On January 15, 1965, President Lyndon B. Johnson telephoned the Reverend Martin Luther King Jr., seeking his assistance. Just six months earlier, Johnson had pushed through the historic and comprehensive Civil Rights Act of 1964, which, among other things, sought to create equal opportunity in employment. Now Johnson was determined to pass a voting rights bill that would help protect the right to vote for America's black citizens. Civil rights activists like King had spent years rallying and lobbying for such legislation. In fact, when Johnson telephoned, King was in Alabama, where he hoped to bring attention to the fact that only 2 percent of black adults in Selma were legally eligible to vote.[1] Johnson called King with a request: he needed the reverend to develop a galvanizing message about black disenfranchisement that week and to "get it on radio, and get it on television, and get it in the pulpits . . . every place you can." If the message spread quickly, Johnson believed that he would be able to push a voting rights bill through Congress. Johnson told King that the passage of this legislation would be "*the greatest breakthrough of anything . . . the greatest achievement of my administration.*"[2]

America in the 1960s was undoubtedly marked by the African American struggle for civil rights. Organizations such as King's Southern Christian Leadership Conference, the National Association for the Advancement of Colored People (NAACP), and the Student Nonviolent Coordinating Committee entered courtrooms and took to the streets to protest the lack of civil rights for African Americans. Unable to ignore this momentum, policy makers took action.[3] Between 1957 and 1960, President Dwight D. Eisenhower signed two civil rights acts that were designed to assist African American voters. In 1963 President John F. Kennedy began a series of policy meetings to discuss employment discrimination. Johnson resumed this work after Kennedy's death, making the issue of African American civil rights an administrative priority.

Specifically, the Johnson administration helped to usher in a series of policies and practices that, although formally inclusive of other minorities, were targeted mainly toward African Americans.[4] For example, the 1965 Voting Rights Act focused primarily on outlawing the preclearance practices that southern states used to bar African Americans from voting. Additionally, the Equal Employment Opportunity Commission (EEOC) mainly processed claims involving African Americans.[5] Moreover, African American communities received much of the funding from several of Johnson's Great Society policies, such as his Model Cities Program.[6] Throughout his tenure in office, Johnson would state that the issue of black civil rights was his, as well as the nation's, most pressing domestic concern.[7]

Policy makers were not the only ones to pay attention to the issue of black civil rights. Foundations also sought to aid the African American struggle by providing funds to organizations such as the NAACP and the National Urban League. In 1966 the Ford Foundation established a Division of National Affairs, whose primary goal was to provide grants to "black-oriented" organizations.[8] This effort stemmed in part from Ford Foundation president McGeorge Bundy's belief that "full equality for all American Negroes [was] the most urgent domestic concern of this country."[9] Other foundations shared the sentiment. In an analysis of grant-making data reported by the Council on Foundations, political scientist Christine Sierra found that between 1960 and 1970, foundations provided more than four hundred grants to African American organizations and causes; by comparison, only seventy went to Native American and Mexican American organizations combined.[10]

Nationally renowned academics helped to sustain the nation's focus on African American communities by penning studies and reports. Among the most prominent of these scholars was Gunnar Myrdal, who decades before had received a grant from the Carnegie Corporation of New York to produce the landmark text *An American Dilemma: The Negro Problem and Modern Democracy.*[11] In the 1960s Johnson's Great Society team included Daniel Patrick Moynihan, a Harvard social scientist, who drafted a widely circulated report on the state of America's poor black families. Labeled the "Moynihan Report" by the press, the text received much early support from policy makers throughout Washington.[12]

The collaboration between policy makers, activists, foundations, and academics helped make the issue of African American civil rights a defining one for the 1960s. Black civil rights activists not only organized important, large-scale protests and marches but also helped policy makers push through civil rights legislation. Policy makers hired social scientists to advise them on the state of black America. Foundations funded the work of social scientists and also contributed to the coffers of black organizations, enabling them to further develop a national agenda for African American civil rights.

Civil Rights for Mexican Americans and Puerto Ricans

Even though the 1960s civil rights discourse was mainly about African American issues, this did not mean that other groups were not equally aggrieved. Along the US-Mexico border, Mexican American families lived in shantytowns where houses lacked running water and public schools lacked electricity.[13] Mexican Americans also faced severe levels of racial discrimination across the Southwest, where they were systematically segregated.[14] They were barred from entering all-white public and private spaces, and Mexican children were often relegated to all-Mexican schools.[15] Conditions for Mexican Americans were so poor that early on Dionisio (Dennis) Chávez, a Democratic senator from New Mexico, had collected hundreds of press reports and letters documenting instances of discrimination against Mexican Americans and used them to convince bureaucrats and congressional leaders that Mexican Americans should be deemed a protected minority for the purposes of civil rights policy.[16]

For their part, Mexican American leaders developed a variety of civic organizations, including the American GI Forum (AGIF) and the League of United Latin American Citizens (LULAC), that advocated the benefits of Mexican American integration while trying to bring government attention to their issues. Their members were often second-generation-plus Mexican American citizens whose main focus was on garnering state resources for civic projects that could help create a robust Mexican American middle class.[17] Among their leaders were World War II veterans such as Hector P. Garcia, Vicente Ximenes, and Edward Roybal, who throughout the 1960s lobbied federal government entities, including the EEOC and the US Commission on Civil Rights, for bilingual education, Mexican American voting protections, and equal representation in federal and state employment.[18] In the Southwest, where the press often associated Mexican Americans with poverty and cultural backwardness, these organizations identified their members as "Spanish American," "Hispano," or "Spanish Speakers" to seem more upwardly mobile.[19]

Chicano organizations appeared during the mid-1960s, often in reaction to the integrationist stance of established groups. These nascent groups were not well funded or well established, but they attracted much attention because they used militant tactics and described Mexican American communities as internal colonies that needed to shed the yoke of assimilation.[20] Chicano organizations, with names like La Raza and the Crusade for Justice, grew quickly in the late 1960s and used protests and walkouts to galvanize a youthful, working-class constituency that had become inspired by, on the one hand, the efforts of César Chávez and the United Farm Workers and, on the other hand, the protests of black cultural nationalists. Chicano organizations tackled not only traditional issues like bilingual education and poverty but also ones that were seemingly more radical. For example, some Chicano organizations lobbied for the formal return of southwestern lands to Mexican American ownership, contending that the US government had stolen these lands by not honoring the 1848 Treaty of Guadalupe Hidalgo, which had given Mexican citizens the right to retain their property.[21]

The Chicano movement differed from the integrationist movement in language and perspective. While groups often shared some goals—such as the desire for bilingual education—they differed in their interpretation of what the goals meant for Mexican Americans. Integrationist groups saw the goals as opportunities to enter the middle class, whereas Chicano organizations saw them as steps toward self-determination.

Amid these political factions lay César Chávez's farmworkers' movement. Like King, Chávez preached nonviolence and collective action. He used this message to publicize the dire, and sometimes deadly, working conditions of Mexican immigrant farmworkers. Yet, unlike King, Chávez did not have many direct ties to powerful policy makers and did not receive direct phone calls from the president about congressional legislation.[22]

Despite the flush of activity in the Southwest, however, a variety of factors kept Mexican American organizing efforts from garnering national attention. Among the most important was the fact that Mexican American communities and their organizations were concentrated in the Southwest, far from East Coast policy makers, foundations, and academics. As a result, policy makers often found it easy to dismiss Mexican American claims as "regional" issues that were subject to state-level attention, not federal intervention.[23] In addition, government officials also pointed to the issue of immigrant assimilation to justify their inaction vis-à-vis Mexican Americans. They claimed that Mexican American concerns were ordinary immigration issues that would be resolved over time; like European American immigrants before them, Mexican Americans simply needed time to assimilate.[24]

The African American civil rights movement also overshadowed Mexican American organizing efforts. Put simply, African American groups were larger and better organized than Mexican American ones, and as such, their issues received much more media and government attention. Indeed, in 1968 the US Commission on Civil Rights reported that the "high drama and nationwide visibility of the [African American] civil rights movement" had "obscure[d] the more localized protests of Mexican Americans."[25] This, the report contended, had led national policy makers, including those in the Office of Civil Rights, a division of the US Department of Health, Education, and Welfare (HEW), to overlook the fact that the conditions of Mexican American communities were deteriorating despite the recent implementation of various civil rights and social welfare programs. These sentiments were further reinforced as professional associations and the press commented on the issue and began using monikers like "the Invisible Minority" and "the Minority Nobody Knows" in reference to Mexican Americans.[26]

If federal policy makers gave Mexican Americans only marginal attention, they virtually ignored Puerto Ricans, even though they also faced documented conditions of poverty and discrimination.[27] In 1960 about 36 percent of Puerto Rican families in the United States lived under the poverty line, compared to 15 percent of white families.[28] Puerto Ricans also had lower levels of educational attainment than did whites, and Puerto Rican children were often relegated to segregated schools.[29] And like other minority groups, Puerto Ricans were subject to blatant racism, often correlated with skin color, that excluded them from employment and housing opportunities.[30]

Like the Mexican American organizations, Puerto Rican groups varied in their orientation and focus. In the 1960s, Puerto Rican leaders founded several civil rights organizations, such as ASPIRA, which empowered young Puerto Ricans by encouraging them to engage in public service and obtain a higher education. ASPIRA clubs opened throughout New York in the 1960s and slowly spread to nearby states.[31] During this time, the upsurge in student activism gave new life to the decades-old issue of

Puerto Rican independence. Student activists, for example, formed the Puerto Rican Student Forum in New York high schools and colleges and held teach-ins on the colonized status of Puerto Rico.[32]

The Young Lords, which emerged in the late 1960s, had perhaps the highest profile of these groups. Inspired by the Black Power movement, they protested the impoverished conditions of Puerto Rican communities by staging large-scale marches and taking over public and private buildings. While mainly focused on domestic poverty, the group also mobilized Puerto Ricans around issues of sovereignty, arguing that because Puerto Rico was an oppressed colony of the United States, self-determination was elusive for mainland and island-born Puerto Ricans alike.

For the most part, however, Puerto Rican groups directed their claims to local government officials rather than to those in Washington, DC.[33] In a context in which most civil rights discourse was centered on African Americans, Puerto Rican leaders likely felt that it was best to focus their lobbying efforts on locally elected officials and to request resources from city and perhaps state governments.[34] The relatively small and concentrated size of Puerto Rican organizations also likely kept them out of the national civil rights spotlight.

In effect, the African American struggle for civil rights had created a situation in which the efforts of black leaders inspired Mexican American and Puerto Rican activists but also overshadowed them. Mexican Americans particularly felt outnumbered and outorganized, and as the 1970s approached, they searched for new ways to attract national attention to their issues.

The Mexican American Push for National Recognition

By the mid-1960s Mexican American organizational leaders had become restless and displeased with the Johnson administration. The leaders of integrationist groups felt that, even though they had led efforts to mobilize Mexican American voters through the Viva Kennedy and Viva Johnson Clubs, their communities were being ignored when it came time to apportion the community grants and resources built into Great Society programs.[35] LULAC, AGIF, and other integrationist groups even stepped out of their more conservative stances and planned a protest in Washington to call attention to Mexican American issues.[36]

These frustrations erupted in the spring of 1966. Mexican American leaders had gotten word that the White House was hosting a conference on civil rights. Of the three thousand invitees slated to participate at the event, only eight were Mexican American.[37] Enraged, Mexican American leaders sought to bring up the issue during a March EEOC conference planned in Albuquerque. In attendance were about fifty representatives from integrationist and activist Chicano organizations. Aside from discussing the White House conference issue, Mexican American leaders also planned to discuss the fact that only 3 of 150 EEOC staff members were Mexican American. This, they argued, was part of a pattern of prioritizing African American concerns within the White House and the EEOC. The day of the meeting, however, all but one EEOC commissioner failed to show up.[38] Feeling that their community had been slighted once again by the federal government, almost all of the integrationist and Chicano leaders walked out in disgust and disappointment.[39]

The following year in February, the leaders of several Mexican American organizations, from LULAC and AGIF to the newly formed Mexican American Political Association, issued a formal press statement demanding that Johnson convene a White House conference specifically on Mexican American issues. Julian Samora and Herman Gallegos were among those who asked for a Mexican American conference. Samora, an academic activist, was the first Mexican American in the country to receive a PhD in sociology. As a tenured professor at the University of Notre Dame, he had published reports on the plight of Mexican Americans, and he had ties to both integrationist and Chicano activists. Herman Gallegos, a community organizer who worked on a project funded by the Ford Foundation in Oakland, also had close connections with academics and foundation officials.[40]

Both Samora and Gallegos were at the White House shortly after the statement was released, to attend a meeting on rural poverty. They hoped to mention the conference to Johnson personally, but had to settle for sending a message to the president through an aide. The aide reported this to Johnson in a memo and warned that ignoring such requests could adversely affect his administration. Johnson's response was emblematic of his disregard for Mexican American concerns. He scrawled back, "Keep this trash out of the White House."[41]

Yet there was one issue that Johnson could not ignore: the 1968 election was looming, and Johnson's ability to secure the Mexican American vote had become tenuous. Several Mexican American leaders had developed a liking for Robert Kennedy, who had become César Chávez's highest-profile supporter. Kennedy had joined Chávez on his Delano march, he was Catholic, and he was not shy about stating publicly that the federal government had ignored Mexican Americans.[42] By contrast,

Johnson's evasion of Mexican American demands for a White House conference, his reluctance to appoint a Mexican American EEOC commissioner, and his refusal to support Chávez's efforts had alienated several Chicano and integrationist groups alike.[43] Moreover, Johnson's popularity was dwindling by the late 1960s. The Vietnam War was becoming increasingly unpopular, and Johnson was worried about his reelection prospects.[44] Any and all support was essential, and Johnson's aides began warning the president: "Mexicans are a major political factor in five states and [the administration] should not risk losing them."[45] By late February 1967, Johnson decided that he could not afford to keep turning his back on Mexican Americans.

To be clear, it was not that Johnson did not recognize the plight of Mexican Americans. Having come from Texas, he had personally witnessed their second-class status. In public he sometimes recalled his time as a schoolteacher in the central valleys of Texas, where he taught the poor and often malnourished children of migrant farmworkers.[46] What concerned Johnson, though, were the possible consequences of granting concessions to the Mexican American community. The president believed that if he extended the concept of minority rights much beyond the African American community—by, for example, creating a conference on Mexican American civil rights—other ethnic groups would demand similar treatment.[47]

Nonetheless, political developments within the Mexican American community made ignoring Mexican Americans risky for Johnson. Some organizations began shifting further left and publically chastised Johnson. Among the most prominent was the Mexican American Political Association (MAPA), established in 1960, which counted among its members Herman Gallegos, Julian Samora, Ernesto Galarza, and Bert Corona. Galarza, like Samora, was an academic who had experience in community organizing. Corona, like Gallegos, had ties to foundations but also had much experience organizing grassroots community campaigns. In late 1966 MAPA issued an official statement opposing the war, arguing that the White House needed to pay attention to domestic civil rights concerns before it meddled in international affairs.[48]

The Inter-Agency Committee on Mexican American Affairs

With Mexican American frustrations reaching fever pitch and the 1968 election looming, Johnson appointed Vicente Ximenes as the first Mexican American EEOC commissioner in April of 1967. Ximenes was a

World War II veteran and a member of AGIF, and he had been one of the coordinators of the 1964 Viva Johnson campaign. Despite his lack of experience in domestic policy, Ximenes's integrationist politics and his proven political efforts on behalf of Johnson made him an attractive appointee. Besides, Ximenes came from a prominent middle-class Mexican American rancher family in Texas, and his father, a Democratic leader, was a longtime acquaintance of Johnson's.[49]

On the day that Ximenes was sworn in as EEOC commissioner, Johnson announced that Ximenes would also chair a new interagency committee that would "assure that federal programs [were] reaching the Mexican Americans."[50] The Inter-Agency Committee on Mexican American Affairs (IMAA) was established by executive order and was composed of the heads of various departments, including the secretary of the US Department of Agriculture and the secretary of HEW. The committee would advise these departments about how to best serve Mexican Americans, and it would be strategically located in Washington, DC.

As the chair of the IMAA, Ximenes had to deal with several issues. The first was that the Johnson administration was losing support among Mexican Americans. Organizational leaders chastised Johnson for taking three years to appoint a Mexican American EEOC commissioner, and they voiced doubt that the administration was taking the issues of Mexican Americans seriously. By that time Johnson had ignored Mexican Americans' calls for a White House conference for more than a year.

Second, the IMAA had limited power. As an interagency committee, it could make recommendations to other federal agencies, but it had no authority to enforce them. In addition, the IMAA's small budget made it difficult to plan and carry out large-scale projects. Finally, Ximenes had to deal with the fact that the IMAA's members were heads of other bureaucracies, who at best were perturbed by Ximenes's presence and at worst resented the idea that an outsider could make recommendations for their departmental efforts. Ximenes would soon find it difficult to convene a full meeting of the IMAA.

With these limitations in mind, Ximenes started his tenure at the IMAA by planning a series of Mexican American workshops and "hearings" to be held in El Paso in October 1967.[51] Although Mexican American leaders had specifically called for a conference at the White House, probably because it would have greater symbolic value, Ximenes pressed on with the Texas event at Johnson's request.[52] Planning for the event forced Ximenes to make several politically consequential decisions. First, he had to choose whom to invite. The range of Mexican American groups made this a difficult decision. Large organizations like LULAC and the

AGIF, of which Ximenes was a card-carrying member, could be invited, but what about the groups that had opposed the Vietnam War, such as MAPA? What about the emerging Chicano power groups, including La Alianza, which had accused the federal government of stealing land that had been granted to Mexican families by the Treaty of Guadalupe Hidalgo?[53] And what about Chávez and the United Farm Workers, whose members seemed to support Robert Kennedy?

Ximenes knew that he would have to include a significant number of Mexican American leaders if the event were to be seen as credible, but he feared that the conference could amount to a public grilling of the Johnson administration. Other embarrassing developments might occur, including demands by Chicano groups for Mexican American self-determination or for an official investigation of the land grant issue. Indeed, at the time that Ximenes was planning the conference, Chicano leaders such as Rodolfo "Corky" Gonzáles, author of "I Am Joaquin" (a poem that was instrumental in establishing a Chicano identity), and Reies López Tijerina of La Alianza were galvanizing youth in the Southwest.[54]

In the end, Ximenes sent out more than fifteen hundred invitations, mainly to integrationists and academics, but also to some Chicano leaders.[55] César Chávez turned down his invitation, stating that he was waiting for the Johnson administration to support farmworker unions. Gonzáles also turned down his invitation but traveled to El Paso nonetheless. Ximenes would later issue a statement indicating that he had invited "solutions oriented" leaders who focused less on the problems facing Mexican Americans and more on developing viable policy solutions.[56]

The event took place October 26–28 and consisted of a series of panels on different issues led by Mexican American leaders and Johnson administration officials. Invitees were preslotted into certain workshops and panels on, for example, bilingual education and labor.[57] Johnson was initially scheduled to end the conference with a speech followed by a question-and-answer period. On the final day of the event, however, organizers announced that the question-and-answer session would be canceled. Instead, participants would travel by bus to the US-Mexico border to attend a treaty-signing ceremony involving Johnson and the president of Mexico.[58]

Despite Ximenes's efforts to be inclusive, many activists were infuriated by the event. Several were upset that Ximenes had not invited important land grant activists such as Tijerina, and others argued that the conference was structured from the top down, with little input from Mexican American leaders themselves. They also contended that the elimination of the final question-and-answer session essentially undermined the ability of Mexican American leaders to get their points across to Johnson. Hundreds of invitees walked out on the final day before the treaty signing and joined leaders, including Galarza, Gallegos, Gonzáles, and Corona, who were picketing the conference.[59]

The disaffected Mexican American leaders headed to a nearby hotel where Gallegos had rented a large ballroom for a rump conference. Dubbed the gathering of "La Raza Unida," they opened the event with shouts of "brown power" and "Chicano power." Galarza read a supportive message from Chávez, who congratulated the rump conference participants for standing up to "perfumed sell outs."[60] At the hotel, the activists ratified "El Plan de La Raza Unida," which laid out the rights of "La Raza"—fair housing, bilingual education, equal employment opportunities, and enforcement of the land grants—and called on Mexican Americans to determine their own political destiny.[61] In effect, the rump conference provided members of different Chicano organizations as well as disillusioned scholars such as Galarza with an opportunity to convene and unite against the Johnson administration.

By January 1968, Ximenes and his staff knew that the IMAA was in danger of becoming a political liability to Johnson. The El Paso event had provided a public stage for government criticism and had resulted in a backlash movement against the administration's efforts. News media outlets on both coasts had reported on the Mexican American leaders' negative reactions, exacerbating the embarrassment.[62] Given that the presidential election was only months away, Ximenes knew he had to do something quickly to show that the administration's efforts to aid the Mexican American community were credible. With little time left, Ximenes set to work compiling a series of reports on the needs of Mexican American communities. These reports emphasized how Johnson's bilingual education and job training programs could help Mexican Americans integrate and reach parity with Anglo Americans. The reports, however, did not use the emerging language of "Chicano power" and self-determination, nor did they mention land rights or colonization.[63]

For all of its difficulties, the IMAA was able to achieve some gains for Mexican Americans. Ximenes argued that by the end of 1968, the IMAA had pushed the US Department of Labor (DOL) to fund employment programs in Mexican American communities, had pressured the US Postal Service and other federal agencies to hire more Mexican Americans, and had helped persuade the US Department of Agriculture to establish programs for migrant farmworkers.[64] It was difficult to tell, however, if this had been the work of the IMAA or the normal course of government action. When Johnson left the White House at the beginning of 1969, the purpose of the IMAA, created less than a year and a half earlier, would be seriously reconsidered.

Nixon and the IMAA

In January 1969 Richard Nixon entered the White House. During his campaign Nixon had promoted the notion of "black capitalism" as his solution to black urban unrest. African American communities, he argued, would benefit most not from receiving funds through antipoverty programs but from receiving the technical opportunities necessary to help jump-start black entrepreneurism.[65] Nixon had also promised that he would follow the pattern set by Johnson and appoint a black special adviser who would promote African American interests in the White House. Within a month of winning the presidential election, Nixon appointed Robert Brown to his White House staff.[66]

For their part, Mexican American leaders had spent years requesting one of their own in the White House. Johnson had steadfastly refused this request, fearing that the appointment of a Mexican American aide would prompt similar demands from other ethnic groups.[67] Nixon did not instate a Hispanic assistant either, and as he entered the White House, the question of whether to maintain the IMAA became pressing.

In many ways the IMAA was a political liability for Nixon. His advisers considered the El Paso conference an embarrassing episode that had served only to provide a forum for Mexican American leaders to criticize the federal government.[68] During its short tenure, the agency had incurred the wrath of Mexican American leaders, who argued that it was a token committee that had not effected any real change in southwestern communities. Mexican American leaders stated that the IMAA had done nothing to increase the number of Mexican Americans in top positions at the EEOC and the Office of Economic Opportunity, and that HEW grants still bypassed Mexican American barrios. Moreover, Mexican American leaders rightly pointed out that the IMAA did not have the power or the resources to enforce its recommendations.[69]

At the same time, Nixon recognized that Mexican American militancy was on the rise. During the campaign, Martin Castillo of the US Commission on Civil Rights cautioned Nixon's staff that the rising tide of Chicano protests in the Southwest could reach levels previously witnessed in African American communities.[70] Moreover, a report on Mexican Americans by the Civil Rights Commission noted that Mexican American students had boycotted several Los Angeles high schools in 1968, that Mexican

American leaders supported land grant claims, and that Mexican American college students were organizing protests throughout the Southwest. These efforts, the report argued, were evidence of a new, unified "Raza" identity endorsed by younger leaders who were bent on a "more active and aggressive assertion of rights."[71]

As Nixon's advisers assessed the situation during the early months of the new administration, they received comments from fellow Republicans. From California, GOP congressman Burt Talcott reminded Nixon's staff that the Mexican American vote was important to California Republicans and that the IMAA should be supported and staffed with Mexican Americans who were "friendly, non-violent, moderate Republicans."[72] Daniel Patrick Moynihan, Nixon's urban affairs adviser, circulated a staff report that equated the renewal of the IMAA with future Mexican American support.[73] Although Nixon had received less than 10 percent of the Mexican American vote, the message was clear: an effective IMAA, perhaps along with a White House conference, could turn things around for Republicans in subsequent elections.

In response, Nixon's administration took some steps to cater to Mexican Americans during his first year in office. In 1969 Nixon appointed Hilary Sandoval, a Mexican American businessman from El Paso, as the director of the Small Business Administration.[74] In turn, Sandoval set up a variety of small-business loan programs in the Southwest. In addition, Nixon and his administration appointed seven other Mexican Americans, most of them Republican, to agency staffs, almost equaling the number of Mexican Americans appointed during the Johnson administration.[75] Thus, even before Moynihan penned his controversial 1970 memo in which he suggested that the administration give blacks a dose of "benign neglect" so that officials might focus on other minority groups, Nixon's advisers had begun to equate federal appointments and policies with potential Mexican American votes.[76]

The question of the IMAA, however, was not easily resolved. Nixon's staff knew that the agency could easily provide a target for criticism if it remained ineffective. In addition, there was the question of whom the committee would serve. In a memo, one of Nixon's advisers speculated that supporting anything from a committee to a conference solely for Mexican Americans might incur the wrath of other "Spanish American" groups.[77] Other advisers argued that an agency dedicated to one particular ethnic group would generally be unwise because there would inevitably be claims from others.[78]

Nonetheless, in June 1969 Nixon tapped Martin Castillo to lead the

IMAA. Although a registered Democrat, Castillo had reportedly campaigned for Nixon in 1968 after meeting him in a televised appearance in Los Angeles.[79] Yet instead of issuing an executive order to extend the IMAA past its 1969 expiration date, Nixon stepped back and allowed the issue to be decided by Congress. By that time Senator Joseph Montoya (D-NM) and Congressman Edward Roybal (D-CA) had taken an interest in the IMAA, and they presented bills that would renew the committee for five years.

"Not Interested in Long Names": Congressional Hearings and the Concerns of Puerto Ricans

As 1969 reached its midpoint, Congress started its consideration of the IMAA's fate. Present at the June hearings, however, were not only IMAA personnel and Mexican American leaders but also Puerto Rican community leaders, who had two important supporters: Senator Jacob Javits (R-NY) and Senator Abraham Ribicoff (D-CT). Javits had secured the support of prominent Puerto Rican New Yorkers for his 1968 reelection bid, and he was a member of the subcommittee that initially reviewed Montoya's bill.[80] More important was Ribicoff's participation. He was chair of the Senate subcommittee that would oversee the bill, and he came to the meetings prepared with several letters from his Puerto Rican constituents.[81] In effect, both senators were determined to use the IMAA hearings to secure resources and assistance for their Puerto Rican constituents.

Ribicoff called the hearings to order and set the tone by stating that the committee's purpose was to focus "on the living conditions, problems, and needs . . . of the Spanish Speaking population"—in other words, not just Mexican Americans.[82] IMAA officials did not seem initially perturbed, for during their testimony they often switched among several terms: *Mexican American, Spanish American, Spanish surnamed,* and *Spanish speaking.* Indeed, in their publications IMAA officials often used the label "Spanish American" to refer to Mexican Americans.

During the hearings IMAA personnel testified about the agency's activities and budget. The agency's interim director touted a long list of its achievements, including convening the El Paso conference, working with the DOL to establish manpower and training programs in the Southwest, successfully persuading federal agencies to hire more Mexican Americans, and working with HEW to establish training and education

31

programs for migrant farmworkers.[83] In addition, IMAA officials provided statistics and reports that showed that Mexican American communities still lagged behind whites on income and education measures.

The East Coast congressmen were impatient, however, and they soon asked about the IMAA's efforts among other Spanish-speaking communities. Sensing that Ribicoff and Javits were not too thrilled about the IMAA's Mexican focus, former IMAA chair Ximenes quickly added that the agency sometimes reached out to help other groups, especially Puerto Ricans. Subcommittee members pressed Ximenes on the issue, with Ribicoff arguing that Puerto Ricans probably felt "downgraded" within the Mexican American organization.[84] Ximenes responded that the IMAA worked closely with the Puerto Rican Forum, with a group of Puerto Rican businessmen in New York, and with a number of other Puerto Rican "organizations that came to our committee and asked for assistance and help."[85]

Several Puerto Ricans leaders, including two officials from New York City, testified immediately after Ximenes. They argued, however, that even though Puerto Ricans and Mexican Americans shared some similar concerns, such as bilingual education and urban poverty, the IMAA had done little to assist their communities.[86] To support their argument, they mentioned that while more than two thousand people attended the 1967 conference in El Paso, only six Puerto Ricans had been invited. "We were well received by our Mexican friends, but it was not our conference," one Puerto Rican leader stated.[87] They also mentioned that the IMAA's staff was composed almost entirely of Mexican Americans who, despite sympathizing with Puerto Ricans, focused their efforts on the Southwest. In effect, the Puerto Rican leaders contended that the IMAA did exactly what its name implied: it assisted Mexican Americans and only Mexican Americans. They demanded that Congress either create a similar committee for Puerto Rican affairs or broaden the scope of the IMAA.

Puerto Rican leaders and their congressional allies were not presenting an outlandish demand. Like Mexican Americans, Puerto Ricans were identified as a protected minority under the Civil Rights Act, and both were sometimes, though not consistently, grouped together as "Spanish Americans" under some civil rights policies.[88] If Mexican Americans had representation in the White House, Puerto Ricans argued, so should they. From their point of view, the only open question was whether Puerto Ricans would have a separate form of representation or whether Congress would restructure the IMAA to give it a broader, multiethnic mandate.[89]

Probably realizing that legislation supporting a Mexican American organization would not be approved by East Coast senators like Ribicoff and

Javits, Montoya submitted an amendment to his bill that would broaden the organization and change the IMAA's name to the Interagency Committee on Hispanic American Affairs. During Martin Castillo's testimony, Ribicoff asked whether he would be opposed to the name change. In a long-winded answer, Castillo replied that the term *Mexican* was an important "word of pride" for Mexican Americans and that the term *Hispanic* was acceptable only to an older generation hailing from New Mexico, Senator Montoya's home state. "The generic term 'Hispanic' is not representative of the Southwestern Spanish Speaking community," Castillo argued, referencing the fact that the term was used primarily by more upwardly mobile Mexican Americans in states like New Mexico to assert a European identity and distance themselves from working-class Mexican immigrants.[90] Ximenes expressed his distaste for the term *Hispanic* as well, arguing that the majority of Mexican Americans in the Southwest preferred *Mexican*.

Both Castillo and Ximenes resisted the push to broaden the IMAA. Although they were not opposed to helping other groups, they believed that a name change would lead the agency away from its primary focus on Mexican American issues. At the same time, however, Castillo and Ximenes recognized what Senator Montoya had seen—that East Coast politicians would not support an agency that was dedicated to assisting only Mexican Americans in the Southwest. To overcome this, Ximenes suggested that the term *Mexican American* could stand for a variety of Spanish-speaking groups. This notion had recently been inserted into IMAA literature as the organization's staff prepared for the congressional hearings. For example, the IMAA's 1969 brochure included the following:

There are others in the United States who have the same features, background, language and surnames [as the Mexican Americans]. For example, there are Puerto Ricans, Spanish Americans (from Spain), Central Americans (from Costa Rica, Panama, etc.), and South Americans. Therefore, among the Spanish-speaking Americans—the second largest minority group in our country—we find a great diversity in origin yet a great commonality in traditions and language. They have also shared the same problems and experiences as citizens of the United States and in this report the term "Mexican American" is used as a general designation.[91]

Not surprisingly, Puerto Rican leaders supported a broadening of the IMAA, but they were not enthusiastic about using *Mexican American* as a generic label. They noted that, like *Mexican American*, the term *Puerto Rican* was a symbol of great pride. Ribicoff stated, however, that a name like the "Interagency Committee for Mexican American and Puerto

33

Rican American Affairs" would be too long: "We want to be practical and achieve as much as we can. Nobody likes long names."[92] He proposed that Ximenes and Castillo discuss the issue with the Puerto Rican leaders and arrive at "the broadest possible term."[93]

Militancy Concerns and the Future of the IMAA

The name question would not be resolved until after the IMAA bill was reviewed again in late September. In the meantime, the House Appropriations Committee reviewed the IMAA issue to determine the agency's budget for the rest of 1969 and, potentially, 1970.[94] The main concern during these hearings had to do with militancy. During the testimony of the IMAA director, committee chair Daniel Flood (D-PA) asked IMAA leaders directly, "Are you forming a bloc? Are we financing the formation of a bloc?"[95] Flood was worried about reports of militancy from Puerto Rican and, especially, Mexican American groups. The *New York Times* had published stories about Puerto Rican student protests and sit-ins in New York City in 1968 and 1969, and Flood feared that these movements could soon become a sustained nationalist threat.[96]

Congressmen were also concerned about Mexican American militants. In the hearings, representative Robert Casey (D-TX) asked whether the IMAA supported the recent spate of unrest in Texas. He noted that Mexican Americans in a south Texas town had recently nailed a manifesto to the courthouse demanding more resources for their community:

The thing I do not like to see and I do not think you do either is where [Mexican Americans] try to advance their cause, not by a positive but by what I call a negative approach, start calling some of the local officials gringos and start making picket signs to that effect, down with the gringos and things of that nature.[97]

IMAA officials were eager to use the issue of militancy to their advantage by arguing that their office could help defuse such unrest. During the congressional testimony, IMAA officials contended that the lack of attention from the federal government and private foundations alike had made Mexican Americans "more and more militant." They explained that this neglect had recently "solidified" Chicano militancy and encouraged protest. Puerto Ricans, they averred, were also "very definitely" on the verge of becoming militant. The IMAA could remedy this because it could persuade "people to present their demands in an across-the-table manner by means of conciliation."[98]

A few months later the House held its own hearings. By this time the Senate had passed the bill that changed the name of the IMAA to the Cabinet Committee on Opportunities for Spanish Speaking People (CCOSSP). The new name was probably a compromise that avoided not only the ethnic-specific names favored by IMAA and Puerto Rican leaders but also the term *Hispanic*, which Montoya advocated. In his impassioned plea for the bill, Roybal tied control of the growing militancy of Mexican Americans to CCOSSP:

The militants in our community are on our backs almost every moment of the day. And the question that is being asked of me, members of Congress, and other elected officials is, "Is it necessary for us to riot? Is it necessary for us to burn down a town before the Government looks at our problems objectively? What are we to do if our community is not recognized?" Those of us who represent the Spanish-speaking communities have quite a problem on our hands. We do not want to see the violence of Watts erupt in East Los Angeles or anyplace else, and I hope that this will never come about. But the answers must be found, and I believe that one of the answers is the establishment of [CCOSSP].[99]

Roybal finished his statement by encouraging the House to act on a historic opportunity to help "the Spanish Speaking." Soon afterward, he and several other Democratic and Republican congressmen, mainly from the Southwest, voiced their support for the bill.

Before the bill could be passed, however, East Coast congressmen brought up one final question: who exactly were "the Spanish Speaking"? The language of the CCOSSP bill mentioned "the Spanish Speaking," but never defined precisely who these individuals were. The issue was less about nationality, for it was clear that Puerto Ricans and Mexican Americans would be covered, and more about assimilation. Thus, one congressman wondered whether the Spanish speaking would also include those who had intermarried with Anglos and, for example, had Irish surnames. In addition, he asked whether CCOSSP would represent someone of Latin American descent who "was reared . . . and educated in this country and did not speak the Spanish language."[100]

Roybal answered that the provisions of the legislation would not apply to those who had "assimilated into the life stream."[101] Castillo also clarified that the term *Spanish speaking* applied to Mexican Americans, Cuban Americans, Puerto Ricans, and other Latin Americans and their descendants who had not assimilated. Moreover, both Roybal and Castillo also noted that perhaps, one day, when "the Spanish Speaking" no longer faced barriers to success, CCOSSP would be phased out.

In effect, Roybal and Castillo argued that the "Spanish Speaking" identity was an ephemeral one that was connected to upward mobility. Specifically, Spanish speakers were those who suffered from discrimination, poverty, and unemployment. Those who had assimilated, however, were a different matter because they might not suffer from these conditions. Yet, for all its qualifiers, this definition of "the Spanish Speaking" remained vague. How much Spanish should one speak? How poor should one be? And what did *assimilation* mean? The discussion had an element of irony because Castillo, who identified himself as a "Spanish Speaker," was a European-educated lawyer who did not speak Spanish fluently and who came from a well-established and prominent New Mexican family.[102]

The final version of the bill that was passed in late November included a provision that created a CCOSSP advisory committee that would be appointed by the president and would be reflective of Mexican American, Puerto Rican, and Cuban American groups equally. The bill extended the life of the committee for five years and increased its budget. On December 31, 1969, President Richard Nixon signed the bill "con gusto" and officially named Castillo the committee chair.[103]

Balancing Demands for Representation through CCOSSP

Castillo and his staff entered 1970 with an expanded budget and a mandate to assist the broad Spanish-speaking community. As his first task, Castillo set about designing a CCOSSP agenda that could cater to the country's large Mexican American population but also consider the needs of Puerto Ricans. Anxious that CCOSSP might prioritize Mexican American issues, Puerto Ricans and their supporters wrote to Nixon and his staff asking for equal representation. Less than a month after the committee's establishment, the governor of Puerto Rico wrote to Nixon: "Now that the concept of the committee has been broadened to include Puerto Ricans, and because they are completely unrepresented at the moment, I should like to have your agreement in principle that Puerto Ricans be given priority for all vacancies within [CCOSSP]."[104] The governor was a fellow Republican who had campaigned for Nixon in 1968, and in his letter he enclosed the résumé of a Puerto Rican associate for consideration. Governor Nelson Rockefeller of New York also sent Nixon a letter expressing concern that CCOSSP staff included only "one Puerto Rican."[105] Despite this pressure, questions about Puerto Rican representation on

CCOSSP would resurface continually throughout the committee's life span.

Castillo faced several obstacles from the onset. Most pressing was the fact that CCOSSP still had no real authority to enforce its recommendations. Moreover, although its budget had increased, CCOSSP's financial and regulatory limitations restricted the committee's role to that of ombudsman. Take, for example, the issue of high school dropout rates among Spanish-speaking students. The only action CCOSSP could take would be to try to convince HEW to channel resources to Spanish-speaking communities. HEW was not obliged to follow through on CCOSSP's recommendation, however. In addition, there were no guarantees that CCOSSP would receive any credit if HEW did help Spanish-speaking communities as a result of CCOSSP's work. In fact, HEW eventually developed its own internal task force to aid Spanish-speaking communities, which allowed the department to argue that CCOSSP was superfluous.

So what can a committee with no authority and a restricted budget do? It creates reports. Castillo spent much of 1970 canvassing the problems of the Spanish-speaking population.[106] The thinking was that if CCOSSP and the problems of Spanish speakers were to be taken seriously within the federal government, each issue would first have to be documented thoroughly in an official government report. Unfortunately, the committee needed nationally representative data on the Spanish-speaking population to write these reports, and government agencies by and large lacked this type of information. The government's main data collection agencies, such as the Census Bureau, HEW (which oversaw the National Center for Health Statistics and the National Center for Education Statistics), and the DOL, regarded Mexican Americans and Puerto Ricans mainly as white, considering them together with Anglos. Without "Spanish Speaking" unemployment data collected by the DOL, for example, CCOSSP would have a difficult time penning reports that would convince government agencies to fund job training programs in cities like Los Angeles and New York.

Recognizing that data would be a crucial aspect of their lobbying efforts, Castillo and his predecessor, Ximenes, began by lobbying the Census Bureau as early as 1969.[107] As a result of this and pressure from other sources, the bureau relented and included a Spanish-origin question on the 1970 sample census form.[108] The data gleaned from the sample enumeration allowed CCOSSP to create comprehensive reports and to channel its resources to specific geographical areas. CCOSSP began publishing its first large reports in late 1970.[109]

Yet gaining access to data only resolved some issues, for CCOSSP still had a difficult beginning. First, support for the committee was weak, at best. Mexican American organizations had little hope that a committee operating under a Republican administration could produce results for Spanish-speaking communities. When a White House conference on Mexican Americans did not materialize despite Nixon's campaign promises, even the integrationist groups became disillusioned with the committee.[110] In addition, because Nixon had received complaints from the GOP about Castillo's Democratic affiliation, Moynihan suggested to Castillo that he maintain a low profile. In effect, Castillo's Democratic affiliation "infuriate[d] Mexican American Republicans" as well as southwestern GOP congressmen.[111]

CCOSSP's second obstacle was that it was often ignored by the administration. During its first year, Castillo asked several times to meet with Nixon but was always turned down. His efforts to organize a Mexican American conference at the White House were also shunned. At one point Castillo warned Nixon's staff that delays on a Mexican American conference and neglecting CCOSSP would feed rising militant tendencies among Chicano activists.[112] Despite Castillo's pleas, Nixon never met with CCOSSP and, worse, failed to appoint an advisory group for the committee as was mandated by law.[113] Faced with these conditions, Castillo resigned in January 1971.

Instead of immediately appointing Castillo's successor, Nixon kept the position vacant for more than eight months, signaling his ambivalence toward the committee. In February 1971 one of Nixon's assistants wrote an in-depth assessment of CCOSSP, describing the committee as a "an unfortunate story of misfires, inaction, and bad luck."[114] There was, however, some optimism: given that Nixon would be running for reelection in 1972, Nixon's aides encouraged him to "get some good, tough-minded people that could turn this neglected machinery around."[115]

Organizations, elected officials, and community leaders flooded the Nixon administration with concerns about CCOSSP. Some, like Roybal and newly elected congressman Herman Badillo (D-NY), a Puerto Rican, accused the president of neglecting Spanish speakers by keeping the CCOSSP chairmanship vacant.[116] Most, however, saw it as an opportunity to promote coethnic candidates. Puerto Rican organizations wrote letters that argued that since CCOSSP's staff was almost entirely Mexican American, a Puerto Rican should be appointed as chair.[117] Mexican Americans wrote to advocate for a Mexican American replacement. One California organization even suggested that replacing Castillo with a non-Mexican could lead to riots in Los Angeles.[118]

By the summer of 1971, Nixon's staff began to notice that the CCOSSP vacancy was threatening the president's image in Spanish-speaking communities. Nixon's advisers warned that Spanish-speaking Americans felt as if they were playing second fiddle to other minorities, especially African Americans. One adviser noted that "most of this population is strategically located in politically doubtful states." Angering these citizens, the advisers cautioned, could compromise Nixon's reelection.[119]

In August 1971, Nixon selected Henry Ramirez, a Mexican American from Southern California, to chair CCOSSP. An educator from the same area in which Nixon grew up, Ramirez had little experience working in the federal government, but he was part of a small, yet growing, group of Mexican American Republicans in the Southwest. Nixon held a private conference with CCOSSP staff members to tell them about the appointment. He said that he understood that Spanish-speaking communities had "not had their fair shake" in government, and he noted that although CCOSSP members had not seen any "follow through" from his administration in the previous year, he hoped that the committee would take a more active lobbying role. "Don't wait until the wheel squeaks—or something gets blown up in Los Angeles," he warned.[120] In addition to appointing Ramirez, Nixon also selected a CCOSSP advisory team that fall. The nine-member group was composed of four Mexican Americans, including the publisher of California's foremost Spanish-language daily newspaper, *La Opinión*, three Puerto Ricans, and two Cuban Americans.[121]

The new presence of Cuban Americans at CCOSSP, however, revived an old debate about whether the Cuban community shared the same concerns expressed by Mexican Americans and Puerto Ricans. During the 1969 congressional hearings, Castillo had argued that Miami was "loaded with doctors, lawyers, accountants, and dentists" who were "the cream of the intellectual Cuban community" and thus did not experience the poverty and education problems that Puerto Ricans and Mexican Americans did.[122] And in appropriations hearings in July 1969, an IMAA official had noted that Cuban Americans were "a different breed of people who are governed by special legislation"—the Cuban refugee policy—"and came over as professionals."[123] The implication was that Cuban Americans had a higher class standing than Mexican Americans and Puerto Ricans. While they may have come to the United States as refugees, many had college degrees and were able to set up businesses and establish a middle-class lifestyle within a relatively short period.[124] This higher standing, IMAA officials had argued, made Cubans fundamentally different from Mexican Americans and Puerto Ricans.

Nonetheless, probably because of the broadened CCOSSP mandate and his ties to Cuban Americans in Florida, Nixon appointed two prominent Cuban American businessmen to the council. One described himself as a "close friend" of Charles "Bebe" Rebozo.[125] The Cuban American appointments quickly became headline news in the major Spanish-language newspapers in Miami, which reported that the Cuban community had finally achieved representation in Washington.[126] For his part, Ramirez did not wish to contradict Nixon, and he soon accepted the new Cuban presence at CCOSSP.

In fact, Ramirez was more concerned about the Puerto Rican issue. When he was appointed, Ramirez restructured the committee and dismissed the Puerto Rican who had held the number two position. Javits and other elected officials from New York complained to Spanish-language newspapers that Ramirez was leaving the Puerto Rican community without representation.[127] About fifty Puerto Rican activists from New York traveled to Washington, intent on forcing Ramirez either to reinstate the Puerto Rican or to replace him with another Puerto Rican from the East Coast.[128] In addition, Puerto Rican groups and elected officials sent letters to Nixon's staff demanding more Puerto Rican representation on the committee.[129] Fearful of further negative publicity, Ramirez took action quickly. He selected Rey Maduro, a Puerto Rican from New York who had lived in the Southwest, to be CCOSSP's second-in-command.[130]

Taking a lesson from these incidents, Ramirez also decided to hire special assistants to be liaisons to different communities. A Puerto Rican special assistant was hired to communicate with Puerto Ricans in New York, and a Cuban American was given a similar role in Miami. These assistants would, in theory, help Ramirez advocate for different projects and policies. Rey Maduro was placed in charge of day-to-day staff operations. With these changes, Ramirez created an office that attempted to provide representation for the three largest Spanish-speaking groups while maintaining a separate administrative staff to carry out national, panethnic projects.[131]

During his first year, Ramirez also focused on revamping the committee's image. Although the incidents surrounding the CCOSSP dismissals had produced flak from the Puerto Rican community, Ramirez and others on Nixon's staff had been working for some time to improve CCOSSP's, as well as Nixon's, image among Spanish speakers. To that end, CCOSSP hired a Spanish-language advertising agency in New York to help the committee develop radio and television commercials to publicize its accomplishments. The goal was to communicate to Mexican Americans,

Puerto Ricans, Cuban Americans, and other Spanish speakers that they had an advocate in the White House.[132]

In addition, Ramirez also planned a series of open forums with leaders of the Spanish-speaking community. These meetings would be held in Chicago, New York, Dallas, and other cities with high concentrations of Spanish speakers. The first was held in Chicago and was attended mainly by Mexican American and Puerto Rican community leaders. Although Ramirez hoped the event would turn things around for CCOSSP and provide an opportunity to showcase the committee's new direction, the meeting went downhill quickly. Chicago leaders accused CCOSSP of ignoring their communities, contending that CCOSSP only focused on the Southwest. Even though Ramirez tried to dispute the claim by pointing to CCOSSP's national advocacy efforts, the event did not end well.[133] HEW staff eventually complained to Nixon officials that CCOSSP was unorganized and that the Chicago meeting had been an embarrassment to the administration.[134]

Ramirez quickly put a hold on subsequent meetings.[135] For the rest of 1971, the committee stuck mainly to conducting closed-door regional meetings with select organizational contacts, writing reports, and exposing disparities in employment for Spanish speakers within the federal government.[136] CCOSSP also engaged in various advocacy projects within the Nixon administration: it lobbied several government agencies to collect more data on the Spanish-speaking population, persuaded the Department of Agriculture to provide more loans to Spanish-speaking farmers, and convinced the DOL to funnel resources into manpower training programs in New York and Texas.[137] Issues that had been deemed militant, such as the land grant issue and the idea of Puerto Rican sovereignty, however, were ignored entirely.[138]

The Spanish-Speaking Vote in 1972

By the spring of 1972, CCOSSP and its shortcomings had been moved to the back burner as Nixon and his staff geared up for the 1972 presidential election. The Republican National Committee (RNC) had commissioned a study on Spanish speakers and was convinced that Nixon could secure a larger percentage of this population's vote in key states such as California, Texas, and Florida than he had in 1968.[139] The study was the first of its kind on Hispanic politics and used the newly released data on the "Spanish Origin" population included in the 1970 census to detail how Spanish speakers were stratified socioeconomically across different regions. The study also included data from an RNC-financed national survey on the political values of Spanish speakers. Puerto Ricans, the study reported, were most worried about drugs and poverty, while Mexican Americans were concerned with education and immigration issues. Cuban Americans were interested in foreign policy.[140] The study concluded that the RNC should create different campaign strategies for each of these groups.

For his part, Nixon assembled a team, which nicknamed itself the Brown Mafia, to help secure the Spanish-speaking vote. Although a small number of Mexican Americans in the Southwest, including Henry Ramirez, had organized "Viva Nixon" campaign events in 1968, the 1972 effort represented Nixon's first coordinated attempt to secure this constituency. Led by Alex Armendariz, the reelection team began by organizing three campaigns: one for Puerto Ricans, one for Cuban Americans, and one for Mexican Americans.[141] In addition, the Nixon campaign purchased several campaign buses, known as "Amigo Buses," and had them roam the Southwest and targeted areas on the East Coast to publicize the resources that CCOSSP had helped to funnel to these areas.[142] The Amigo Buses in the Southwest broadcast mariachi music for the mainly Mexican American population, and buses on the East Coast played Caribbean salsa to attract Puerto Rican and Cuban American voters.[143]

CCOSSP was important to the Brown Mafia not simply because it had a track record that could be publicized, but also because its staff could be commissioned as spokespersons for Nixon. During the summer and fall of 1972, Ramirez made several campaign speeches for Nixon.[144] CCOSSP's public information officer, the person in charge of working with Spanish-language media, was also detailed to work for Nixon's campaign.[145] The use of CCOSSP staff for reelection efforts was questionable because the committee was intended to serve as a nonpartisan advocate for the Spanish-speaking population. This did not seem to trouble Nixon's staff. Indeed, when a staff member warned that campaign assignments were dangerously infringing on CCOSSP's resources, a Nixon campaign staffer responded, "So what."[146]

CCOSSP also helped Nixon's reelection efforts by creating Spanish-language radio broadcasts. The monthly recordings, which highlighted the committee's efforts and the gains that Spanish speakers had achieved under Nixon, were distributed to hundreds of Spanish-language stations. Although Democratic congressmen wrote angry letters to Ramirez, arguing that these recordings exaggerated CCOSSP's achievements and took credit for projects implemented by congressional action, CCOSSP continued to distribute the programs past the election.[147]

In fact, Spanish-language media were an important tool for Nixon's re-election campaign. Nixon's team worked closely with Spanish-language advertising agencies and produced several advertisements for radio. The Brown Mafia even created a Spanish-language commercial that was aired nationally on the emerging Spanish-language television firm, Spanish International Network. The commercial stressed that the Nixon administration had appointed more Spanish-speaking citizens to government positions than any other president in US history.[148]

The ads that appeared in Spanish-language newspapers published in Los Angeles during the two campaigns reveal an important shift in terminology.[149] In 1968 Mexican American Republicans purchased ads advocating Nixon's efforts on behalf of "Mexican Americans." For example, one ad noted that Nixon "knows firsthand the problems facing the Mexican American community."[150] By 1972 his campaign ads used only "Hispanic" and "Spanish Speaking." One full-page ad that ran in several papers mentioned CCOSSP and noted that Nixon has "recruited Hispanics to serve in his administration and these individuals are implementing programs that directly affect the lives of the Spanish Speaking."[151]

In the end, Nixon's push to secure Spanish-speaking voters paid off handsomely. Staff officials estimated that Nixon received about 35 percent of the Spanish-speaking vote in the 1972 general election, more than five times the percentage he had received in 1968.[152]

The End of CCOSSP

CCOSSP continued its advocacy work through 1973. It lobbied for the hiring of more Spanish speakers in federal agencies and held several hearings in different regions that were, for the most part, closed to the public. In addition, it worked closely with the Office of Minority Business Enterprise, now run by former Brown Mafia member Armendariz, to identify sectors that lacked Spanish-speaking entrepreneurs. Between late 1972 and the end of 1973, CCOSSP also persuaded various federal agencies to appoint Spanish-speaking liaisons to work directly with CCOSSP. At the same time, CCOSSP continued to issue reports on topics of interest to Spanish-speaking Americans, such as bilingual education, conditions for migrant farmworkers, and healthcare access within Spanish-speaking communities.[153]

CCOSSP, however, faced a new form of criticism. By mid-1973, Democratic elected officials were accusing CCOSSP of having funneled resources and services to the Nixon reelection campaign. In July, the House

Government Operations Committee held hearings on CCOSSP's partisan activities and grilled Ramirez about his political efforts on behalf of Nixon. Ramirez denied engaging in unethical activities and said that he could not recall exactly how many meetings he had attended or the number of memos he had received from Nixon's reelection campaign team.[154] Democratic congressmen from Spanish-speaking districts continued to press the issue. Henry González (D-TX) contended that CCOSSP members had made political speeches against his campaign, and others argued that Ramirez had distorted the facts by crediting Nixon for congressional efforts.[155] It did not help that one of the few Democratic members of CCOSSP's advisory committee, Hilda Hidalgo, submitted her resignation letter and accused CCOSSP senior staff of spending most of the fall of 1972 campaigning for Nixon.[156]

The accusations of partisan activity soon spilled over into larger discussions about CCOSSP's purpose and effectiveness. Some congressmen thought that the committee existed simply for the sake of bureaucracy and that it had lost touch with its original mandate. Others argued more diplomatically that a committee whose main purpose was to lobby Congress could never be seen as highly functional because it could not provide proof of its effectiveness.[157] Even former members of the Brown Mafia implied that CCOSSP was ineffective.[158] Although CCOSSP could claim that it funneled resources to, for example, schools in south Texas, in reality this would be the work of government agencies. The only tangible fruit of CCOSSP's work was its reports.

Reaction from the Spanish-speaking community was mixed. At CCOSSP congressional hearings, there were groups that called the committee invaluable, as well as those who argued that it had not been effective at all. Patterns of support and criticism did not seem to vary by ethnic group. In the same session in which the AGIF lauded CCOSSP's accomplishments and argued that "the Spanish Speaking need [CCOSSP] because . . . it is working and producing [results]," a Mexican American association argued that CCOSSP "has failed to live up to expectations" because it was "designed to fail."[159]

Accusations of ineffectiveness and partisan activity became more pronounced as the Watergate scandal unfolded and Nixon's prospects of remaining in office became bleak. By mid-1974, national papers implied that CCOSSP was linked to a pay-to-play scandal that had gripped Nixon's Office of Minority Business Enterprise. Stories in the *New York Post* and the *Los Angeles Times* stated that CCOSSP might have funneled resources only to those Spanish-speaking organizations and entrepreneurs that pledged loyalty to Nixon's reelection.[160] The finger-pointing escalated, and in September 1974, Ramirez submitted his resignation letter to President Gerald Ford.[161] In December 1974, a bill designed to extend CCOSSP past its five-year mandate failed on the floor of the House of Representatives.[162] When it was clear that CCOSSP would close its doors, Maduro issued a statement arguing that the committee "was the only vehicle that the Spanish Speaking had at a national level that could document their needs."[163] Its demise, he contended, was a huge loss for the Spanish-speaking population.

For all its difficulties, though, CCOSSP did have an important impact on research. Since its initial establishment as the IMAA, the committee had made the collection of statistical data on the Spanish-speaking population a priority. Committee members lobbied the Census Bureau, the DOL, and other federal agencies to convince them to stop labeling Spanish speakers as white. These efforts, coupled with the information published in CCOSSP's reports, sensitized other federal agencies to the notion that Spanish speakers comprised a social group that was distinct from Anglos. In this way, CCOSSP promoted the notion of a separate, Spanish-speaking panethnic group.

At the same time, however, CCOSSP's research efforts also helped the committee legitimate its existence. When, for example, senators argued that CCOSSP should be dissolved because a similar organization did not exist for Italians, CCOSSP staff were quick to provide statistics and reports that highlighted not only the sheer size of the Spanish-speaking population but also this population's socioeconomic standing vis-à-vis Anglo or European Americans.[164] Over time this research fed into a self-sustaining process: the more that CCOSSP lobbied for data on the Spanish-speaking population, the more reports it could produce on Spanish speakers and the more resources it could secure to continue lobbying for more data.

By the time that CCOSSP was dissolved, the Census Bureau had begun collecting Spanish-origin data, and several other agencies, including the HEW, had set up a series of task forces to discern how to best collect data from Spanish-speaking Americans.[165] Moreover, several agencies had instituted permanent Spanish-speaking community representative positions whose task was to assure that departments were collecting data on and providing resources for Spanish speakers. The Executive Office of the President instituted something similar. A few months before CCOSSP expired, Ford created the Office of Hispanic Affairs, headed by Fernando De Baca, which took over many of CCOSSP's advocacy tasks. Most important, Ford's Office of Hispanic Affairs continued CCOSSP's work by implementing a series of meetings with the Office of Management and Budget as well as the Census Bureau to develop a strategy for standardizing the data collected on the Spanish-speaking population by different government agencies.[166]

By the mid-1970s, CCOSSP had also helped institutionalize the idea that Spanish speakers constituted not simply a bureaucratic category but also a national political constituency. CCOSSP members took a lead role in organizing the Spanish Speaking Advisory Committee for the RNC, which held its first national conference in 1974.[167] The Republican National Committee formally recognized the Republican National Hispanic Assembly in 1976.[168] And during his 1976 presidential campaign, Ford followed many of the same strategies put in place by CCOSSP and Nixon's reelection team, including reaching out to Mexican American, Cuban American, and Puerto Rican voters with messages tailored for each group.[169] Later, Jimmy Carter would also assemble a team to appeal to Spanish-speaking voters, and Ronald Reagan would create advertisements that argued that his party shared the "Hispanic American" commitment to hard work and family.[170]

Conclusion

The history of the IMAA and CCOSSP reveals processes of co-optation that emerged as state and ethnic leaders alike struggled to define the needs of Mexican American and Puerto Rican communities and negotiated ways of doing so. Fearing the rise of militancy and sensing the opportunity to win more votes, both Johnson and Nixon created agencies that would purportedly represent Mexican American and Puerto Rican needs within the federal government. This resulted, however, not simply in the redirection of federal resources, but also in the construction and legitimation of a new administrative category that lumped together the issues of Mexican Americans, Puerto Ricans, and Cubans under a single classification. This co-optation process comprised three steps. First, elected officials came to recognize the demands of Mexican Americans, and to a certain extent Puerto Ricans, as both a threat and a political opportunity. Second, a formal government body—first the IMAA and then CCOSSP— was established to not only represent but also reframe the issues of the aggrieved. Third, CCOSSP publicized the idea of Spanish-speaking issues across government agencies, helping to institutionalize the panethnic administrative category within official government reports.

Although the process of co-optation began when activists started to make claims on the federal government, it was only when the Johnson and Nixon administrations could identify potential political gains that they began to respond to activists' demands. Johnson, like Kennedy, largely ignored the demands of Mexican American leaders during the early and mid-1960s, even though both initially courted the Mexican American vote. Johnson did not see the benefit of co-optation until mid-1967, just in time for the 1968 election. This, probably in combination with escalating Mexican American militancy, led to the establishment of the IMAA.

The renewal of the IMAA in 1969 became an opportunity for some government officials across the country to appease their constituencies and gain political favor. Congressmen jockeyed with the executive office over how to define the Spanish-speaking population. Elected officials from the East Coast saw Mexican Americans as part of a larger group that included Puerto Ricans. Javits, Ribicoff, and Rockefeller, all elected officials with large Puerto Rican constituencies, pressed the IMAA to reach out to Puerto Ricans. Puerto Rican leaders, for their part, lobbied their congressmen, thus legitimating the congressmen's demands and accelerating the transformation of the IMAA into CCOSSP.

As Nixon's team began using CCOSSP to establish a strategy for winning the Spanish-speaking vote in the 1972 election, the idea that Spanish speakers were a political constituency as well as a minority group became increasingly accepted. CCOSSP came to represent a constituent category, not just a set of grievances. On the one hand, CCOSSP constituents were depicted as a minority whose civil rights had been violated; on the other hand, they were represented as a bounded group with specific political tastes and needs.

For their part, CCOSSP bureaucrats focused on rearticulating the demands of Mexican Americans and Puerto Ricans alike. Specifically, the committee concentrated on issues that best fit the institutional capabilities of the federal government, such as bilingual education, housing, unemployment, and the administration's agenda—particularly minority entrepreneurship. As a result, it never addressed the more militant and abstract questions of Chicano and Puerto Rican self-determination. And by claiming to cater to the Spanish-speaking population as a whole, CCOSSP could skirt the more radical ethnic-specific issues like Mexican American land grant claims and Puerto Rican independence.

Once it had created an agenda, CCOSSP set about publicizing Spanish speakers as the nation's "second largest minority." It accomplished this, however, without ever really defining who Spanish speakers were. Thus, instead of outlining which Latin American or immigrant groups would be covered by CCOSSP, or defining what assimilation meant, CCOSSP officials used lofty narratives about culture to define their constituency. For example, in its reports, radio programs, and publications, CCOSSP reiterated that America's Spanish speakers were united by a common language and a "common Hispanic culture straddling over 400 years."[171] CCOSSP officials also linked their terminology to American notions of upward mobility and claimed that Spanish speakers were united by a common immigrant desire to achieve socioeconomic parity with other groups. For CCOSSP the concept of "the Spanish Speaking" was more than a bureaucratic category; it formed an American constituency that sought equal membership in US society.

Let us, however, consider a counterfactual set of events. Suppose that Johnson had not created the IMAA but, rather, developed a forum that allowed all of those interested to voice their grievances and political demands. Although this might have seemed a waste of time and resources from Johnson's perspective, it could have allowed other issues and narrative frames to become prominent. Thus, there might have been important backing for the more militant "Chicano" land grant issues. Additionally, there could have been discussions about Puerto Rican sovereignty—and even talk about reparations for both Puerto Rican and Mexican American groups.

This alternative is not too far-fetched. In 1971 Puerto Rican and Mexican American leaders gathered in Washington for a unity conference. Although there was raucous arguing on both sides, the final manifesto of "Spanish Speaking" demands included recognition of the land grants and Puerto Rican independence.[172] More important, conference participants depicted themselves as unified not simply by language, but by their experiences of discrimination and colonization and a common history of domination and oppression vis-à-vis Anglo Americans.[173]

In effect, IMAA and CCOSSP officials, working with members of Congress, stifled alternative interpretations of panethnicity. These bureaucrats obscured more militant expressions about oppression and self-determination, and they never suggested that Mexican Americans and Puerto Ricans could be united by their common experience of colonization. Instead, they broadened the notion of "the Spanish Speaking" to include Cubans and others and emphasized a Hispanic unity through language. Even those statesmen who became weary of CCOSSP and were more sympathetic to the cultural nationalist claims of Chicanos and Puerto Ricans ended up helping reinforce a more benign, panethnic narrative. Indeed, Roybal, who often criticized CCOSSP's attachment to Nixon's policies, never really questioned the use of the Spanish language as the basis for a panethnic classification.[174]

Ultimately, the notion of a category for "the Spanish Speaking" did not emerge from a single advocate or agency. Instead, it emerged from a classification struggle in a new political field occupied by state officials and activists. By developing government agencies and endowing them with the symbolic power to articulate group issues and needs, Johnson and Nixon attempted to disarm militant factions and absorb the demands of Mexican Americans and Puerto Ricans. Ximenes, Castillo, and Ramirez were given authority to advocate on behalf of all Spanish speakers and to create reports that defined "Spanish Speaking" issues. These representatives ultimately depicted "the Spanish Speaking" as an American minority bent on achieving the American dream. In doing so, elected officials were able to define a constituency and develop a bureaucratized category that could extend and further legitimate, instead of threaten, government policies.

Yet co-optation on its own was not sufficient. Much more work had to be done before Hispanic panethnicity could become the basis of national political and market organizations. And much more effort had to be expended to make Hispanic panethnicity seem like a natural by-product of history rather than a tactic in the federal government's strategy. The next chapter thus examines more closely how activists bought into the idea of panethnicity, and how they worked to connect the Spanish-speaking/Hispanic category to collective identity narratives.

TWO

The Rise of a Hispanic Lobby: The National Council of La Raza

While the White House and Congress were busy devising a "Spanish Speaking" government agency, activists were responding by experimenting with new forms of organization. African American issues dominated discussions of civil rights at the time, and Mexican American and Puerto Rican activists observed the development of the new agency with both hope and suspicion. The label "Spanish Speaking" signaled that the federal government had begun to take seriously the fact that Mexican American and Puerto Rican communities lacked resources and that their experiences were distinct from those of European immigrant communities. Activists suspected, however, that policy makers would remain focused on African American issues and would not follow through with support for Spanish speakers' causes. As activists tried to gain traction within the civil rights movement, some saw the need for a panethnic, Hispanic organizational structure.

This chapter reveals how these changes unfolded by focusing on the rise and transformation of the National Council of La Raza (NCLR), the nation's foremost "Hispanic" civil rights advocacy organization. NCLR, originally named the Southwest Council of La Raza, was established as a Chicano organization in the late 1960s, a time when there were virtually no national, panethnic organizations. By 1990 the

Table 1 Changes in the National Council of La Raza, 1970–90

	1970	1990
Agenda	Protest activities—i.e., protesting local instances of discrimination against Chicanos Programs—i.e., funding and implementation of job training programs and day-care centers	Policy analysis and research Technical assistance to Hispanic community organizations Media programs about Hispanics Legislative advocacy/lobbying
Structure	Regional—California, Texas, New Mexico, Arizona, Colorado	National—including constituent affiliates in Puerto Rico
Funding	Ford Foundation	Federal government grants, philanthropic foundations, corporate foundations
Identity	Mexican American, Chicano	Hispanic, Latino, Hispanic American

organization had evolved into a Hispanic advocacy group that provided resources for Mexican American, Puerto Rican, and Cuban American constituents alike. Table 1 provides a detailed snapshot of these organizational changes.

This chapter argues that issues of resource procurement and networks were at the core of NCLR's transition. Put simply, NCLR found that it could best secure more resources from state and private grant-making agencies if it could frame its constituency as a sizable *national*, rather than regional, minority group that stretched from coast to coast. To make its claims about panethnicity seem credible, NCLR built networks with federal bureaucrats, especially those within the Census Bureau, and learned to incorporate CCOSSP reports as well as Hispanic census data in its grant applications. Over time, NCLR's networks also extended to Spanish-language media executives, who helped activists create national cultural projects that could promote the notion of a Hispanic community. By 1990 NCLR had become the nation's foremost Hispanic advocacy organization and a central player in what would develop into a national field centered on the idea of Hispanic panethnicity.

To be sure, NCLR was not the first organization to espouse the idea of panethnicity. Some small local organizations in more diverse cities like New York attracted Puerto Ricans and Cubans alike, and some well-established southwestern organizations, such as the League of United Latin American Citizens (LULAC), had emphasized for decades that persons of Latin American descent were bonded by a shared Spanish culture.[1] Yet many of the local panethnic organizations were short-lived, and broader organizations like LULAC spoke about panethnicity but remained focused on Mexican Americans in the Southwest.[2] By contrast, NCLR was the first organization to embody the notion of panethnicity and actively court Puerto Rican, Mexican American, and Cuban American constituents at a national level.

The Establishment of the Southwest Council of La Raza

The late 1960s were both exciting and frustrating for Mexican American activists in the Southwest. On the one hand, the African American civil rights movement had inspired a new cohort of young activists to expose the high levels of poverty and discrimination that Mexican American communities endured. These student and grassroots groups organized protests and joined higher-profile organizations, such as César Chávez's United Farm Workers, to bring national attention to the Mexican American condition. For the most part, these young activists called themselves "Chicanos" and promoted a cultural nationalist discourse that used Aztec symbolism to remind others of their indigenous, not simply Spanish, roots and to decry the seemingly colonized status of Mexican American communities. Just as Native American communities had been colonized and displaced by European settlers, they argued, so too had Mexican communities been colonized by the United States during its westward expansion. Labeling the more established "Spanish American" activist groups, such as LULAC, as sellouts for emphasizing assimilation and a connection to Spain, Chicanos drew a clear racial line between Mexican Americans and the descendants of European migration. For Chicanos, Mexican Americans constituted a "*raza*," a distinct racial minority that had been persecuted and stripped of its southwestern lands.[3]

At the same time, government officials began establishing ties with certain, arguably more conservative, Mexican American civic leaders. As we saw in chapter 1, President Lyndon B. Johnson named Vicente Ximenes, a member of LULAC and the American GI Forum (AGIF), as the head of a newly established Inter-Agency Committee on Mexican American Affairs (IMAA) in 1967. The new agency was created to serve as an advocate for Mexican American issues within the federal government and, putatively, to steer federal monies to southwestern barrios.

These political developments triggered new political agendas, organizations, and networks, helping to diversify Mexican American politics. On one side were the Chicano groups that were led by youth and student leaders and were aimed at consciousness-raising. On the other side were the more established and conservative integrationist groups that sought to promote social mobility through government alliances.

The late 1960s, though, were also a time of frustration. The Johnson and the early Nixon administrations paid more attention to African American than to Mexican American causes, which discouraged Mexican American groups across the political spectrum. Herman Gallegos, a prominent activist involved in both integrationist and Chicano organizations, claimed publicly that the Chicano walkouts and protests in the late 1960s always went unnoticed because rioting in African American communities captured the attention of policy makers:

Every time we walk out in Albuquerque, we're clouted by something happening in Selma or Montgomery. . . . We are invisible to the eyes of public officials in this country. . . . [Every] time we have a legitimate set of complaints to present to city hall Watts is burning or Rochester is burning and the federal money [goes] to black programs.[4]

Mexican American scholars and researchers echoed this disappointment. Julian Samora, the nation's first Mexican American sociology professor, published a monograph in 1966 titled *La Raza: Forgotten People*, which argued that Mexican Americans suffered from socioeconomic inequality and government neglect.

In the late 1960s, Samora, working with Herman Gallegos and others, secured a planning grant from the Ford Foundation and established the Southwest Council of La Raza (SWCLR). As an academic, Samora had worked on a few Ford-funded research projects and had ties to foundation officials. As a researcher and community organizer, Gallegos had previously worked on an urban development project funded by the Ford Foundation. In June of 1968, these two men received what would amount to a total of $630,000 to develop an organization that would assist Mexican American communities. The grant was part of a larger disbursement that the Ford Foundation made to Mexican American leaders in the Southwest, including those who established the Mexican American Legal Defense and Education Fund (MALDEF) in 1967.[5]

Given that so much national attention was focused on African Americans, why did the Ford Foundation provide funds for Mexican Americans? There are two important reasons.[6] First, Samora used his research on Mexican Americans to persuade foundation officials. Although the study presented in *La Raza* had been hindered by a lack of adequate census data, the book and other similar reports called national attention to conditions in Mexican American communities.[7] Second, by the late 1960s, the federal government had taken a step toward acknowledging these conditions by creating the IMAA, which sought to frame Mexican Americans as a distinct American minority group.

Samora and Gallegos established SWCLR six days after receiving the grant. The organization's name was likely inspired by the title of Samora's book. In *La Raza*, Samora noted that government labels such as "Spanish Speaking" and "Spanish Surname" excluded a large percentage of Mexican Americans. "Spanish Speaking" implied that the community was limited to those who spoke Spanish, even though many second- and third-plus-generation immigrants had attended schools where Spanish was not allowed and thus lacked Spanish fluency. "Spanish Surname" implied that the community did not include Mexican Americans with surnames that did not sound Spanish. Samora argued that the term *La Raza*—literally, "the race"—was the most inclusive, embracing Mexican Americans, undocumented Mexican residents, and self-described Chicanos of all surnames and language abilities.[8]

The people whom Samora and Gallegos invited to join SWCLR's executive board spanned the Chicano-integrationist spectrum. Self-described Chicano activists such as Maclovio Barraza, an organizer with the AFL-CIO, Bert Corona, the president of the Community Service Organization, and Alex Mercure, a student activist in New Mexico, sat alongside relatively more conservative integrationists such as Albert Peña, an elected official from Texas.[9] Miguel F. Barragán, another Texan, was a Mexican American Catholic priest and member of the Catholic Bishop's Committee on the Spanish Speaking (which at the time was focused mainly on Mexican Americans, especially migrant farm laborers); Barragán opened the first board meeting, on June 16, with a prayer.[10]

At that first meeting, the group discussed using the Ford Foundation money to develop an umbrella organization that would disburse grant money and provide other assistance to community groups across the Southwest. SWCLR's constituents would be the community organizations that received SWCLR's assistance rather than dues-paying members. This configuration was unique: other groups had a rank-and-file membership or engaged in direct service. The board also decided that SWCLR would have an executive director—Gallegos—and an administrative staff that would be based in Phoenix, Arizona.

A large organization like SWCLR, one that funded community groups through foundation grants, had never before been established for Mexican Americans, so the board's first goal was to determine how SWCLR could make a contribution that would not reproduce the efforts of other organizations. SWCLR leaders thought hard about what organizational structure could best help alleviate inequality for Mexican Americans.[11] Two questions drove these discussions: What kind of activities would SWCLR support? Which community groups would receive SWCLR funds?

Samora envisioned a group that would have a "broad structure" and would assist neighborhood organizations engaged in direct services.[12] Board member Bert Corona, in contrast, wanted SWCLR to help establish Mexican American councils that would "meet regularly to discuss common problems and to plan a strategy for combating the establishment." He and other board members imagined an organization that would provide funds for demonstrations and consciousness-raising efforts at the local level. The power to determine community needs would reside with the community affiliates, not with SWCLR leadership or the Ford Foundation.[13]

Some board members, however, feared that Corona's vision would estrange the Ford Foundation, and they appealed for more moderate projects like job training programs. The issue quickly created factions within the leadership and developed into discussions about the organization's identity. The rifts escalated, and in 1969 some board members who favored consciousness-raising and protesting resigned. In a later interview, Bert Corona described the reason for his, and others', disaffection:

Despite all of the talk of the grassroots organizing, [the Southwest Council of La Raza] in fact represented organization from the top. . . . [SWCLR leaders] were beholden to the Ford Foundation. This limited the effectiveness and autonomy of the group and steered it towards an establishment perspective.[14]

The program that ultimately emerged from these early rifts balanced social service projects with protest-based activities. Between 1969 and 1973, SWCLR funded bilingual education programs in Oakland, job training programs in Los Angeles, and day-care centers in San Antonio. Over time, its social service mandate evolved to include research projects as the board realized that it would need data on the Mexican American population to determine what projects would have the greatest impact.[15] SWCLR also organized walkouts and activist conferences. In 1969 it helped stage a walkout at a National Institute of Mental Health conference to draw attention to the lack of resources being directed to Mexican American mental health issues. Similar walkouts were coordinated to protest the poor quality of public schools in Mexican American neighborhoods. Further protest-based activities included a voter registration program designed to raise consciousness about the importance of voting. In addition, SWCLR provided community affiliates with resources to organize conferences. For instance, it funded a series of "Chicano student conferences" in California and Texas that aimed to "iron out major ideological differences" among Chicano student groups.[16]

Indeed, SWCLR learned to balance direct service and protest-based projects as it attempted to situate itself at the center of Mexican American politics in the late 1960s. Its structure as an umbrella organization made it unique, and its commitment to social service helped the organization maintain ties with more established groups on both ends of the political spectrum. However, SWCLR did not simply promote a centrist discourse; rather, the organization cultivated both seemingly nationalist and conservative discourses to relay its goals and perspectives to different audiences. For example, consider a speech made by Henry Santiestevan, SWCLR's first executive director, to Chicanos about "La Raza":

Chicanos share . . . the imposed burden of being acquired by conquest. The dead hand of old conquerors still holds them in the bony grip of hostile attitudes, ranging from personal prejudice to institutionalized racism. . . . They have been contained in the bleakness of poverty, forced to live in the blighted centers of urban deterioration and to accept the shambles of an inferior education system. . . . It is time for La Raza to take its place on the national scene.[17]

SWCLR leaders, however, were also mindful of the organization's backers, and thus they used a more moderate discourse in their correspondence with Ford and other grant-making agencies.

Yet the Ford Foundation was not always pleased with SWCLR's protest-based activities, and it took some steps to shape the organization's agenda. For example, in an early 1969 letter, a Ford official warned SWCLR that links with the Mexican American Youth Organization (MAYO) would not be viewed favorably. MAYO, a nationalist group, had recently been tagged as militant and violent by some congressmen because its members had nailed a manifesto of demands onto a Texas courthouse door.[18] Up to that point, SWCLR had provided MAYO with funding to create a Chicano youth conference. Fearful of negative publicity, the Ford Foundation warned that the relationship between the two organizations and the "apparent advocacy of violence" would not be tolerated.[19] Much of this pressure stemmed from the Ford Foundation's own troubles with Congress and the Nixon administration, which were pressuring the foundation to desist from funding nationalist projects. Although McGeorge Bundy, the Ford Foundation's president, attempted to resist by arguing that cultural nationalist groups were focused mostly on providing vital services and resources in their communities, the foundation eventually shifted course.[20]

Aside from the question of nationalism, the Ford Foundation was also concerned about SWCLR's structure. The foundation had hoped that SWCLR would evolve into a national civil rights advocacy organization similar to the NAACP or the National Urban League, which also received Ford Foundation funding. These more established groups, however, had hammered out their agenda several decades earlier, received multimillion-dollar grants, and were recognized as the nation's foremost civil rights organizations. By contrast, SWCLR had a limited budget and lacked institutional presence, and it had spread itself thin by supporting too many projects. SWCLR simply couldn't compare to the more established African American organizations. The nascent group was trying to discern its identity and establish itself within the arena of Mexican American politics.

Nonetheless, SWCLR grew rapidly. By late 1972 the organization was sponsoring thirteen community affiliates and funding programs in cities such as Albuquerque and Phoenix.[21] Juggling commitments to community affiliates, an emerging research agenda, and even some financial investments, the organization soon realized that it needed to diversify its funding portfolio and garner resources from other grant-making agencies to keep its programs running. Fortunately, by that time Richard Nixon had been reelected and members of CCOSSP had promised that his administration would steer more funds to Mexican American communities. With these possibilities in mind, SWCLR turned its gaze toward the nation's capital.

National Status and a Broader Constituency

Sensing the importance of the national scene, SWCLR's board members had voted to change the organization's name to the National Council of La Raza in late 1972[22] and began plans to move its headquarters to Washington, DC.[23] A year later, Santiestevan, who had been the executive director since 1970, resigned and was replaced by Raul Yzaguirre. Yzaguirre hailed from San Juan, Texas. Even though he was only thirty-four when he was appointed, he had vast experience working in community activism and civil rights advocacy. Yzaguirre was a veteran who had received a BA from American University with the assistance of the GI Bill. After graduating, he had helped to establish the National Organization for Mexican American services (NOMAS), which was one of the first Mexican American groups to ask the Ford Foundation for a grant (it was turned down).[24] Additionally, Yzaguirre had established Inter-Agency Research, which specialized in creating policy reports on Mexican American communities.

Yzaguirre was a likely candidate because he had experience with and sympathy for integrationist as well as Chicano groups. As a member of AGIF, he had links to the more conservative groups and probably understood the importance of acculturation for Mexican Americans' social mobility. Yet, having come of age in the 1960s, he had also been influenced by African American civil rights protests, and he sympathized with the aims of some Chicano nationalist organizations.[25]

The move to Washington, DC, came as the organization was grappling with tough questions about its constituency. During the early 1970s, the executive board and the staff held a series of meetings about the relationship between NCLR and its constituent community organizations and the relationship between NCLR and the grant-making agencies on which it depended. These discussions ultimately led to a series of new programmatic statements expressed in amendments to the group's constitution, the development of a corporate structure, and the adoption of a Hispanic corporate identity.

From Community Development to National Lobbying

By 1973 NCLR represented thirteen affiliates.[26] Five were community affiliates that SWCLR had established in 1968 and financed heavily. The rest were newer affiliates that NCLR had added to expand its coverage and to prove to the Ford Foundation that it was growing and becoming a leader within Mexican American politics. At the same time, NCLR began finding it expensive to support its growing constituency.

Yzaguirre and his staff decided that the best way to address the financial issue would be to alter NCLR's relationship with its affiliates. For the five charter affiliates, the organization would continue to fund their projects, provide local-level technical assistance, and help with federal grant procurement. For newer affiliates, NCLR would provide only grant-writing and technical assistance. The move to Washington placed NCLR executives close to the agencies that disbursed federal resources, and NCLR believed that it could best help new affiliates by facilitating their access to these funds. By positioning itself as an information broker instead of a grant maker to new affiliates, NCLR could expand its constituency in a cost-effective manner.[27]

NCLR executives understood, however, that the organization's new structure had a disadvantage: once community organizations learned how to win federal grants on their own, they would no longer rely on NCLR for support. Its success could lead to its demise. Board members pondered the issue as they tried to hammer out a new agenda for the organization. The issue came to a head in the mid-1970s, when board members suggested that NCLR follow the path of some African American organizations and focus more on policy research and lobbying. In 1977 one executive board member stated bluntly that although NCLR affiliates had needed NCLR funding "maybe ten years ago," they now

probably have better experts on [their] local staff than we have on the national level. . . . We have to start moving on the national scene. . . . There is no *national* Chicano organization that can really focus in on the national scene. I say we need "sophisticated hell raising." With the administration, with Congress . . . [because] we are going to need a hell of a lot of money for our people. [And] though those dollars won't specifically be channeled through this organization, but because of the results of this organization, that money is going to be channeled to those local affiliates.[28]

By focusing on lobbying, NCLR could still assist community organizations, but on a broader level. NCLR's leaders concluded that forging networks with elected officials, testifying before Congress, and creating lobbying campaigns would eventually produce more resources for Mexican American communities. In addition, the new focus could help the organization to gain prominence on a national level. Most other Mexican American organizations were still based in the Southwest, and they focused on regional or state politics. NCLR could become the voice of the Mexican American community in Washington, DC.

Lobbying in Washington for Mexican American causes remained difficult, however, because African American issues still had prominence in the discourse on minority rights. The NAACP and the National Urban League had established themselves in Washington decades earlier, and both had a larger and more sophisticated lobbying apparatus than NCLR had.[29] Their efforts were bolstered by black congressional representatives who made African American civil rights a priority. In comparison, NCLR and MALDEF, which had been established in Washington for less than a year, had only a handful of Mexican American congressional representatives to turn to. In fact, in 1975 black congressional representatives outnumbered Mexican American representatives more than threefold.[30]

Another reason NCLR found it difficult to obtain support for its causes was that many policy makers considered Mexican Americans a regional, rather than a national, minority. Although NCLR could gain the support of some southwestern representatives, the broader group of representatives from the Northeast, South, and Midwest tended to ignore the organization's efforts. NCLR activists tried to shift this perception. In congressional testimony delivered in the summer of 1975, an NCLR representative chided Congress for viewing African American issues as national but Mexican American issues as "not national in scope, but regional in nature."[31] He then went on to cite the number of Mexican Americans living in the Midwest, Northwest, and South, and declared that NCLR's constituency was a national minority that rivaled the size and scope of the African American population.[32]

In effect, NCLR had to find a way to reframe itself and its constituents as *national*. During a fateful 1977 meeting, one member suggested that this could be accomplished if NCLR's lobbying efforts were carried out on behalf of the broader Hispanic community, because while Mexican Americans were clustered primarily in the Southwest, Hispanics were found on both coasts. Lobbying on behalf of Hispanics, the member continued, would not only benefit NCLR and Mexican Americans vis-à-vis federal grant-making agencies but also provide real help to other communities that were not connected to state resources:

We are the only organization in the country that has a full staff in Washington, D.C. So by that mere fact, if nothing else, we can become a key coordinating element on what is happening in the entire Chicano [and] Latino community throughout the country.[33]

Another member agreed and stated that NCLR could take advantage of a historic opportunity to become a spokesperson for *"the entire Hispanic community."*[34]

In effect, NCLR's lobbying shift steered it toward a panethnic agenda. The notion of Mexican American was simply too regional, and NCLR believed that it could gain better access to government funds if it could frame its constituency as national. And soon after NCLR made this shift, its leaders launched a major campaign to present Hispanics as a national constituency. In an op-ed piece published in the *Washington Post*, Raul Yzaguirre argued that Hispanics resided "throughout the nation":

[NCLR] has been trying for some time to call national attention to the rapid growth and potential impact of Hispanic Americans on the nation's future. . . . [Yet, until] now, the Latino community has been relegated to regional coverage. In reality, we are a national entity deserving of national coverage and concern.[35]

Let us consider for a moment, however, whether NCLR could have simply remained an organization focused on Mexican Americans. By 1974 this would have been a bit difficult to do in Washington for various reasons. As mentioned in chapter 1, by then CCOSSP and some congressmen, such as Edward Roybal (D-CA), had already spearheaded a movement to develop a category for "the Spanish Speaking." Through their efforts, other government agencies had begun to see not only Mexican Americans but also Puerto Ricans and Cubans as part of a broader underrepresented minority group that deserved special protections. Thus, to the extent that government grant-making agencies, such as those in HEW, considered Mexican Americans as minorities, they likely had already begun to see them as part of the broader "Spanish Speaking" community.

Indeed, had NCLR simply stayed in the Southwest and focused on regional politics, it could have created a disaggregated umbrella structure that focused on lobbying state or municipal agencies for resources. This would have allowed it to tap into state and local funds and carry out local projects in cities throughout the Southwest. Yet the move to Washington placed NCLR within a different political field altogether. In this broader field of minority politics, federal grant-making agencies likely drew on the larger administrative categories advanced by the state, and NCLR found itself having to adjust to new expectations about who minorities were and where they resided.

Panethnic Identity and Organizational Structure

NCLR leaders quickly realized that there were advantages to adopting the notion of Hispanic panethnicity. The most important was that after the 1970 census, the Census Bureau had begun to release reports and data on the "Spanish Origin" population—a category that included Mexican Americans as well as Cuban Americans and Puerto Ricans. By the mid-1970s NCLR had started using the newly developed Spanish-origin data to apply for grants from various government agencies and to create policy reports. For example, one of NCLR's reports from 1975 on Hispanic voter registration noted that Census Bureau data showed that "40 percent of all Spanish Origin persons were never registered to vote in 1974."[36] Reports like these were used to lobby for resources for projects that were targeted toward this population, such as Spanish-language voter information campaigns and registration drives.

To be sure, data on Hispanics were not necessarily abundant, and those government agencies that did collect such data, among them the Census

Bureau, provided no guarantee that they would do so consistently. Although CCOSSP had persuaded the Census Bureau to add the question about Spanish origin for the 1970 census, the agency could not assure activists that the category would be used on the 1980 census. Moreover, other agencies that CCOSSP had tried to influence, including the Department of Health, Education, and Welfare (HEW) and the US Department of Labor, still collected data on this population only intermittently.[37]

Additionally, several other government agencies simply refused to report on the Hispanic population. Although the US Department of Agriculture released regular reports that mentioned the relative differences between white and black farmers, it never provided data on Spanish-speaking farmers.[38] Perhaps most frustrating for NCLR and other activists was the fact that the Office of Management and Budget's *Social Indicators* report, which was designed to aid policy makers, reported on black and white differences across a variety of dimensions, but placed information on the Spanish-speaking population within the "white" category.[39]

Sensing that the availability of national data would be important for reinforcing panethnic claims, NCLR joined a campaign to help institutionalize "Hispanic" as a category across government agencies. In 1973 Roybal submitted a bill that would require all government agencies that collected racial data to collect information on "the Spanish Speaking." In support of this effort, NCLR representatives testified before Congress that "Hispanic Americans" were a disadvantaged minority group that deserved representation in data sets and government reports. In addition, an NCLR representative submitted a copy of one of NCLR's reports, *Impact of Limits of Federal Statistical Data/Information Policies on Hispanic Americans*, to the *Congressional Record*. The report argued that federal agencies were masking the inequality experienced by "Hispanic Americans" by not extracting their data from that of white European Americans.[40] A year later, in 1976, Congress passed the Roybal Act (PL 94-311).

By 1975 NCLR had become a political advocate for the notion of panethnicity, and it had also adopted the use of the term *Hispanic*. This had more to do with numbers than semantics. In testimony before Congress, NCLR representatives argued that the terms *Spanish Speaking* and *Spanish Origin* underestimated the larger Hispanic population because the terms were based on language use and a Spanish connection, respectively. Those who could not speak Spanish or those who refused to trace their ancestry to Spain, such as the growing number of Chicano nationalists, would not identify with the more restrictive terms. *Hispanic American* was broad enough to encompass the entire Latin American diaspora in the United States.[41] In effect, NCLR was pushing for an expansive definition of its constituency, and it was leading a charge to resurrect the term, which IMAA officials had rejected a few years earlier.

During this time NCLR started its transition to a panethnic organization by strategically allocating its resources to Puerto Rican and Cuban American organizations. NCLR's first northeastern affiliate was the East Harlem Council for Human Services, a Puerto Rican organization that received grant money to establish a job training program. NCLR found it easier to attract Puerto Rican than Cuban American affiliates. Because Puerto Ricans had been engaged in community development during the early 1970s, they already had an array of community service organizations that searched for the very resources and grant monies that NCLR could provide.

The recruitment of Cuban American organizations was more difficult for several reasons. On the one hand, Cuban American communities boasted very few social service organizations, in large part because their civic leaders were focused on foreign policy issues.[42] Moreover, the social service organizations that did exist were often suspicious of NCLR's agenda. For all of its panethnic discourse, NCLR was mainly Mexican American, and Cuban American leaders in Miami did not support the close ties between the governments of Mexico and Cuba. This stance toward Mexico often spilled over into animosity toward Mexican American organizations.[43] It did not help that some Chicano and Puerto Rican nationalists had begun to incorporate Cuban revolutionary symbols, such as the image of Che Guevara and the writings of Fidel Castro, into materials generated within their organizations.[44]

A broader discourse about class and social mobility also made it difficult to attract Cuban American affiliates. Put simply, some argued that Cuban Americans belonged in a different category because they had a higher educational and class status than did Mexican Americans and Puerto Ricans.[45] Under these circumstances, it was hard for NCLR to justify the establishment of Cuban American affiliates to either potential Cuban American networks or its own Mexican American and Puerto Rican constituency. NCLR thus held off pursuing Cuban affiliates until it could devise an organization that both accepted a disadvantaged minority status and focused on community service rather than foreign policy.[46]

In the late 1970s, NCLR found its opportunity as community advocates began forming organizations to help Cuban refugees. These Cubans were different from those in the early waves of émigrés—they were less likely to have descended from Cuba's elite Spanish families and more likely to be laborers with darker skin and fewer white-collar skills. Cuban Americans such as Guarione Diaz and Arnhilda Gonzalez-Quevedo quickly established social service organizations to help these refugees, and they soon turned to NCLR for resources. NCLR responded by providing funds for English-language classes, job training programs, and housing assistance projects.[47] By connecting with these lower-profile organizations, NCLR leaders could sidestep the broader issue of foreign relations and still claim to represent Cuban Americans, which allowed them to present NCLR as a national Hispanic organization.

Defining Hispanic Panethnicity

Equally important, NCLR embarked on a cultural campaign to define Hispanic panethnicity. In 1977 it changed the name of its newsletter from *Agenda* to *Agenda: A Journal of Hispanic Issues*. All of the articles, even if they were about Mexican Americans, would use the term *Hispanic* in some way. For example, *Agenda*'s May–June 1977 special issue was titled "Hispanics in the Arts," even though all of the articles were about Mexican American muralists. The articles in this issue used the terms *Hispanic* and *Mexican American* interchangeably.[48]

Initially, NCLR sought only to popularize the term *Hispanic* and connect it to the idea of an underrepresented minority. These efforts were most prominent in NCLR's Census Bureau lobbying. Indeed, during the 1970s, members of NCLR met with officials from the bureau to persuade them to classify "Hispanics" as distinct from whites. These efforts were broadcast in NCLR's newsletter, with NCLR leadership arguing that the Census Bureau should categorize Latino subgroups as "Hispanic Americans" because this would best convey their national minority group status. For example, Yzaguirre wrote:

The underlying problem is one of a conflict between the utilization of an ethnic [panethnic] classification for the Hispanic-American and the utilization of a national origin [subgroup] classification. . . . In redefining the Hispanic American identifier on the level of [subgroup] nationality, [federal agencies] place that sector of the population on the level of other national origin subgroups, rather than the level of a minority group. There is a difference between a minority group and a national origin group—a difference recognized in terms of national economic and social policies as well as a lengthy, broad ranging legal history relative to civil and minority rights.[49]

In effect, NCLR argued that the institutionalization of a broad panethnic term like *Hispanic American* would help to define Mexican Americans, Puerto Ricans, and others as national minorities, not simply as immigrant groups that were similar to European immigrant communities. Without a panethnic identification, the article continued, the Latin American diaspora would be perceived as disparate subgroups whose needs could be met through immigration legislation rather than civil rights policy.

It was not until 1978, however, that NCLR began to tackle the issue of what Hispanic panethnicity actually meant. Until then, NCLR leaders had argued that Latin American subgroups were part of a broader minority group and thus shared experiences of discrimination and underrepresentation, but they had never explained exactly *how* Hispanics were united. NCLR leaders tackled this question by applying for a grant from the National Endowment for the Humanities (NEH) to fund a series of articles by Puerto Rican, Mexican American, and Cuban American writers about the meaning of panethnicity. The articles focused on four themes—roots, language, culture, and character—that together underscored "the likenesses and the basic common heritage that all Hispanics share."[50] In a letter to the NEH, an NCLR executive stated that the articles spoke "to the entire Hispanic population" rather than specific segments of it "by not simply concentrating on Mexican Americans."[51] The project culminated in fifteen articles that were published in *Agenda: A Journal of Hispanic Issues* in 1979.

How did the NCLR-sponsored articles define *Hispanic*? An examination reveals a few broad topics: diversity, racial mixing, language, family, religion, immigration, and inequality. Most important was the idea that Hispanics were not homogenous but a diverse group with different cultures, accents, and phenotypes. One article, titled "Reflecting on Common Hispanic Roots," noted that Hispanics were "a people of different colors and hues."[52] This diversity was described mainly by contrasting Mexican Hispanics, who were primarily of Spanish and Indian extraction, with Caribbean Hispanics (Puerto Ricans, Dominicans, and Cubans), who were primarily of African and Spanish descent. These differences, some articles argued, translated into everyday cultural traditions. Hence, one article stated:

[The] traditions of Puerto Rico and Cuba are a blend of African and Spanish folk practices adapted to their new island homes, while [those] of Mexico [are] more of a blend of the Indian and Spanish folk traditions, melded and adapted in the highland valleys of New Spain.[53]

Other articles argued that language differences among Latin Americans had been shaped by Native and African influences. One piece contended that the reason that Mexicans call turkeys *guajolotes* and Puerto Ricans call them *pavos* was because *guajolote* stemmed from the Nahuatl

(Aztec) word for turkey. Elements of Nahuatl, the article continued, had been incorporated into Mexican Spanish in part because indigenous communities in Mexico, unlike those in Puerto Rico, had not been immediately slaughtered by the Spanish during the conquest.[54]

What is interesting is that the NCLR articles never mentioned the different political and class issues that actually fractured these subgroups. Diversity was discussed in terms of foods, customs, and skin tone, but not in terms of Republican or Democratic leanings or socioeconomic status. Thus, there was never any mention, for example, of how the status and education of Cuban exiles who arrived in the United States before the 1980s placed them in a higher socioeconomic class vis-à-vis Mexican labor migrants. NCLR's focus on cultural diversity allowed it to ignore issues of class diversity and political differences.

Despite the emphasis on diversity, many of the panethnic articles also sought to underscore cultural uniformity and similarity. Thus, one article concluded:

The specific ethnic composition of Chicanos, Puerto Ricans and Cubans [is] different . . . but they share a common yearning for ethnic affirmation. Their folk heroes and types are not the same, yet they are comparable. Their artistic expression . . . is varied yet similar. It seems to me that the next step is to make sure that the similarities overshadow the differences, for only by cultivating a spirit of community can the greatest cultural aspirations of all Hispanics find fulfillment in a country in which they are a minority.[55]

The commonalities were usually identified as family and family traditions, religion, and the experience of migration. Several articles thus mentioned that Hispanics shared a devotion to popular religion and noted that there were only slight differences between Mexican American and Cuban American beliefs and values.[56] The most important commonality, however, was the experience of inequality. The articles consistently noted that Hispanics had been victims of discrimination and were less well-off than other US population groups.[57] At the same time, however, they also noted that Hispanics had not been deterred by such inequality, for they had developed a sense of social justice that was expressed through a communal striving for upward social mobility.[58]

In effect, the definitions employed to make these arguments of difference and cultural similarity were often inconsistent. One article mentioned that Mexican American families gave importance to their paternal lineage, whereas Puerto Ricans had a "more matrifocal tendency."[59] Another article, however, noted that the Puerto Rican and Mexican American tendency to maintain a patriarchal family structure had to do with a similar "hacienda" culture that developed in nineteenth-century Mexico and Puerto Rico.[60] NCLR's publicity efforts ultimately showed that, rather than having a uniform description of Hispanic panethnicity, the organization struggled with, and was often ambiguous about, what exactly made Hispanics Hispanic.

Despite NCLR's inability to explain exactly how Latin American subgroups were united, the notion of Hispanic unity was important because it provided the organization with the opportunity to represent a vast national constituency. The strategy apparently worked, for as NCLR evolved, it became more successful at diversifying its funding. By 1980 only 3 percent of its budget was funded by the Ford Foundation; the rest came mainly from federal grant-making agencies.[61]

The Forum of National Hispanic Organizations

The move to Washington and the new emphasis on lobbying for "Hispanic" civil rights motivated NCLR to help establish the Forum of National Hispanic Organizations (FNHO) in late 1976. That year NCLR convened an initial group of representatives from twelve professional, artistic, political, and community organizations. Although most organizations were based in the Southwest and focused on Mexican Americans, Cuban American and Puerto Rican groups such as the Association of Cuban American Government Employees and the National Conference for Puerto Rican Women also joined the FNHO early on.[62]

Why did NCLR help establish the FNHO? Given that NCLR's budget and membership were growing, why did it create a national coalition, and, more important, why did this coalition include non-Mexican groups? Two significant factors contributed to the establishment of the FNHO. The first was that African American groups had created a similar organization a few years earlier. In 1972 activists established the National Black Political Convention, which convened in Gary, Indiana. There, African American lobbying groups created an agenda of black policy issues that they presented to the Democratic and Republican parties.[63] The goal of the agenda was not only to spell out the needs and expectations of the black community but also to force the major political parties to commit to meeting some of these needs. Additionally, the convention provided an opportunity for African American leaders to devise a unified response to current political developments.[64]

In effect, NCLR and other groups understood the political value of the

African American agenda, and they were determined to follow the lead of black groups. At a 1979 FNHO planning meeting, members often referred to the structure of "national Black leadership" organizations as they tried to hammer out what their organization would look like.[65] By 1984 the FNHO had created a "National Hispanic Agenda" that reiterated many of the policy issues and recommendations outlined in the black agenda. The section on media, for example, called on political parties to "support the formation of a Hispanic equivalent to the National Black Media Coalition."[66]

Yet the African American model of organization was not the sole reason the FNHO was established. As we have seen, by the mid-1970s organizations had begun to recognize the need to present themselves as leaders of a national minority. Groups like AGIF, for example, had begun to advocate for a coalition movement that could help to bring national, rather than simply regional, political attention to Hispanic communities.[67] FNHO leaders also knew that certain issues, such as census enumeration and bilingual education, affected Cuban Americans, Puerto Ricans, and Mexican Americans alike and thus could be resolved most effectively through national efforts.[68]

The FNHO started by staging an open conference in 1976 for Mexican American, Cuban American, and Puerto Rican organizational leaders. The purpose of the conference was to explore wide-ranging concerns, and participants were invited to discuss any issue of importance to their constituencies. Discussion topics included strikes by the United Farm Workers (UFW) and the exploitation of workers in Central America by the United Fruit Company. NCLR took a lead role because the coalition's mission aligned with NCLR's existing work on behalf of Hispanics and because NCLR was one of the few Mexican American organizations with an office and full staff in Washington, DC.

Over time the organization developed a national agenda around eleven policy domains, which included political empowerment, economic development, arts and humanities, employment, administration of justice, and housing. It did this by hammering out a system in which member organizations were encouraged to submit concept papers to the FNHO secretariat concerning one national issue. In addition, members were instructed to choose an important local issue and reframe it as a national one. For example, the UFW shifted the focus of a complaint that striking farmworkers were being beaten by law enforcement by rephrasing the issue as "Police Brutality in the Hispanic Community."[69]

Repackaging local issues as national concerns became an important strategy for retaining non-Mexican organizations in the FNHO. Early

on, Puerto Rican leaders were skeptical of the FNHO's ability to go beyond Mexican American issues and represent the interests of other subgroups. These complaints seemed to fizzle when policy reframing became
a standard practice.[70] Non-Mexican groups also likely remained in the
FNHO because it was not a demanding commitment. The FNHO executive board met sporadically, sometimes only four times per year, and the
convention was held only once every four years.

Although the FNHO focused on eleven distinct policy domains, its
reports coalesced around a single concept, "Hisparity," which the FNHO
defined as "a call for parity for Hispanics in the social, political, and economic mainstream of the United States."[71] The term suggested that all
Latin American subgroups were united by a common culture and common experiences of disadvantage. By pairing arguments about inequality
with those about culture, the FNHO could obscure internal differences
among its members and present its agenda as representative of a cohesive
national panethnic group. This tactic is exemplified by the sentence cho-
sen to open the FNHO's 1980 report on its housing policy: " '*Mi Casa es Su
Casa*' declares that which is fundamental to a Hispanic: my home, grand
or humble, is a thing of value which I can share with pride."[72] The report
goes on to advocate for an increase in federal funding for community
revitalization programs in Hispanic barrios.[73] Statements that maintained
that Latin American subgroups had a shared culture were commonplace
by the time of the FNHO's conference in 1984.

By the late 1980s, the FNHO had gained national publicity and attracted high-profile Hispanic leaders such as Henry Cisneros, the mayor
of San Antonio. The reports issued by the FNHO continued to describe
Hispanics as a community united by both culture and the experience of
disadvantage, and NCLR continued to be an important organizer for and
member of the FNHO, even though the 1980s would prove to be a time
of tremendous change.

The Growth of Corporate Funding

In 1982 NCLR's funding was dramatically reduced when President Ronald Reagan instituted a series of budget cuts that severely diminished
resources for community development grants. These cuts threatened
NCLR because about 96 percent of the organization's funding now
came from government grant-making agencies.[74] NCLR employed a
staff of nearly a hundred, and it had taken on more policy and community development projects than ever before.[75] The cuts were so

draconian that NCLR leaders took loans from staff and board members to meet the organization's expenses.[76] Years later Yzaguirre described the years following the cuts as "the most difficult period of my life."[77]

To survive, NCLR leaders had to quickly devise a new funding strategy. The organization had three options: it could shrink and remain dependent on the federal government, it could increase its dependence on the Ford Foundation, or it could begin to court corporations for funds. They chose all three. NCLR trimmed its budget and reduced many of its programs. It turned to the Ford Foundation for funds, but this time it also asked other organizations, such as the Carnegie Corporation of New York and the Rockefeller Foundation, for resources. This second strategy was successful for two reasons. By 1980 NCLR had already become the nation's foremost Hispanic advocacy organization and had gained status through its presence in Washington. Foundations were thus more familiar with NCLR than they were with any other Hispanic organization. Moreover, by 1980 the Census Bureau had instituted a Hispanic category in the US census, and an abundance of data on the Hispanic condition was now available. NCLR capitalized on this by citing census data in its grant applications, contending that Hispanics were disadvantaged.

NCLR also turned to corporations for revenue for the first time. This strategy became extremely important not only because corporate contributions provided a new source of funds but also because corporate money seemed to come with less oversight. Government and foundation monies were usually given for particular programs, and the grants often strictly stipulated how each dollar could be spent. In addition, applying for a foundation grant could be costly. NCLR leaders often had to expend resources on data analysis or grant writing to create a competitive grant application, leaving the organization in the red until the funds came through. By contrast, NCLR found that corporate contributions could be solicited with less effort and that corporate funds could be spent with greater discretion.[78]

With this in mind, NCLR leaders aggressively courted corporations such as General Motors and Gulf Oil during the early 1980s. To be clear, NCLR had not devised a new strategy. In effect, NCLR followed the lead of African American groups such as the NAACP and the National Urban League, which had courted corporations since the 1970s.[79] Yzaguirre had extensive ties to these African American organizations and probably learned some tactics from them.[80] By 1985 more than 50 percent of NCLR's budget came from the corporate sector.[81]

Yet how was NCLR able to create connections or networks with corporate foundations in the first place? One answer becomes apparent when we examine the changes in the NCLR executive board. When the board was established, it was composed mainly of activists and scholars. The longest-serving board chairperson, Barraza, who served from 1968 to 1976, was a prominent labor union activist. When Barraza resigned, Juan Patlan, the director of an NCLR affiliate, took his place and stayed in the position for about five years. In 1981 Gilbert Vasquez was named chairman. Unlike the previous two chairs, Vasquez was a prominent businessman and also well connected: he was later appointed to the executive board of the 1984 Olympic Organizing Committee.

Further connections to the corporate world also came through ties that NCLR developed with an emerging group of media marketers. Specifically, NCLR turned to Alex Armendariz, a former member of Nixon's 1972 "Brown Mafia" reelection team who was now the owner of a firm that promoted the nascent notion of a Spanish consumer market. As a Hispanic marketing professional with experience working in a state grant-making agency, Armendariz was well positioned to help NCLR link to corporate America.[82] In addition, NCLR hired other Hispanic marketers to set up meetings with corporations that advertised on Spanish-language television.[83] Hiring Hispanic marketers as consultants proved a successful strategy. By the summer of 1981, these links had facilitated meetings between NCLR staff and the Washington representatives of several different Fortune 500 corporations.[84]

Yet it was one thing to establish contact with the corporate world; it was another to convince corporate foundations to contribute money to NCLR causes. For this, Armendariz and other consultants suggested that NCLR form a "nationwide corporate committee" composed of business executives who could advise the organization on which projects would be suitable for corporate funding.[85] The committee would function as an interface between NCLR and the corporate world. In addition, the marketers advised NCLR staff to appoint Hispanic corporate executives to positions on the NCLR board.[86]

These suggestions seem to have been followed. A few months after NCLR staff met with marketing consultants, Vazquez became the first businessman to be appointed executive board chair. NCLR also created a corporate advisory council.[87] Over time, this council grew to attract executives from powerful corporations, including Coca-Cola, Gulf Oil, and General Motors. In fact, Donald Rumsfeld of Gulf Oil eventually became an active and influential member of the council.[88]

Despite these changes, corporate executives often balked at the idea of giving money to a Hispanic organization, particularly when other organizations, especially African American ones, were also asking for funds. "Corporations [have supported] certain interests for years!" complained one executive. "Suddenly the Hispanic movement coalesces and money has to be taken from one faction to provide funding for Hispanic interests."[89]

NCLR leaders addressed these concerns by using census data. Throughout the early 1980s, NCLR leaders delivered presentations to corporations that described the education, employment, and income needs of Hispanics in America.[90] In doing so, NCLR leaders implied that Hispanics were a large, underserved population whose needs and size rivaled those of African Americans.

More important, NCLR conveyed to corporations that Hispanics constituted not only a distinct minority but also a consumer market. Upon the advice of marketing consultants, NCLR stressed to corporations that Hispanics were also consumers who were ripe for the picking. Thus, in letters to corporations, NCLR would often remind these firms that providing money for Hispanic causes would create a mutually beneficial relationship. For example, one corporate solicitation letter reminded potential donors that Hispanics represented "a $60 billion reserve of largely untapped purchasing power and human resources."[91] Another promised that reaching out to Hispanics would produce a new revenue stream:

Everybody's talking about it . . . THE HISPANIC MARKET. . . . Enough talk. . . . Stand up and participate . . . in the 1980 National Council of La Raza's Affiliate Conversion Center in Albuquerque New Mexico on July 23–26 1980. . . . Hispanics live in different cultural environments from their Anglo-American counterparts, yet their needs, desires and aspirations are, for the most part, the same. If you are looking for a chance to test your Hispanic advertising ideas in the most cost-effective method possible, we urge you to purchase a page of advertising space in our convention brochure. An ad in our brochure is an effective way of reaching the Hispanic leadership and building good will for your product or service. . . . A commitment on your part will yield results that will create a new profit center for you.[92]

The message was clear: contributions to Hispanic causes could translate into publicity and purchasing dollars from Hispanic consumers.

By the mid-1980s the idea of a Hispanic consumer market had become an important tool for NCLR leaders as they sought to lure long-term corporate contributions. They suggested that the Hispanic market was a viable one because Hispanics were numerous and had distinct cultural tastes and practices. Speaking at a 1982 corporate convention, Yzaguirre

reminded businessmen of what an investment in the Hispanic community could yield:

Purchasing Power. [Hispanic] ability to inject dollars into the system is conservatively
estimated to be $60 billion dollars per year. Hispanics have been shown to be very high
in brand loyalty, i.e. you do right by us and we'll do right by you.[93]

NCLR's strategies seemed to have been well received in the corporate
world. Corporations soon became important contributors to the organization's coffers, and executives themselves often pointed to NCLR's
structure as a model that others should follow. As one corporate executive noted:

Corporations are not used to Hispanics and are confused by the lack of homogene-
ity among Hispanics. *For example, Hispanics are Puerto Ricans, Mexican-Americans, and
Central Americans. Corporations don't understand why the different Hispanic groups within
a given community can't work together as one. That way the corporations could give one
grant to cover the whole community.*[94]

By the mid-1980s NCLR had become an important promoter of panethnicity and Hispanic marketing within the broader arena of minority
politics.

The Hispanic Market and Corporate Responsibility

The relationship between NCLR and corporate America, however, was
not always free of tension. Although the organization learned to use
the notion of a Hispanic market as a way to entice corporations, it also
learned to use it to penalize them. This strategy was mainly employed
toward corporations that NCLR felt consistently discriminated against
Hispanics.

These efforts began in the late 1970s, when the AFL-CIO called for
a national boycott of beverages produced by the Coors Brewing Company, alleging that the company employed unfair labor practices and
discriminatory hiring procedures.[95] Soon thereafter, NCLR and Mexican
American organizations began pointing to Coors's hiring discrimination
against Hispanics in the Southwest and began asking its members to refrain from purchasing Coors products. The potential loss of the Hispanic
market was especially acute for Coors because much of the company's
profit came from the Southwest (which, coincidentally, had the highest

percentages of Mexican American immigrants). Market research indicated that "Hispanics" in the Southwest drank about 46 percent more malt liquor than other groups. Thus, in an interview for *Advertising Age*, a Coors sales manager later noted that Hispanics had made the corporation a leader in the California malt liquor market: "You [couldn't] be No. 1 in California without the support of Hispanics."[96]

Despite the importance of the Hispanic market for its sales, Coors refused to revisit its Hispanic hiring practices. In response, NCLR coordinated an official meeting with five FNHO members: the US Hispanic Chamber of Commerce, the AGIF, the National Image Inc., the Cuban National Planning Council, and LULAC. Bringing these groups together was momentous because it enabled NCLR to turn a regional issue—hiring discrimination in the Southwest—into a national one. The coalition, known as the Hispanic Association for Corporate Responsibility (HACER), threatened Coors with a prolonged *national* Hispanic boycott.

In October 1984, HACER signed a pact with Coors and agreed to publicly ask its members to end their boycott of the brewer's products.[97] The agreement called for Coors to "devote $350 million over five years to Hispanic jobs and distributorships and to contract with Hispanic owned banks, suppliers, insurance companies and others."[98] In addition, the brewery also agreed "to spend 8.9 million on advertising and promotions" that projected "a positive image of Hispanics."[99] By the end of 1985, Coors had seen its sales increase by 14 percent, and it publicly noted that its sales in the "Hispanic community" had almost doubled.[100] By 1986 Coors had become the tenth largest advertiser in Spanish-language media. Indeed, *Advertising Age* called the sales jump "one of the most dramatic marketing turnarounds in modern corporate history."[101]

The creation of HACER and the signing of the Coors pact were an important step in NCLR's evolution. The organization's leaders had learned how to leverage the idea of Hispanics as a panethnic consumer market in a way that could threaten corporations and spark an economic movement. Soon thereafter, HACER began to target more companies for "fair share" agreements. In these agreements it asked for contributions to certain Hispanic causes and for improved Hispanic hiring practices in exchange for the association's support and the assurance that it would not call for a national boycott.[102]

By the mid-1980s NCLR was turning to corporations and corporate philanthropies for most of its funding. Key to securing this help was the idea that Latin American immigrants comprised an important, undervalued consumer market. Although the relationship between corporations and the activist groups under the NCLR umbrella was not always amicable, NCLR learned to use Hispanic consumerism as a tool both to entice and to pressure corporations.

Popularizing Hispanic Panethnicity through Media

NCLR's presence on the national scene increased during the late 1980s, and by 1990 it had become the leading Hispanic civil rights organization in the country. Others certainly took notice. In the early 1980s, a group of educators, activists, and administrators sought NCLR's help to establish what would later be known as the "National Hispanic University."[103] George H. W. Bush spoke at most of NCLR's affiliate conferences while he was vice president, and during his presidency NCLR leaders were invited to the White House for meetings to discuss topics such as immigration and bilingual education.[104] Moreover, by 1990 NCLR had built an extensive network in the corporate world. Some of these corporate connections, like ties with Donald Rumsfeld and Alex Armendariz, linked NCLR to the federal government, while others linked it to Spanish-language media. These links essentially allowed the organization to diversify its sources of funding. These ties also made NCLR leaders cautious, however. By 1985 they were reminding staffers to refrain from using terms like *Aztlán* and, to some extent, *Chicano* when describing the organization.[105]

Despite NCLR's national visibility, its leaders still needed to find a way to publicize the notion of panethnicity to Hispanics and non-Hispanics alike. Indeed, NCLR leaders could use the idea of panethnicity to gain prominence in Washington and to garner money from grant-making agencies, yet it still needed Hispanics themselves to identify as Hispanic in order to seem credible. NCLR executives tackled the issue by developing a media campaign and using corporate contributions to establish a Raza Production Center, which created broadcast programs about Hispanic history and culture. One of its projects was a television series titled *Latin Tempo: The National Hispanic TV Magazine.*[106] An entertainment news show, *Latin Tempo* was aired in southwestern and eastern television markets. It broadcast interviews with famous US Hispanics, such as actor Anthony Quinn and golfer Lee Trevino, and Latin American and Spanish personalities.[107] *Latin Tempo* showcased who Hispanics were by piecing together interviews and segments that featured personalities with different Latin American origins. A typical *Latin Tempo* show would, for example, include three segments: one with a Mexican wrestler, another with a Cuban American business owner in Miami, and a third with a Spanish pop singer. The series ran through the mid-1980s and was supported with commercials purchased by corporations whose members held seats on NCLR's corporate advisory council or by companies that were looking to tap into the Hispanic market.

During the mid-1980s NCLR also created a series of documentaries, called HispanUS, about the US Hispanic population. These films were financed with contributions from corporations and broadcast on English- and Spanish-language television.[108] Yet perhaps NCLR's most ambitious publicity project was the National Hispanic Quincentennial Commission (NHQC) in 1983. Created as a response to President Reagan's "Christopher Columbus Quincentennial Jubilee Act," which established a commission to organize festivities pertaining to Columbus and his voyages, the NHQC would "promote the role that Hispanics have played in the Americas since Columbus."[109]

Indeed, NCLR recognized early on that the NHQC could help debunk stereotypes about Hispanic "foreignness." At the time, the United States was embroiled in debates about undocumented migration, and nativist sentiments had culminated in a series of legislative proposals that would eliminate bilingual education, finance mass deportations, and militarize the US-Mexico border. In early organizing meetings for the commission, Yzaguirre spoke at length about the need to highlight the positive contributions of "Hispanic Americans" in US history and to show the nation that, like other groups, Hispanics were part and parcel of American history.[110] The NHQC's first project was to create a series of pamphlets, papers, lectures, and museum exhibitions about Hispanics in American history. One popular cultural tidbit was Hispanic Trivial Pursuit, a board game designed by the NHQC that used a series of questions about Hispanics in US history. Some questions in Hispanic Trivial Pursuit were:

How many Hispanic-Americans have received the Medal of Honor? (Answer: 37)

Which famous performer . . . recorded "Babalou" in 1941? (Answer: Desi Arnaz)

Name this Mexican-American tennis legend who never once took a lesson, yet taught himself to play the game of tennis [and went on] to be the National Champion of grass, clay and indoor courts in 1949? (Answer: Alberto Salazar)[111]

The materials produced by the NHQC soon attracted the attention of educators across the nation. Several wrote to the NHQC and NCLR during the late 1980s and early 1990s requesting the materials for classroom use. Many of these letters came from non-Hispanic whites. For example, Margaret Holland, a high school teacher in Maine, wanted to purchase

Hispanic Trivial Pursuit for the course she taught on US history.[112] Similarly, Sally Norton, a librarian in Indiana, asked for copies of NHQC pamphlets for a display about Hispanic heritage.[113] The NHQC also received a request for materials from Patricia King, a staff librarian at Radcliffe College who wanted to include information on Hispanic women in a library exhibition on women and work.[114] And John Gueguen, a political science professor from Illinois State University, wrote to the commission requesting materials for his course on American politics. The professor's interest was so great that he sent his course syllabus to Yzaguirre, asking for his opinion on what should be included in a section on Hispanics and the American political tradition.[115]

Through the NHQC, NCLR sought not only to disseminate information about Hispanics but also to historicize Hispanics as a panethnic group. This reflected a trend in NCLR discourse to make Hispanics part of American history. A speech given by Yzaguirre at a conference about corporate philanthropy exemplified this strategy:

In every war since the War of Independence, Hispanics have fought bravely for this nation. From the Civil War to the Vietnam Conflict, a recurrent phenomenon has occurred. Hispanics [tend] to be the first in and the last out. During the Civil War, Major Benavides led his Mexican-American troops in battle months after General Lee had surrendered. Vietnam was not a popular war, but a Hispanic was the first American to be captured in Battle, a Hispanic was the first American to escape captivity and the last marine to evacuate Saigon was a Hispanic. Despite documented cases of failure to award the congressional medal of honor to Hispanics who had rightfully earned [it], our community still received more congressional medals of honor awards proportionally than any other group.[116]

By historicizing Hispanics, NCLR could frame Hispanic panethnicity as an American identity and, at the same time, create the impression that panethnicity was a timeless, natural cultural propensity shared by Latin American subgroups.

Of course, not all agreed with NCLR and its stance on panethnicity. Although they did not direct their comments specifically at NCLR, critics objected to the notion of Hispanic panethnicity because they believed it was artificial and thus developed by government officials and self-interested political leaders, or because it disguised the importance of national identity among Latin Americans.[117] Some commentators suggested, furthermore, that those who used the term *Hispanic* had internalized a label that was imposed by the government.[118]

The charge that panethnicity was an artificial construct was difficult to deflect, if only because there were no surveys that asked subgroups whether they felt panethnic and no studies that examined which identity subgroups preferred. The first survey on Latin American self-identification was not carried out until 1989, and the results were not published until the early 1990s.[119] Nonetheless, NCLR buffered itself from criticism in a couple of ways. First, it pointed to the rise of civic organizations espousing the notion of panethnicity. By the late 1980s, there were several state, academic, community, and professional organizations that claimed to represent a panethnic Hispanic constituency.[120]

Second, NCLR reiterated that panethnicity was complementary to ethnic identity—the two notions were not mutually exclusive. The organization's position was that Hispanics were a diverse group composed of different ethnonational populations. One could be Mexican and Hispanic or Puerto Rican and Hispanic. To emphasize this point, NCLR continued to celebrate ethnic-specific events such as Mexican Independence Day and the Puerto Rican Day Parade, and it accepted affiliates that were ethnic in focus.

Other critics, however, argued that the notion of Hispanic panethnicity overlooked the fact that Latin American subgroups were united by a colonial past and history of oppression, not simply a common language or a historical tie to Spain. These critics did not deny that a bond existed between the subgroups but instead took issue with what that bond was. Those leveling this charge tended to be grassroots and protest-oriented organizations, which preferred the term *Latino* to *Hispanic* to signify panethnicity. *Latino*, they said, referred to the people of Latin America and highlighted how these communities were united in their struggle to shed the yoke of Spanish imperialism.[121] To many, NCLR's use of *Hispanic* and *Hispanic American* seemed too conservative. The organization's response was simple: it used both terms. NCLR was wedded to the idea of panethnicity, not necessarily to a particular label. By the late 1970s, it often used *Latino, Raza,* and *Hispanic* interchangeably to signal the notion of panethnicity.

Despite these efforts, it is not clear how effective NCLR was at buffering itself from criticism. The organization probably continued to be rebuked by some, but it also likely received praise for its ability to garner resources for different Latino subgroup communities. What is certain is that NCLR's strategies allowed it to engage with its critics and still expand its boundaries. By noting that panethnicity was complementary to national identity, it avoided excluding those who preferred their national identity. Moreover, by picking up other panethnic terms, NCLR linked its definition of panethnicity with others' definitions. For NCLR, subgroups were united because they spoke Spanish, had a connection to Spain, came from Latin America, had a common history of being colonized, or—probably most important—because they shared a common culture. Indeed, ambiguity would come to be an important tool that NCLR—like CCOSSP before it and several other organizations after it—would use to obscure what made Hispanics Hispanic.

Conclusion

Between 1960 and 1990, NCLR transformed from a small regional organization to one of the nation's foremost Hispanic civil rights advocacy groups. Along with CCOSSP, NCLR became an important advocate of the notion of panethnicity, and within the field of minority politics, it spearheaded the notion that Mexican Americans, Puerto Ricans, and Cuban Americans could work together as one community. For NCLR, the Hispanic community was defined by its common struggle to overcome discrimination, disadvantage, and inequality. And by 1990, NCLR had taken to spreading this message everywhere—from the congressional floor and the White House to corporate boardrooms and the media.

Factors such as the expectations of state grant-making agencies, the development of Hispanic census data, and networks with Hispanic marketing executives were key to NCLR's transition. In the late 1960s, NCLR's leaders faced a major framing obstacle. State bureaucrats at the time perceived Mexican Americans as a regional, southwestern population worthy of state, but not necessarily federal, government assistance. Until then, federal agencies had mainly dealt with African American groups and therefore conceived of minorities as national, not regional, entities. NCLR's focus on Mexican Americans, then, would prove difficult to maintain as it lobbied federal agencies. NCLR's transition into a panethnic organization thus helped it sidestep the regional frame, because Hispanics were a national minority group comprised of southwestern Mexican Americans, northeastern Puerto Ricans, and southeastern Cubans alike.

Moreover, NCLR found ways to use the newly released "Spanish Origin" census data to substantiate its panethnic claims. The data gave contours to NCLR's panethnic claims, providing information about where Hispanics lived, how much money they made, and how many years of schooling they had obtained. NCLR used these data not only in its grant applications but also in its press releases and publicity information as a way to argue that its constituents were a large, broad group that rivaled the size of the African American community. By using census data that grouped Mexican American, Cuban American, Puerto Rican, and other subgroup information together, NCLR leaders could argue that Hispanics would soon outnumber blacks and thus insinuate that the amount of state resources a minority group received should be proportionate to its size.

NCLR also used the idea of panethnicity to garner resources from private corporations. Like government grant agencies in the 1970s, corporations in the 1980s mainly provided resources to African American causes. The idea of Hispanic panethnicity became a useful tool for NCLR because it could be tied to the notion of a national Hispanic consumer market. Thus, during the early 1980s, NCLR met with corporate charities and conveyed to them that contributions to Hispanic causes would translate into positive publicity among Hispanic consumers. This notion probably seemed attractive to corporations since it implied that there existed a sizable untapped constituency that had distinct consumer tastes and practices.

It is useful to imagine an alternative scenario in order to elucidate how the notion of panethnicity was tied to the acquisition of resources. In effect, one might argue that NCLR could have shed its regional image by forging an alliance with Puerto Ricans on the East Coast. Thus, instead of becoming panethnic, NCLR could simply have become a multiethnic organization that represented two distinct nationalities. Given that Cubans were mainly focused on Cuban independence during the late 1960s and early 1970s, and that many perceived Cubans as an upwardly mobile professional group, the idea of a Mexican American and Puerto Rican alliance would not have been far-fetched. In fact, such an alliance was spearheaded in the early 1970s under the same premise, and a group of cultural entrepreneurs even published a Mexican American and Puerto Rican magazine called *Chicano-Riquena*.[122]

Yet a successful agenda based on a Mexican American–Puerto Rican identity would have been difficult for NCLR for several reasons. First, the notion would have been at odds with the trend within government agencies to see Latin American subgroups as part of a larger Spanish-speaking group. By that time CCOSSP had institutionalized the notion of "the Spanish Speaking" within individual grant-making federal agencies. Moreover, some in Congress were suspicious of Puerto Rican–Mexican American alliances because they feared such ties would lead to a political bloc. Second, forging a Puerto Rican–Mexican American identity would have made it difficult for NCLR leaders to access census data in the 1970s. During that time, the Census Bureau released data mainly on the "Spanish Origin" population and only sporadically provided data on individual Latin American subgroups.[123] Although this would change by the late 1980s, census reports primarily depicted Latin American groups as part of a larger Hispanic/Spanish-origin category. Finally, a Puerto Rican–Mexican American identity would not yield a constituency sizable enough to compete with African American groups for funding. Although Cuban Americans were not a large ethnic group, every last potential constituent counted. Indeed, Yzaguirre often argued that Puerto Ricans living in Puerto Rico should be counted in the US Hispanic minority population. This would, of course, make the Hispanic population larger than that of African Americans.

The history of NCLR, though, is not simply about access to resources; it is also about how the resources were expended. To situate NCLR as a broad-based organization, its leaders strategically allocated resources to non–Mexican American affiliates. They picked these organizations carefully, making sure to attract Puerto Rican groups in New York and not those that were located, for example, on the West Coast. Moreover, it sought out Cuban American affiliates headed by more moderate leaders who were concerned with domestic affairs and not necessarily foreign policy. NCLR was able to retain these affiliates by respecting their political turf. One Cuban affiliate explained this relationship by noting, "We [have] an understanding. . . . [The] ethnic group with the most population in the area [has] priority to organize and to provide services."[124] In other words, NCLR would provide funding to these ethnic-specific affiliates without necessarily requiring them to provide services outside their own ethnic group. This made NCLR a broad, panethnic umbrella group with ethnic affiliates. Later, as cities became more diverse—particularly with the influx of Dominican and Nicaraguan immigrants into New York and Miami, respectively—NCLR affiliates did become more panethnic in their service structure, but this was never a stipulation for receiving NCLR funds.

Above all, NCLR's transformation would not have been possible without the networks that helped NCLR leaders define the organization's identity at every step. Indeed, because some of its founders, such as Samora, were academics, NCLR leaders had access to Ford Foundation resources early on and could establish NCLR as a community advocate. Equally important were their connections to government officials, such as Roybal and Armendariz, who motivated NCLR leaders to consider a panethnic identity. The organization also maintained important connections to the corporate world and to a variety of Spanish-language media marketers and consultants. These connections not only solidified NCLR's panethnic orientation but also helped NCLR leaders learn how to speak about Hispanic consumers and a US Hispanic market.

Some important ties spanned different sectors and provided NCLR with several kinds of resources. For example, Armendariz oversaw Nixon's efforts to increase his support among Spanish speakers during his reelection campaign in 1972, and he was also appointed to federal grant-making agencies by the Nixon and Ford administrations. In the late 1970s, Armendariz established his own Hispanic marketing firm, and shortly thereafter NCLR hired him as a consultant. It is likely that Armendariz's government and market experience were valuable resources for NCLR leaders. Another example is Antonio Guernica, who worked briefly with NCLR in the early 1970s. By the late 1970s, he was a prominent Spanish-language media executive. In that capacity Guernica oversaw meetings between media executives and Census Bureau officials and assisted in publicizing the 1980 census on Spanish-language television. In the mid-1980s NCLR hired Guernica to consult on its Hispanic media projects. NCLR's networks were key in helping the organization make the transition to a panethnic identity.

By 1990 NCLR had successfully established itself as the nation's foremost Hispanic civil rights advocacy organization. It had close ties with state legislators, corporate businessmen, Hispanic marketers, Census Bureau officials, and several community groups across the country. It oversaw a multimillion-dollar budget and sponsored programs for Mexican American, Cuban American, and Puerto Rican communities alike. Perhaps most important, by 1990 NCLR had become a leading producer of policy reports and publications about Hispanics in America. These reports used census data to outline the issues and conditions of the Hispanic community and to further institutionalize the idea of Hispanic panethnicity. The next chapter focuses on data and reveals the series of negotiations that allowed a Hispanic census data statistic to emerge in the first place.

THREE

"The Toughest Question": The US Census Bureau and the Making of Hispanic Data

It is one thing to classify a population and another to count it. For Mexican American and Puerto Rican activists in the late 1960s, these issues were inherently related. On the one hand, they needed the US Census Bureau to provide an accurate count of their communities in order to make claims on federal resources. By then several government programs, especially those that aided minority groups, used census data to distribute funds to poor communities.[1] In addition, minority groups often found that census data offered the best way to prove to the Equal Employment Opportunity Commission that they were underrepresented in certain employment sectors.[2] A census undercount in a southwestern barrio, for example, could translate into fewer community development grants and fewer resources for bilingual job training programs.

Yet community leaders needed the bureau to also classify their communities as Mexican Americans and Puerto Ricans. Activists argued that these national-origin classifications, rather than the bureau's standard "white" racial classification, best represented their groups. For activists, the demands were not simply about identity, they were also about exposing inequality and claims making. If the bureau would count a person of Mexican descent as Mexican

American, and not simply as "white," activists would be able to use these data to show, for example, that Mexican Americans had higher unemployment and even higher poverty rates than whites and blacks in certain regions.

For census officials in the 1960s, however, the business of classification and enumeration had to be as scientific as possible. Officials had spent much of their energy since the 1920s honing statistical measures and trying to develop more objective procedures for collecting data. From their perspective, capitulating to the demands of political activists could threaten the seeming validity of much of the ethnic and racial data already collected. Moreover, the issue of Mexican American and Puerto Rican classification presented a slippery slope. If the bureau gave into activists' demands, it would have no basis on which to resist future demands from other groups.

In addition, bureau officials recognized that complex issues related to ethnic and racial identification and labeling would have to be resolved before they could modify classification practices. Did an upwardly mobile, light-skinned, fourth-generation American of Mexican descent who identified himself as simply "Spanish" count as Mexican American? What about the daughter of an Irish American father and a non-Spanish-speaking Mexican American mother who identified herself not as Mexican but as "Tejana"? Did individuals have to have been born in Puerto Rico to be counted as Puerto Rican? Did either group have to speak Spanish? These and several other questions about identity plagued the bureau.

This chapter examines the conflicts, negotiations, and compromises that led to the addition of the Hispanic/Spanish-origin category on census forms for the 1980 decennial enumeration. Vincent Barabba, census director at the time, noted that development of the measure constituted "the toughest question" that he faced during his tenure at the bureau.[3] The negotiations were marked by intense fights, as officials' notions of scientific objectivity clashed with activists' political interests, but they also included important moments of cooperation. In the process, census officials shifted their focus from trying to devise objective measures of race and ethnicity to generating scientifically reliable identity classifications.

Objective and Valid Measures in the 1970 Census

In October 1967 President Lyndon B. Johnson's newly established Inter-Agency Committee on Mexican American Affairs (IMAA) held a conference for Mexican American community leaders in El Paso, Texas. As we saw in chapter 1, the event was billed as an opportunity to voice grievances to the Johnson administration. About two thousand activists attended the event, and among their major concerns was the lack of local-level census data on Mexican American communities. Whether the issue concerned education, employment, discrimination, or poverty, speaker after speaker lamented that federal agencies, especially the Census Bureau, produced data and reports that classified Mexican Americans as simply white. This practice, they argued, masked the dire conditions within southwestern communities because it grouped Mexican American data with Anglo American data. Exasperated by the situation, one conference attendee noted with frustration that Mexican Americans should have their own social category because their "dark skin," "mispronounced names," and distinct culture made them "lousy Anglos."[4]

It was not that the Census Bureau completely ignored Mexican Americans, however. It was true that census officials classified this community as white and lumped their data together with those of the descendants of European migration. Yet this decision emerged after experimentation with a series of other measures. For the 1930 census, at the request of Congress, the bureau had added "Mexican" as a racial classification, providing respondents with the opportunity to identify as white, Negro, Mexican, or one of an array of Asian nationalities.[5] The category was eliminated for the 1940 census after Mexican American advocacy groups and Mexican diplomats protested.[6] The American government had just forcefully repatriated upward of one million Mexican-origin residents, many of whom were Mexican American citizens, and activists and diplomats feared that census data gathered specifically on "Mexicans" could be used to unfairly target and repatriate more individuals.[7] In addition, the bureau discovered that the category had generated a high degree of respondent error because a significant number of second- and third-generation Mexican Americans, who identified themselves more narrowly as Tejano, Californio, or Spanish American, were not classified as "Mexican."[8]

In the 1940s census officials continued to classify Mexican Americans as racially white, but they also tabulated measures on place of birth, parents' place of birth, and mother tongue to approximate the Mexican American population. In addition, for the 1950 census, the bureau developed a question to identify respondents with Spanish surnames. To make the measure objective—and reduce the level of subjectivity that had occurred in 1930—census enumerators did not ask respondents if they had a Spanish surname. Instead, the bureau generated a list of eight thousand of the most common surnames found in Mexico City telephone directories. Puerto Rican and Cuban phonebooks were also consulted. See US Department of Commerce, "Comparison of Persons of Spanish Surname and Persons of Spanish Origin in the United States" (Washington, DC: Government Printing Office, 1975). If respondents had a last name that was on the list, they were classified as "Spanish-surname"; if their names were not on the list, they were not. Because most Mexican immigrants and their descendants were concentrated primarily in the Southwest, the surname question was limited to census forms sent to California, New Mexico, Colorado, Texas, and Arizona.

There were, however, important limitations to the bureau's estimates of Spanish surname, language, and nativity. Because the surname question was only asked in the Southwest, a second-generation Mexican immigrant living in Chicago, for instance, or any second- or third-generation Mexican American without a "Spanish surname" and reporting limited Spanish-speaking ability was categorized as simply white.

For activists these measurement practices were also problematic because they did not yield local-level data. Unlike questions on race, which were included on all census forms and thus yielded "100 percent data"—data on all Americans—the surname, language, and nativity questions used to parse out people of Mexican heritage were employed only on a sample basis, and these data were tabulated only minimally. If, for example, activists wanted information about Mexican Americans and immigrants in Houston, they would have to ask the bureau to tabulate Spanish-surname data from its sample surveys. This could easily take several years, and the data did not always yield local-level information on other important characteristics such as employment. In contrast, groups like the National Urban League and the NAACP could request data from the bureau about blacks and receive the information quickly because the question about race was included in all surveys and was tabulated promptly.

In addition, activists complained that the bureau's measures yielded different outcomes. Not all Mexican Americans spoke Spanish, not all had Spanish surnames, and not all who had Spanish surnames spoke Spanish—and so on.[9] Several Mexican American leaders called on the bureau to abandon the language and surname measures and to create instead a single self-identification question for Mexican American respondents.[10] By the late 1960s, activist groups were, in effect, calling on the bureau to resume practices it had discarded after the 1930 enumeration. With such a category in hand, activists hoped to be able to delineate the disadvantaged status of America's Mexican community.

Activists voiced their concerns to the IMAA, which in turn set up several meetings with census officials to discuss the issue. In these meetings, the IMAA asked the bureau to include a Mexican-origin self-identification question on all census surveys, not just on the long forms used for the sample census. The bureau resisted the change. The 1970 decennial census was less than two years away, and officials believed that its questions about language, surname, and nativity were more objective estimates of the Mexican American population.

Census officials became more flexible, however, after the IMAA and activists took their concerns to the Congressional Subcommittee on the Census in 1969. During the hearings, activists accused the bureau of reproducing inequality by not providing the data that activists needed to prove that Mexican Americans were living in poverty, suffered discrimination, and had lower levels of education than did whites and blacks. Activists had an important ally at these hearings in Senator Edward Roybal (D-CA), who argued that the bureau needed to create a more comprehensive self-identification question that would adequately capture the number of Mexican Americans in the Southwest.[11]

Puerto Rican activists had even greater difficulties with the data gathered by the Census Bureau. Mexican American activists at least had access to information about individuals with Spanish surnames in the Southwest, but similar data were not available for Puerto Ricans because the question was not asked on the East Coast. Puerto Ricans were classified as white unless enumerators classified them as black. As a result, short form census data and reports were useless to Puerto Rican activists for lobbying purposes. As they and their New York congressional allies also began to demand classification changes, the pressure on the Census Bureau intensified.[12]

In December 1969 the IMAA was formally replaced by the Cabinet Committee on Opportunities for Spanish Speaking People (CCOSSP). Its mandate was to advocate on behalf of all Spanish speakers, including Puerto Ricans and Cuban Americans. In the fall of that year, those working in the IMAA had increased pressure on the bureau to revise its questionnaires. The bureau insisted that it was simply too late to change the short form, which was the only form that could provide 100 percent data at the local level. Mexican Americans, Puerto Ricans, and Cuban Americans would still have to mark "white" as their racial designation on the short form. The bureau did agree, however, to insert an additional Spanish-origin question on one of the two long forms, which would be distributed to 5 percent of Americans.[13] The new question read:

Is the person's origin or descent:

Mexican	Central or South American
Puerto Rican	Other Spanish
Cuban	No, none of these

The addition of this question represented an important concession for bureau officials. Instead of using what they believed to be straightforward and objective questions about nativity, language, and surname, they would now use—albeit on a small percentage of the bureau's questionnaires—what they considered to be a more subjective question about ethnic self-identification. This, officials feared, could generate a high level of respondent error. At the same time, however, the addition represented a victory for census officials. Because the Spanish-origin question was distinct from the question about race, the bureau retained the ability to continue counting Mexican Americans, Puerto Ricans, and Cuban Americans as white. This would allow it to keep its data on race more or less commensurate across decades. CCOSSP and activists hoped that the new Spanish-origin question would provide more accurate information on how Spanish speakers identified themselves, but because the question would be used on only one of the long forms, the data would provide little local-level information.

The Bureau and the 1970 Legitimacy Crisis

Yet even before the 1970 census numbers were released, various Mexican American advocacy organizations began protesting that the enumeration had undercounted Mexican Americans.[14] Their protests centered on two arguments. First, although a Spanish-language instruction guide was available to all who requested it, the census form had not been translated into Spanish. Second, Mexican American leaders argued that Mexican American families, especially those that lived in garages, basements, migrant camps, and other places that lacked formal addresses, were systematically overlooked.[15] In New York, Puerto Rican activists lobbed similar complaints at the bureau, contending that Puerto Rican families had been grossly undercounted.

When the bureau finally released its counts of Mexican Americans and Puerto Ricans, activists and community leaders found major discrepancies between census estimates and data collected by state agencies. With the support of elected officials, especially mayors, these activists alerted the press, and soon accusations of an undercount made headlines in the *New York Times* and the *Los Angeles Times*.[16]

Before long, activists' claims were supported by independent reports that compared census figures to other data. CCOSSP cross-referenced the Spanish-origin data that the bureau had released with data from state and federal agencies. CCOSSP's report concluded that the number of Spanish-origin persons in the United States was about 30 percent higher than the 1970 census estimate.[17] Using a similar approach, a group named the Mexican American Population Commission of California (MAPCC) argued that the bureau had undercounted Mexican Americans in California.[18] The US Commission on Civil Rights would later issue a report, *Counting the Forgotten*, that called the bureau's estimates of the Spanish-origin population "disastrous."[19]

La Confederación de La Raza Unida v. George Brown

Criticism of the Census Bureau reached a boiling point in 1971, when the Mexican American Legal Defense and Education Fund (MALDEF) filed a class-action lawsuit in federal district court in California on behalf of Mexican Americans seeking to prohibit the bureau from publishing its reports and data on the Mexican American population.[20] MALDEF's suit, *La Confederación de La Raza Unida v. George Brown*, quickly received the backing of CCOSSP and the US Commission on Civil Rights.[21] In their motion for a preliminary injunction, plaintiffs claimed that they had been denied a number of rights without due process of law, including their right to be fairly enumerated. In requesting the injunction, MALDEF stated that publication of census data would cause Mexican Americans "great and irreparable harm" since the census data would be used in "disbursing federal funds to the poor and minorities, in allocating federal jobs to minorities, in apportioning Congressional districts, as well as in formulating remedies in employment discrimination cases brought under Title VII of the Civil Rights Act of 1964."[22] The court deposition and documents lodged with the court reveal that the issue of the undercount was intimately related to the issue of Mexican American ethnic and panethnic identification.

Robert Gnaizda, MALDEF's lead attorney, relied primarily on two types of evidence for the case: accounts from residents and studies that cross-checked census data with California Department of Education data. The first type of evidence supported the argument that improper procedures had been used to count the Mexican-descent population. Gnaizda gathered depositions from several Mexican Americans and Mexican immigrants that detailed the difficulties they had had with enumerators. The testimony included statements such as these:

> The person who contacted our family could not relate to us in our tongue. So I did not return the questionnaire.[23]
> The person who contacted us was Anglo and did not attempt to help fill out the questionnaire. [He] just gave it to us and left.[24]
> I . . . received a census [long] form in 1970 but was unable to understand it because it was in English and because it was very complex.[25]

During the pretrial hearing, Gnaizda argued that Mexican Americans and Mexican immigrants were more likely than other groups to throw out their census forms because of the significant language barrier. Additionally, he contended that the language barrier negatively influenced the interaction between census enumerators and respondents.

Gnaizda also described problems with the address lists that the bureau had relied on for mailing the census questionnaires. The 1970 census was the first decennial census in which the bureau pursued a mail-in, mail-back strategy for most US counties. Instead of sending enumerators to canvass neighborhoods, the bureau purchased commercially generated address lists and mailed each household a census form. Gnaizda argued that the bureau had overlooked thousands of Mexican immigrant families because they resided in areas without formal postal addresses. Gnaizda supported this claim with statements from Mexican Americans and Mexican immigrants who testified that they had never received census forms.

During his deposition, Conrad Taeuber, the associate director for the 1970 census, refuted all of Gnaizda's points.[26] To respond to Gnaizda's first claim—that the government's procedures had been improper—Taeuber explained that simply because a person had not returned the census form did not mean that the household had not been counted. Indeed, per the census procedure, an enumerator had been dispatched to visit all households that had not returned a form. When asked what he thought about the testimony concerning the language barrier between enumerators and respondents, Taeuber replied that the statements gave no indication that the plaintiffs had *not* been counted. He explained that in cases where there was a serious language barrier, enumerators were instructed to return later with a translator. If the enumerator and the translator returned but could not establish contact with the head of the household, then enumerators were instructed to obtain the information from neighbors or nearby relatives. Thus, even if a household could not communicate at all with an enumerator, the enumerator may have received the information from a neighbor on a subsequent visit.[27]

Taeuber also addressed Gnaizda's points about the bureau's address lists. He testified that enumerators were instructed to count all persons in the household, regardless of how large the household seemed to be. If a home had a family residing in the garage or another structure, the enumerator was to include this family in the total count. Additionally, Taeuber noted that bureau employees often supplemented the address lists by adding households that were not on the initial list and sending enumerators to survey them.[28] These responses to Gnaizda's questions exasperated the attorney. Essentially, Taeuber was stating that even if someone did not reside in a place with a postal address, did not return the census form, or could not communicate with or never saw an enumerator, he or she might still have been counted.

Gnaizda had one other important type of evidence, however—the independent studies from CCOSSP and MAPCC that compared census data with local data. The MAPCC report was especially damaging because it used county-level data to make its point and because it had been endorsed by prominent Mexican American politicians as well as the US Commission on Civil Rights.[29] Gnaizda pointed out during the deposition that the MAPCC report had estimates for the number of "Mexican Americans" in California that were higher than the bureau's preliminary estimates for "Spanish-origin" or "Spanish-language" residents. When Gnaizda asked Taeuber whether the conflicting tabulations would make him reconsider publishing the census data, Taeuber responded, "No."[30] He noted that before the bureau could reconsider publication of the 1970 census count, census officials

would have to know much more than is given about how [the MAPCC report] was done. How [the report] took into account the fact that [employment and school board data were collected] some 20 months after the U.S. census, and [the Bureau would also have to know] what definitions [of the population] were used.[31]

In effect, Taeuber was invalidating the MAPCC report on two grounds: because it used data collected after the 1970 census, and, more important, because it might have counted a different population.

The issue of definitions—of exactly who had been surveyed by MAPCC—was especially damaging for Gnaizda's argument. At one point Gnaizda asked Taeuber to imagine a hypothetical situation in which a "scientific" census was done of "Mexican Americans" on the same day that the bureau conducted its own census. Gnaizda then asked Taeuber how he would respond if the count from this hypothetical census were different from the bureau's. Exasperated, Taeuber replied:

I'm not sure what you mean by Mexican-Americans. Let me tell you what we have. We will have in the [census] report . . . the number of persons born in Mexico, who are living in the U.S. and California. We will have the number of persons born in the U.S. who have a parent born in Mexico. We will have this figure, the Spanish-language population, and we will have the number of persons who reported Mexican in response to the question of origin. That's who we have.[32]

In effect, Taeuber argued that because the other surveys used different labels, such as "Mexican American," their numbers were not comparable to census data. In other words, any population study that used categories for ethnicity and race that were different from those on the census forms could not be employed to evaluate the accuracy of the Census Bureau's findings.

Essentially, Gnaizda and the Census Bureau were using different terms to identify the Mexican-origin population. For Gnaizda, the Mexican American category was more representative because it included persons who considered themselves Chicanos, Californios, or Raza, and others who might not consider themselves simply "Mexican," as well as those who were of Mexican descent but did not speak Spanish or who did not have a Spanish surname. This large and complex population was counted as simply "white" by the bureau. Yet to Taeuber it did not matter what Gnaizda or other surveys called that population—Chicano, Mexican American, Mexican immigrant; from Taeuber's point of view, these people had been counted, though perhaps not as part of the Mexican-origin, Spanish-surname, or Spanish-language population. For Taeuber, Gnaizda's argument was about labels rather than an undercount. Ultimately, Taeuber did not see Mexican Americans the way Gnaizda, or even CCOSSP or MAPCC, saw them.

Taeuber did admit, however, that perhaps a more uniform definition of who Mexican Americans were would have been preferable. He noted that a more standard definition could have abated the backlash from Mexican American leaders, and he stated that he wished that the bureau had arrived at an

agreed-upon definition of what it is we are talking about. [The Bureau] hear[s] terms like Mexican-American, Chicano, like Spanish-American, like Latin American, like Mexicano, Spanish origin, Spanish speaking. There apparently is no agreement on what it is we are trying to get at. . . . And this in itself creates a problem in the structure of the census questionnaire.[33]

Every lawsuit filed against the US Census Bureau over the 1970 census, including *La Confederación de La Raza Unida,* was eventually unsuccessful. Judges across the country dismissed the cases or ruled that there was no evidence that the bureau had intentionally undercounted certain populations. Yet, soon after these cases were wrapped up, the bureau reported that it had undercounted about five million people. Using vital statistics on blacks and whites from the 1970 enumeration, the bureau estimated that people living in poor urban areas were less likely to be counted. About 7 percent of the black population, the bureau admitted, had been undercounted.[34] Because vital statistics did not exist for the Spanish-origin population, the bureau argued that it could not estimate how many Mexican Americans, Puerto Ricans, or Cuban Americans had been undercounted.

The lawsuits and the admitted undercount did little to improve the public image of the Census Bureau. By 1972 stories of a rumored Spanish-origin undercount were appearing in major periodicals across the country, including the *New York Times.* These news stories reasoned that if blacks had been undercounted, then Mexican Americans and Puerto Ricans had been so as well.[35] In addition, by 1974 the US Commission on Civil Rights had disseminated a report, *Counting the Forgotten,* that alleged that

the Bureau's procedures [had] been insensitive to the Spanish speaking background population . . . [and] as a result, persons of Spanish speaking background were probably undercounted more than . . . the black population.[36]

The report was revealing, although less for the accuracy of its claims than for the way the Commission on Civil Rights chastised the bureau for relying on what it called "confusing" and "disastrous" strategies for measuring the Spanish-origin population.[37] The bureau's different measures (language, surname, ancestry), the report stated, created uncertainty and made it difficult to interpret things like educational attainment. The report caught the attention of Congressman Roybal and the newly elected Puerto Rican congressman Herman Badillo (D-NY), who fired off a letter to George Brown, director of the Census Bureau, asking him to scratch the 1970 numbers and recount the Spanish-origin population.[38] As the pressure for census reform and discontent grew, Nixon replaced Brown with Vincent Barabba, a marketing statistician who had helped run Nixon's 1968 presidential campaign in California.[39]

The Spanish Origin Advisory Committee

Barabba's appointment as director of the US Census Bureau marked a new phase in the bureau's approach to racial and ethnic categorization. Perhaps because of the heightened scrutiny of the 1970 census, the admitted undercount of blacks and the poor, and the fact that the bureau did not wish to be sued in 1980, Barabba began his tenure by instituting a Spanish Origin Advisory Committee (SOAC) in January 1974, just a few months after he was instated. Specifically, Barabba sent letters to "leaders of the Spanish-American community," inviting them to a one-day meeting in March to discuss the planning of the 1980 population census. Barabba described the meeting as an opportunity to gather "Americans of Puerto Rican, Mexican, and Cuban [and] other Spanish ancestry" for the purpose of planning an efficient and adequate 1980 census count.[40] The invitees ranged from community activists to social scientists and government officials. Among them were Gnaizda and Julian Samora, founder of the NCLR.[41] Raquel Creitoff, a second-generation Puerto Rican with ties to the Puerto Rican Studies program at the City University of New York, was also invited.[42] To represent the Cuban American perspective, Barabba invited Arturo Hevia, who had recently established one of Miami's first Cuban community-based organizations.[43]

At the meeting, Barabba described the bureau's need to create a group that could essentially serve as a "channel of communication" between census officials and the "Spanish" community.[44] Barabba stated that officials were not communicating effectively with Mexican Americans, Puerto Ricans, and Cuban Americans because of "differences between the Anglo world and the Spanish world."[45] He described two ways that the attendees could help the bureau improve its count of the Spanish-origin population. First, the leaders could facilitate interaction between the Census Bureau and Spanish-language media and thus help the bureau publicize the importance of being counted. To this end, Barabba had even invited a Miami Spanish-language television personality, Manolo Reyes from WTVJ, to the meeting to discuss the issue.[46] Second, the attendees could assure their communities that census counts were completely confidential and not linked in any way to the government's immigration efforts.[47] This could, of course, help improve census counts among undocumented Mexican immigrants.

The attendees generally supported the establishment of a formal group, which they named the Spanish Origin Advisory Committee, but they also articulated doubts.[48] On the one hand, they felt that the SOAC could help the bureau reduce the undercount of Mexican American, Puerto Rican, and Cuban American communities, which would yield more accurate data and, in the long run, lead to more federal and state resources for these communities. On the other hand, these leaders wondered whether the bureau would implement their suggestions in good faith, or whether the formation of the committee was only a symbolic gesture meant to help the bureau gain legitimacy in the wake of the MALDEF lawsuit.[49]

Despite their suspicions, the "Spanish leaders" that Barabba selected formally established the SOAC in August of 1974. The foundation of the group was aided by a grant from the Ford Foundation, which had recently started to fund research and community organizing in Mexican American areas. At the same time, the Census Bureau began establishing a Black Census Advisory Committee, and it also considered creating an Asian Census Advisory Committee.[50]

For the most part, the SOAC meetings were held in Washington and were open to the public. Depending on the issue and the date, Barabba and other high-ranking officials, including Taeuber, were present. A question-and-answer period for the general public ended each meeting. Although CCOSSP had been disbanded in the wake of the Watergate scandal, its former members, as well as representatives of Mexican American and Puerto Rican community organizations, were present at several SOAC meetings.

Response Rates and Historical Comparability: Race and Spanish Origin

The bureau made clear to SOAC members early on that there had been several problems with the 1970 question. As mentioned earlier, the 1970 question read:

Is the person's origin or descent:

Mexican	Central/South American
Puerto Rican	Other Spanish
Cuban	No, none of these

Much of the problem with the question was that the second generation was likely to check "No, none of these" because terms like *Mexican American* were not included on the form. This pattern was similar to what had occurred in 1930, when Mexican Americans skipped over the "Mexican" race category on census forms. Thus, in its first meeting with the SOAC, the bureau asked for assistance in identifying different labels and categories that it should test to classify the second-plus generation.

What is curious about this initial meeting, however, was the fact that participants dwelled on the issue of labels, but not on the issue of question format. Specifically, census officials and SOAC members focused on how identity labels, such as "Mexican," "Chicano," and "Raza," might affect the Spanish-origin count rather than on whether "Spanish-origin" would indicate a racial group. Indeed, it would be about one year before the issue of race would surface, only to be eventually discarded by census officials. Why? Why did neither group discuss the effect of a two-question format—with one question on race and a distinct question on Spanish origin—versus a combined race/Spanish-origin question format that would allow individuals to identify as white, black, Asian, *or* Spanish-origin?

One reason that the bureau purposely made the 1970 Spanish-origin question distinct from the race question was because the former was inserted on one of the long forms, after the short form had been printed. Given that the bureau had only a few months between the time it agreed to include a self-identifier question and the time it had to administer the census, officials probably simply added on the Spanish-origin question, thus making it distinct from the race question. But the case would be much different for the 1980 census form. This time the bureau promised the SOAC that it would collect Spanish-origin data on all its forms, yielding 100 percent local-level information. Moreover, this time the bureau had ample time to test different versions of the Spanish-origin question.

The short form would have been especially conducive to a combined race/Spanish-origin question for several reasons. Most obviously, a combined question could have saved space on the short form and maintained its succinct, brief nature. There were also important technical reasons for using a combined question. The Spanish-origin question yielded a high nonresponse rate. In several precensus trials for the 1980 census, the bureau consistently found that about 25 to 30 percent of persons who did not consider themselves Spanish-origin—presumably Anglo whites, blacks, and Asians—skipped the question altogether despite the fact that the bureau included a "No, not Spanish-origin" option.[51] This presented a major problem for the bureau because the high level of missing data compromised its ability to draw any statistical conclusions about the characteristics of the Spanish-origin community.

Conversely, there were also serious problems with false-positive answers. Thus, in one particular precensus trial for the 1980 enumeration, census officials noticed that there was an unusually high number of respondents who checked "Mexican American." Upon closer examination, the bureau discovered that these were Anglo whites and blacks who crossed out *Mexican* or circled only *American* in this category. Another unusual finding was the high rate of respondents in the South and in the Midwest who identified themselves as "Central/South American." Through follow-up interviews, the bureau discovered that these respondents had interpreted the category in reference to the US South or to those states in the Central Standard Time Zone: persons in states like Illinois, for example, identified themselves as Central Americans and respondents in states like Texas identified themselves as South Americans.[52] Although these discrepancies may have seemed negligible on sample surveys, they would have proved disastrous for the decennial census because they could have substantially skewed estimates of the Spanish-origin population.

A combined race/Spanish-origin question could have resolved both of these dilemmas because a Spanish-origin category would become mutually exclusive with racial categories. Thus, respondents would be less likely to read into the question factors like geography or nationality. Respondents would simply see the question as referring to race and answer it accordingly. Last, a combined question would also have been preferable because a significant number of persons identifying themselves as "Spanish Origin" consistently either skipped the race question or checked the "Other Race" category. For example, the Oakland census pretest conducted in late 1977 found that the Spanish-origin population had a higher than average nonresponse rate for the race question and, of those who did answer the question, over one-third checked "Other" and wrote in their nationality or terms like *Chicano* in the "Race" box.[53] This suggested that Spanish-origin individuals perceived themselves as racially distinct from whites, blacks, Asians, and Native Americans.

Despite the evidence collected during the census trials, the bureau never seriously considered a single question combining a Spanish-origin category and the standard categories for race. In fact, a combined question was never fully tested in the bureau's trials.[54] Why? Given that the bureau was committed to include a Spanish-origin question on the short form, and that the Spanish-origin question had returned high nonresponse and false-positive rates, why was a combined question never considered for the 1980 census?

One answer might be that the bureau was following the orders of the Executive Office of the President. Some scholars have argued that during the 1970s the executive office, through the Office of Management and Budget (OMB), took important steps to ensure that the Spanish-origin population would be classified as an ethnicity and not as a race.[55] They point to Statistical Policy Directive 15, issued by the OMB in 1977, which defined racial and ethnic categories for all federal agencies collecting demographic statistics.[56] Specifically, it identified whites, blacks, Asians, and American Indians as racial groups and Hispanics as an ethnic group. Additionally, the directive noted that it would be "preferable" for agencies to collect and report race and ethnic data separately.[57]

The idea that the bureau was simply following orders from OMB, however, holds little weight when we consider that Directive 15 was a final outcome of several meetings that took place throughout the 1970s.[58] The Census Bureau was an active participant in these meetings and often advised OMB and other state agencies about how to collect racial and ethnic data. In fact, the bureau had advised the Ford administration on these matters three years before Directive 15 was issued.[59] Indeed, instead of simply following orders, census officials helped to influence OMB's decision to advocate for the two-question format.[60] Thus, in an interview, Barabba later described OMB as more of a "coordinating" body, noting that "it was us in the Bureau in the meetings with [SOAC] who had to decide how to measure and define the ["Spanish Origin"] category, OMB simply gave a broad, general directive."[61]

Others have suggested that it was Congress that forced the bureau to create a separate Hispanic category.[62] In 1976 Roybal had sponsored Public Law 94-311, known as the Roybal Act, after witnessing CCOSSP's struggle to persuade other federal agencies to collect Spanish-origin data. The bill instructed federal agencies that collected data on race to also collect data on the Spanish-origin population. Some have thus suggested that it was this bill that persuaded the Census Bureau to add the 1980 Hispanic/Spanish-origin census category.

There are several historical events, however, that refute the thesis about congressional action. Most obvious was the fact that the US Census Bureau considered the issue well before the Roybal Act was passed or discussed in congressional hearings. Indeed, census officials had pondered the question of a Spanish-origin category as early as 1969, when they first began meeting with CCOSSP representatives. In addition, there is simply no evidence to show that the Roybal bill, or the related congressional discussions, ever outlined or defined what a Spanish-origin category would look like. In fact, the congressmen, activists, and scholars who testified at the PL94-311 hearings often skirted the issue of how the Census Bureau or other federal agencies would define or measure the Spanish-origin population; they spoke mostly about the need to count Mexican Americans, Puerto Ricans, and Cubans, rather than about whether these populations would be defined panethnically, whether they would be measured as a race, or whether other factors like language, citizenship, or surname would be used to define them.[63] Moreover, while the text of Public Law 94-311 mentioned that the Spanish-origin population suffered from "racial discrimination," the bill did not provide a specific statement about whether this population should be measured as a race or as an ethnicity.[64] These specific and complicated issues were left up to the Census Bureau.

Another answer might be that the bureau retained the Spanish-origin ethnic category because it best reflected Mexican American identity. Some scholars have argued that Mexican Americans are effectively a white racial group, suggesting that the bureau's classification communicated a sociobiological fact. They posit that Mexican Americans are an "ambivalent" community because their leaders have historically sought minority group status even though Mexican Americans belong to the white race.[65]

This claim is not unfounded. In his deposition for *La Confederación de La Raza Unida v. George Brown*, Taeuber mentioned that the Mexican American leaders he spoke to in the early 1960s had insisted on keeping their white racial designation.[66] Additionally, an earlier generation of Mexican American activists living in Jim Crow Texas had often argued that their communities were white, but their motivation was straightforward: in an era when segregation was still rampant and a racial line divided the South, these activists sought to place Mexican Americans among the advantaged.[67] This did not mean that Mexican Americans in Texas benefited from the privileges afforded to the white population on an everyday basis—in fact, the opposite was often the case.[68]

These feelings of "whiteness," however, were not held by the SOAC members who advised the bureau in the 1970s. In fact, Samora had written extensively about the structural and social differences between Mexican immigrants and whites. He contended that Mexican immigrants were a product of *mestizaje*: they were neither white nor Indian, but a mixture of both.[69] During one contentious SOAC meeting, Samora argued that the bureau's racial categories—which at that point distinguished among blacks, whites, American Indians, and Asians—were simply "nonsensical" to Mexican immigrants.[70] Other SOAC members, pointing to the fact that at least 30 percent of Spanish-origin survey respondents had selected "Other Race" during census trials (there was no count of how many of the Spanish-origin population had skipped the separate race question altogether), lobbied for a "brown" or "Spanish-origin" racial designation.[71] One member even argued heatedly, "The Bureau is calling Spanish-origin people ethnics while they are calling themselves a race. Spanish people are both; that is, race and ethnicity have become intermeshed."[72] And it was not only the Mexican Americans who were voicing doubts about the white racial designation. Raquel Creitoff, a Puerto Rican community leader from New York, stated that the Census Bureau's existing racial categories were "confusing" to Puerto Ricans, presumably because many did not identify with those strict racial classifications.[73]

The issue became more complicated when the bureau brought in experts to comment on the issue. Nampeo McKenney, who worked for the bureau's Division on Racial and Ethnic Statistics, recalled hiring three anthropologists to conduct focus groups and examine the issue. The results were mixed. "One study deemed [the Spanish-origin population] a separate race, especially if you considered the Mexican Americans . . . but two others found them to be white, especially if you considered Cubans in Florida."[74]

Despite the objections from activists and the scientific shakiness of the two-question format, the bureau decided to retain it. Historical precedence was a weighty factor. Large institutions can change, but they do not change radically, and for the bureau the issue of race and Spanish origin was not clear-cut. In some regions, especially in states like New Mexico, and among some groups, especially Cuban Americans, the Spanish-origin population did check the "white" box even when they were not prompted to do so by enumerators. These respondents might have considered themselves to be racially white, or they may have simply been following the bureau's historical precedence—the reasoning is difficult to untangle.

Moreover, since a Spanish-origin racial category would radically alter the bureau's established classification system, the bureau likely reasoned that it would be easier and safer to simply maintain the status quo and devise a system that would allow it to keep the Spanish-origin category white. McKenney recalled that "it was difficult to decide to change the race question. We found that black and white categories seemed to be reliable and work well [for non-Hispanics]. . . . [I]ncluding the Hispanic category as a new racial category would fundamentally change our methods . . . affecting our ability to compare white data over time."[75] In effect, bureau officials decided that sticking to a two-question format would not only be a safer option under uncertain circumstances but also could preserve the historical integrity of previous census findings.

The second major reason that the bureau made the Hispanic question an ethnic one had to do with statisticians' need to balance the demands of other racial groups. Bureau officials suspected early on that a combined race/Spanish-origin question would affect the counts not only of whites but also of other racial groups. Although the bureau never fully tested a combined question in a census trial, it did test a version in a special current population survey conducted in Pima County, Arizona, in 1975.[76] Leobardo Estrada, a census official at the time, recalled that Barabba called a "pencil and paper–free" meeting soon after the Pima County results were tabulated. In the meeting Barabba contended that the combined race/Spanish-origin question had led to a decrease in the number of whites and Native Americans counted. Such an outcome from the 1980 census could incur the wrath of Native American leaders, and some officials commented nervously that a Spanish-origin racial identifier could also affect black statistics in the Northeast, especially if Puerto Ricans were to choose "Spanish Origin" instead of black. Estrada recalled that officials even feared that the statistics on Asians would be compromised if Filipinos were to identify themselves as Spanish-origin instead of Asian.[77] Because the bureau was trying to avoid the negative publicity it had attracted after the 1970 census, the combined question was scratched and never tested again.

The SOAC did not push the issue further. Estrada spoke confidentially with Mexican American SOAC members to let them know that a new racial category could spark resistance and resentment from other racial minorities.[78] In fact, the question of whether the new category would decrease the number of blacks was so contentious that Barabba met with prominent African American leaders to assure them that the Hispanic classification would not affect the black census count and that blacks would remain the nation's largest minority group.[79] Perhaps because SOAC members felt the need to create alliances with the black and Asian advisory committees, or perhaps because they reasoned that they could not convince the bureau otherwise, SOAC members finally endorsed the two-question format, which established "Spanish Origin" as an ethnic category.

Ultimately, by defining Spanish-origin as an ethnicity, the bureau was able to count some persons as members of two minority groups. Afro-Cubans, for example, could identify themselves as both black and Spanish-origin, which appeased both groups' concerns about the total count. A person who was Cuban Irish would not have to be either Cuban or white; he or she could be both. This option was available only to Hispanics. Persons of Chinese Irish or African Italian descent, for example, would have to choose one racial category.

Developing the Spanish/Hispanic Category

It was one thing to decide that the Spanish-origin question should be distinct from the race question, and thus to imply that Spanish-origin was an ethnicity rather than a race. It was another thing to contend that subgroups comprised a panethnic group. Indeed, the SOAC could have simply endorsed the idea that Cuban Americans, Mexican Americans, and Puerto Ricans were distinct ethnonational groups. But what resulted in the 1980 census, I argue, was a distinct "Spanish Origin/Hispanic" classification that defined subgroups as components of a metagroup. Why the SOAC decided to endorse the idea of panethnicity becomes evident when we examine how the bureau and the SOAC compromised on the issue of sample size and the "Other Spanish/Hispanic" option.

As mentioned earlier, the bureau began producing its first reports on the Spanish-origin population soon after the 1970 census. These reports were often complicated by the different measures used to identify that population and thus included distinct descriptive statistics for "Spanish-Language," "Spanish Origin," and "Spanish-Surname" data groups.[80] Why would the bureau use the 1970 census to report on the Spanish-origin population? The question on the 1970 census asked respondents whether they were of Mexican, Puerto Rican, Cuban, or Central/South American origin. Although there was an "Other Spanish" option, the "Spanish Origin" data category that the bureau included in its reports was a conglomeration of all Latino subgroups, including "Other Spanish." Why would the bureau provide statistics for the Spanish-origin population, instead of, for example, reporting on the age and marital status of Mexicans or Cubans or Puerto Ricans separately?

The 1973 report on persons of Spanish origin provides some important answers. When descriptive tables about distinct Spanish-origin subgroups were provided, they tended to use data mostly on the Mexican-origin population. Tables on educational attainment, for example, reported on the education level of the Spanish-origin population and then provided a separate description of educational attainment for the Mexican-origin. In some cases, the report also provided information on Puerto Ricans separately.[81]

Indeed, much of the reason for combining subgroups into a broad Spanish-origin category had to do with sample size. During one SOAC meeting, Cuban and Puerto Rican members asked the bureau why it had produced reports with statistics on the Spanish-origin population and on Mexicans, but not on individual ethnonational groups. In response, a bureau official pointed out that the 1970 Spanish-origin question had been included on only one of the long forms, which reached a 5 percent sample of the US population. Given this, the official argued, it was difficult to report on the smaller subgroups because the sample size was too small and the standard error often too high to make valid estimates.

Without having oversampled smaller groups, he continued, the bureau could not confidently report on the characteristics of each Spanish-origin subgroup separately.[82] The information on the small subgroups, such as Cuban Americans, would not be lost, he stated, because that information would be aggregated.[83]

In many ways, then, the bureau was already disposed to recognize, at least technically, that Latin American subgroups were part of a panethnic group. Despite this, the bureau itself was still unclear about who was part of this Spanish-origin population. In his notes for his initial meeting with "Spanish leaders" in March 1974, Barabba noted that a main purpose of the committee would be to help the bureau figure out exactly who belonged to the Spanish-origin group.[84]

SOAC members did not really challenge the bureau's interpretation of the 1970 data or its decision to employ a Spanish-origin question. For them, the argument about sample size seemed to suffice.[85] Because the bureau had made a commitment to count Mexican Americans, Puerto Ricans, Cuban Americans, and other subgroups on the short form for the 1980 census, which would yield larger sample sizes and more local-level data, SOAC members probably believed that their issues with data reporting would be resolved.

Moreover, there is evidence that SOAC members were unperturbed by the way the bureau reported on the Spanish-origin population. Indeed, some SOAC members found the aggregate Spanish-origin classification beneficial because the "Other Spanish" category provided an opportunity to include those who did not consider themselves part of an ethnonational group. This becomes clear when we examine the SOAC discussions about the third generation and persons of mixed descent.

As early as 1975, SOAC members inquired about whether the bureau could create a category that could allow Spanish-origin respondents who did not identify with a particular nationality to distinguish themselves from Anglo whites. Although this may not have been an issue for immigrants who had been in the United States for a short time and still identified with their native countries, it was of special concern to leaders of the Mexican American community because some of its members had been in the United States for several generations. One Mexican American SOAC member reported that "there was substantial peer pressure in the Southwest [among the second, third, and fourth generations] not to identify oneself as Mexican."[86] This population would probably prefer to identify as Chicano, Raza, Tejano, or Californio. Puerto Ricans also worried that third-generation Puerto Ricans would identify themselves as Spanish or even Boricua rather than Puerto Rican. In 1978, just before the census was to finalize its coding instructions for race and ethnicity, the SOAC recommended that the bureau retain the "Other Spanish" category used on the 1970 long form, or at least provide a write-in option that could capture these mainly third- and fourth-generation respondents as members of the Spanish-origin population.[87]

Essentially, SOAC members argued that even those who did not identify with a particular Latin American point of origin, such as Mexico or Puerto Rico, should still be distinguished from whites. This had two effects. On the one hand, it extended the idea of the Spanish-origin population beyond nationality and beyond the second generation. On the other hand, this argument suggested that "Spanish Origin" was a real collective identity. One could identify as and feel "Other Spanish" only if there was a Spanish-origin categorical reference that was distinct from individual subgroup identities. Thus, the "Other Spanish" category could indicate that even if the second and third generation did not identify with a Latin American point of origin, they had links with those who did. By arguing that there was something about Spanish-origin identity that went beyond nationality, SOAC members implied that there was a cultural link among Latin American subgroups.

The "Other Spanish" category had another important function: it provided the bureau and the SOAC with a means of categorizing persons of mixed ancestry. As early as 1975, members of the SOAC had argued among themselves about how to categorize respondents who had, for example, one Puerto Rican and one Cuban parent. If these respondents chose not to self-identify as either Cuban or Puerto Rican and no other option was available, they would not be counted as part of the Spanish-origin population. The "Other Spanish" category could capture respondents of mixed heritage because it would not force them to choose between divided loyalties.[88] Although some SOAC members resisted this suggestion and argued that the bureau should find a way to count such respondents as both Cuban and Puerto Rican, the bureau ultimately decided that "Other Spanish" would be the better option. This compromise on mixed ancestry was no doubt shaped by the fact that the bureau had not yet institutionalized a way to efficiently count persons of mixed heritage.

Nonresponse Rates and Subgroup Distinctions: Puerto Ricans in the Far West

The idea that Latin American subgroups might share a collective identity, however, did not override the importance of ethnonational identification for SOAC members. Although discussions about mixed ancestry and the third generation hinted at some underlying bond shared by Latin American subgroups, SOAC members shelved this discourse when officials suggested that panethnic identity was more important than national identity. Indeed, one of the main points of contention between the SOAC and the bureau emerged in 1977 when the bureau considered eliminating the Spanish-origin subgroup categories on the short form.

Between 1975 and 1978, the bureau conducted five major census trials to assess different versions of the Spanish-origin question. It experimented with different wordings and the placement of categories in order to ensure that all respondents, including whites, blacks, Native Americans, and Asian Americans, would answer the Spanish-origin question. Local media were asked to publicize the trials, enumerators were hired, and 100 percent of residents in the test areas were provided with the trial forms. The high nonresponse rates in the first few trials led the bureau to question the use of a separate question for Spanish origin.

In 1977, after consulting its statistical and population advisory committees, and despite extreme disapproval from the SOAC, the bureau tested a new ethnicity question in a major trial in Oakland. This question was distinct from the question about an individual's race and would serve as a substitute for the separate Spanish-origin question. Specifically, the question on the short form asked individuals to check whether they were of European, African, Spanish, or "Other" origin (this would of course compare individuals who hailed from continental categories [European and African] with those who hailed from a national-diasporic category [Spanish]). Using this question meant that the bureau would be able to estimate local-level information for the Spanish-origin population but not for individual groups like Mexican Americans and Puerto Ricans. On the long form, however, respondents would be able to answer the ethnicity question and write in their subgroup information. Thus, a person who was of European origin could write in "Italian American," a person of African origin could write in "African American," and a person of Spanish origin could write in "Mexican American."

Outraged, SOAC members called the bureau's tactics "nasty" and "deceitful." They charged the bureau with ignoring their recommendation to collect Latin American subgroup information on the short form.[89] Bureau officials responded that they were still committed to providing data on the Spanish-origin population but that they had never agreed to provide complete, local-level data on distinct subgroups. Additionally, the bureau argued that the combined question had two important benefits. First, it could solve the problem of the high nonresponse rates for the Spanish-origin question. Non-Hispanics often skipped the Spanish-origin question, and the bureau was hopeful that the combined ethnicity question could appeal to persons of all backgrounds. Second, the bureau reasoned that a combined ethnicity question would be "more fair" to other subgroups—especially Polish Americans, who had recently begun to pressure the bureau to collect data on their community.[90]

The SOAC was not appeased. Members felt betrayed by the bureau and insisted that it collect complete data on subgroups on the short form. Indeed, ethnonational identity still had great importance for Mexican American, Puerto Rican, and Cuban American leaders. During an SOAC discussion in 1977, for example, a Puerto Rican member of the audience spoke out, stating that the combined ethnicity question would not allow for an accurate, local-level count of Puerto Ricans living in the "Far West":

Although the bureaucrats in Washington may not realize it, this [local-level subgroup data collected on the short form] is a matter of grave interest to the Puerto Ricans in the Far West. They are in a peculiar position. They are sandwiched between two powerful minorities—the blacks and the Mexican-Americans. All doors to address their concerns are closed. When they try to go to an agency to demand their rights, they find the Chicanos are in control. [The Puerto Rican] has concluded that the Chicanos fight hard for what they want, but the benefits they win are only for their own people. The Puerto Ricans are left out.[91]

He noted that there were real differences in agendas, needs, and interests among the different Spanish-origin subgroups, and by not providing each subgroup with data about its own population, the bureau weakened the ability of the smaller subgroups, like Puerto Ricans on the West Coast, to lobby successfully for their causes. Mexican Americans on the SOAC were also extremely unhappy with the bureau's insistence on a combined ethnicity question. Vilma Martinez of MALDEF, chairperson of the SOAC, argued that without complete subgroup data, Mexican Americans would not be able to file class-action lawsuits on behalf of disadvantaged Mexican American communities.[92]

Nonetheless, the bureau carried on and tested the combined ethnicity question in its Oakland precensus trial. Yet the results of the trial were disappointing. The combined ethnicity question had elicited an even lower response rate from whites than the Spanish-origin question had.[93] Non-Spanish-origin whites, who would have been expected to check "European American," ended up skipping this question at a higher rate than they had skipped the Spanish-origin question in other trials.

For the last trial, in Manhattan, the bureau switched back to using a separate Spanish-origin question. A new version of the question produced a more reliable response rate. The question still asked respondents to indicate whether they were of Mexican, Puerto Rican, Cuban, or "Other Spanish" origin, but the question now included "No (not Spanish/Hispanic)" as a first option. When non-Hispanic respondents came to the question, they could simply check the first category.[94]

Essentially, the SOAC's reaction to the combined ethnicity question underscored an important aspect of the way that these community leaders conceived of panethnicity. Although their comments and criticisms hinted that there were some commonalities among Latin American subgroups, it was clear that the idea of panethnicity would be acceptable only if it did not negate their ethnonational identity.

Spanish Speakers, Spanish-Origin, Latinos, and Hispanics

By late 1979 the bureau had decided that the Spanish-origin question would employ the identifiers that had received the highest response rates in the census trials. The question would include "Chicano" and "Cuban" but would omit "Central/South American" because of the false-positive answers given in the central and southern United States.

Yet the bureau still faced the issue of how to phrase the question and how to label the new panethnic category. Estrada claimed that census officials had received pressure from the executive office to use the term *Hispanic* somewhere on the census form.[95] As mentioned earlier, OMB's Statistical Policy Directive 15 had mandated that federal agencies collect data on the Spanish-origin population, and although it had not bound organizations to use specific terms, the directive did use the term *Hispanic* heavily throughout.

Moreover, a number of government agencies had expressed early support for incorporating a "Hispanic" label. As early as the fall of 1973, Stanley Pottinger, an assistant attorney general and a section chief of the Civil Rights Division of the Justice Department under Nixon, had written reports on the legal needs of the "Hispanic" population. Having conducted a small study of identifiers for Spanish speakers, Pottinger decided that his staff should use and consistently capitalize the term *Hispanic* in official reports.[96] In October 1974 Pottinger even revised some of President Nixon's official memorandums, advising the executive office that "with few exceptions, the term [*Hispanic*] is well received" and thus should be established as "the appropriate generic term" for the government.[97] Grace Flores-Hughes, a staff member in Nixon's

Department of Health, Education, and Welfare, later claimed that she too had lobbied for the term's use within the department as early as the spring of 1973.[98]

There were certainly other terms that could have been used, but these were rejected because they were either too specific or too general. Indeed, Estrada recalled a meeting with OMB when some on President Ford's staff argued that *Latin American* be used. The representatives of the Census Bureau and others at the meeting rejected the term, Estrada said, because it was too "foreign" and might not capture the second generation. The bureau also rejected the terms *Spanish Surname* and *Spanish Speaking* because they were too specific and often yielded different data. Estrada remembers that the term *Latino* was refused because it seemed tied to the term *Latin*, which could be interpreted as inclusive of all Latin-origin language groups, including French and Italians. And the term *Raza* was perceived as synonymous with *Mexican American*.[99]

Yet the "Hispanic" label was not without problems. It was tied to the notion of *Hispano*, a term used by the purported descendants of Spanish families in the Southwest to distance themselves from Native Americans and other groups. By the mid-twentieth century, having a Hispanic identity in states such as Texas and New Mexico became a way for established families of Spanish and even Mexican descent to distance themselves from poor, undocumented, first-generation Mexican immigrants.[100] Indeed, CCOSSP leaders had resisted relabeling their committee "Hispanic" because some argued that the term *Hispano* was connected to Mexican American shame.[101] Antonia Pantoja, a leading Puerto Rican community activist in the 1960s, noted that the same phenomenon existed among Puerto Ricans in New York: those born in New York often called themselves "Hispanic" or "Spanish" because they felt the need to assimilate and distance themselves from their "Puerto Rican" identity.[102] The term *Hispanic*, although seemingly acceptable to bureaucrats and some community leaders, was not well received by all.

Nonetheless, the term *Hispanic* was introduced on the 1980 census form. The question read, "Is this person of Spanish/Hispanic origin or descent?" and the Census Bureau would later go on to refer to populations as either of Hispanic or non-Hispanic origin. It is not clear if this came about because it was the term that was least problematic or because it had important supporters in other government divisions. What is clear is that by the mid-1970s some activist groups, such as the NCLR, had adopted the term, and census officials hoped that the "Hispanic" label would be received as a valid representation of a distinct panethnic population.

Creating the Spanish-Language Census Form

One of the last issues that the SOAC and the Census Bureau faced concerned the final Spanish-language census form. While this might seem like a simple task requiring the work of a few translators, the issue became complicated as SOAC members considered how local colloquialisms shaped the vocabulary of different Latin American subgroups. Moreover, the issue of class compounded the difficulties. If certain groups, such as Mexican immigrants, had lower levels of education than other groups, such as Cuban Americans, would it be possible to create a common lexicon that each could understand?

For example, the long form asked questions about the respondent's rural surroundings. Vilma Martinez, a Mexican American, objected to the use of the term *finca* for "farm." She suggested the use of *rancho* because it would be more widely understood by Mexican Americans. Luz Cuadrado, a Puerto Rican, however, noted that in Puerto Rico and Caribbean countries, *finca* meant the farm area and *rancho* meant the building. Similar disagreements arose concerning other translated terms such as *head of household, bathroom,* and even *daycare*.[103]

At one point, SOAC members suggested that the bureau use three different Spanish-language long forms that could be circulated locally: a Mexican translation in the Southwest, a Puerto Rican one in the Northeast, and a Cuban one in the Southeast.[104] Estrada was asked to research the issue. He wrote to linguistic experts across the country asking whether a "universal Spanish" form could be achieved. After evaluating their responses, and with the help of a linguistics center in Washington, Estrada and the bureau decided that a single Spanish version of the census long form could be used.[105] They decided that "a universal Spanish did exist . . . except for discrepancies in food, technology, and agricultural descriptors."[106] The long form did not ask about food or technology, but it did ask about agriculture, so Estrada created a Spanish-language question that included three Spanish words for "farm."

The issue of language was important because it underscored the variance within the Spanish-origin population. The fact that the bureau had to spend time investigating whether there could be a "universal Spanish" form shows that it was unsure about whether Latin American subgroups were part of a metagroup. The SOAC was concerned about what these cultural differences might mean for response rates, but the fact that it never insisted on three Spanish forms indicates that it was disposed toward the idea that language could be a unifying characteristic of the Spanish-origin population.

Promoting the Hispanic Category

Once the final Spanish-origin/Hispanic question had been agreed upon, and once a Spanish-language form had been devised, the bureau faced one final task—getting the Spanish-origin population to fill out their census forms. Indeed, throughout their meetings with the bureau, SOAC members spoke candidly about how the bureau would have to exert a special effort to obtain the trust of the Spanish-speaking population, especially undocumented immigrants.[107]

For their part, undocumented immigrants probably feared that the bureau would turn over census information to immigration authorities. This fear was not baseless. In 1930, shortly after the bureau had administered the decennial census with the new "Mexican" race category, President Herbert Hoover ordered a mass-scale deportation of undocumented Mexicans in the Southwest.[108] Although the timing may (or may not) have been coincidental, it exacerbated fear within Mexican American and other communities. Barabba and his staff were conscious of the long legacy of this fear and even took to clipping Spanish-language newspaper articles that encouraged Mexican Americans not to participate in the 1980 census because the data might be provided to immigration agents.[109]

Barabba asked SOAC members to help census officials develop a strategy to publicize the positive aspects of being counted in the 1980 census. Together, the bureau and the SOAC launched a two-part plan. First, the bureau acquired the support of civic organizations, including NCLR, and developed a grassroots campaign to provide information about the census. Second, through contacts with the SOAC, the bureau won the support of key Spanish-language media personnel, especially broadcasters and advertising agents, who agreed to create a Spanish-language media campaign that would encourage participation in the 1980 count.

But aside from response rates, the bureau was also concerned about whether persons of Latin American descent would actually identify themselves as of Spanish or Hispanic origin. The addition of the new Spanish/Hispanic-origin category could only be justified if Mexican Americans, Cuban Americans, Puerto Ricans, and others consistently identified with the label. To ensure this, the bureau had to find community leaders to endorse the idea of a Hispanic community and make the notion of pan-ethnicity seem more like an organic form of cultural identification and less like a bureaucratic construct.

Hispanics at the Grass Roots: Mobilizing Political Organizations

The bureau needed the support of civic organizations because these groups held direct ties to the community and could help to authenticate the new Hispanic category. The bureau soon found that acquiring such support would not be difficult, because many SOAC members had ties to, or were leaders of, these organizations. Samora had founded NCLR; Gnaizda and Martinez were both representatives of MALDEF, which had close ties to NCLR; and Hevia was the head of a prominent Cuban American community organization that was an NCLR affiliate. These SOAC members had agreed to help mobilize a grassroots campaign around the new Hispanic question.[110]

Community leaders were eager to help the bureau because population numbers were a primary consideration when federal and state grants were awarded. From their perspective, the more accurate the count, the better able they would be to claim government resources for their constituencies. Some of the most prominent Mexican American organizations at the time, such as the American GI Forum (AGIF), the League of United Latin American Citizens (LULAC), and NCLR sent representatives to the SOAC meetings. Puerto Rican organizations such as the Puerto Rican Legal Defense and Education Fund and the members of the Cuban National Planning Council also attended some of the meetings.

Perhaps the most organized conduit between the bureau and Hispanic advocacy groups came through the Forum of National Hispanic Organizations (FNHO), a coalition of Mexican American, Cuban American, and Puerto Rican organizations brought together by NCLR to discuss common issues and to coordinate a "Hispanic" agenda.[111] In 1979 the FNHO held a series of meetings with the bureau to discuss the role of the coalition's members in the 1980 census. The FNHO disclosed that several community organizations had already begun to hold public workshops in which community leaders talked about the new "Hispanic" terminology and encouraged community members to respond to the new Spanish/Hispanic-origin question.[112] These FNHO-sponsored workshops were held across the country. The Cuban National Planning Council held sessions in Miami, the Puerto Rican Forum did the same in New York, and AGIF and LULAC held workshops across the Southwest.

Organizations that had multiple chapters also adopted resolutions at their annual conventions to help the census. In 1980 NCLR affiliates adopted a resolution to promote the census in their communities. In the keynote address, "Vamos a Contar! We Are Going to Count in the 1980s!," the speaker linked the census with the aims of NCLR affiliates, stating that "Hispanic" communities had to be counted if their political leaders were to be assured of the necessary demographic and economic data needed to demand resources for bilingual education, job training programs, business development, and fair political representation.[113]

Promoting "Hispanic" on the Airwaves: Mobilizing Spanish-Language Media

While these community forums and national meetings were effective, the bureau also needed a way to connect to the Spanish-origin population on a broader, more massive scale. For advice, it turned to the SOAC, which in turn suggested that the bureau hire a full-time Spanish-language media consultant who could forge networks with key Spanish-language radio, newspaper, and television executives. In effect, the consultant would be in charge of producing Spanish-language census advertisements that could be tailored to different local needs.[114] The idea was not completely novel, for the bureau had a long history of working with media. To publicize the 1970 census, for example, the bureau had solicited the help of the Advertising Council, which created an English-language media campaign about the count and then distributed it to radio, television, and print media groups across the country. At that time, however, no Spanish-language media equivalent of the Advertising Council existed, and Spanish-language media tended to be highly localized and disparate ventures. For example, the country's two largest Spanish-language newspapers, *La Opinión* in Los Angeles and *El Diario* in New York, were not connected to each other through ownership or marketing conglomerates.[115] Spanish-language radio stations also often operated as distinct firms with few links to professional or national organizations.[116] It was not until the late 1970s that sizable Spanish-language media professional organizations such as the National Association of Hispanic Publications and the National Association of Spanish Broadcasters emerged.[117]

Nonetheless, in the late 1970s the bureau hired Armando B. Rendon, who was an early member of NCLR, as its Spanish-language media liaison.[118] Through Rendon, the bureau established contacts with three important Spanish-language media executives: Ed Gomez, Antonio Guernica, and Rene Anselmo. Ed Gomez was one of the country's few Mexican American owners of Spanish-language radio stations. Based in Texas and Albuquerque, Gomez had connected with other Mexican American broadcasters and established the Southwest Spanish Broadcasters Association (SSBA) in 1978.[119] On August 16, 1979, Rendon and Barabba met with Gomez and other members of SSBA.[120] Rendon and his Census Bureau team introduced their idea for a Spanish-language radio commercial, and SSBA agreed to produce it and to persuade its members to air it repeatedly on their broadcast stations.

Anselmo and Guernica were executives at Spanish International Network (SIN), which was at the time the country's only Spanish-language television network.[121] Guernica was head of market research for SIN and was helping to prepare Spanish U.S.A., the country's first national Hispanic marketing survey.[122] Anselmo was SIN's president. Rendon and Barabba presented the bureau's Spanish-language media campaign to SIN executives, asking them to produce and run the bureau's ads on their stations. They agreed, but Guernica and Anselmo had their own ideas for promoting census participation. They wanted to create a series of commercials that would run on SIN stations. The commercials would encourage Spanish-language television viewers to fill out the census forms and, equally important, would emphasize the importance of answering the Spanish/Hispanic-origin question. Additionally, Anselmo and Guernica revealed that they planned to have Spanish-language station managers make the census a topic in their weekly news magazine shows. In Los Angeles, for example, census participation would be spotlighted in a weekly segment. SIN executives also planned to air a special documentary on the role that Hispanics would play in the census. Titled *Destino 80*, this documentary would "explain government procedures and demonstrate how to fill out census questionnaires."[123]

The media efforts launched by SIN would not only convey the importance of census participation but also show audiences how to respond to the Spanish/Hispanic-origin question. Just before census forms were mailed, Rendon and SIN officials broadcast a daylong telethon, replete with Mexican, Puerto Rican, and Cuban musical acts. Rendon recalled that

we had people manning the phones with a hotline number for people to call in. . . . Off to the side we held up the [1980] census form and the camera zoomed in on the Hispanic question, introducing viewers to the new categories.[124]

A number of circumstances undoubtedly contributed to the cooperation of Spanish-language broadcasters. *Destino 80* and the ads promoting the census counted as public service announcements, which helped the networks fill their quotas for their impending renewal applications. However, this was likely not the most important reason for their cooperation, since SIN executives could have aired the advertisements provided by the bureau without spending resources on creating their own commercials, not to mention the documentary and telethon. The major reason that SIN and other media executives were supportive of the bureau's efforts was because the census would provide much-needed consumer data on Hispanics. In the newsletter for the National Association of Spanish Broadcasters, Guernica laid out this argument:

An accurate count of Hispanics in the 1980 Census is a key issue with Spanish broadcasters in that the Census count directly affects station revenue by defining the potential Hispanic audience of the stations and by serving as a basic body of raw data for the development of marketing information and material.[125]

In effect, accurate census data would allow Spanish-language media executives to identify where Hispanics lived and show advertisers the size of the potential audience for Spanish-language media. Furthermore, sample surveys would provide additional information on Hispanic consumer behavior, which could be used to attract more advertising revenue from certain industries.[126]

This mutually beneficial relationship between the Spanish-language media and the bureau had been overlooked during the 1970 census preparations largely because the Spanish-language broadcasting industry was nascent. At the time, the industry included only three full-time television stations and fewer than fifteen full-time Spanish-language radio stations.[127] Additionally, there were virtually no Spanish-language media marketing agencies or Spanish-language consumer data firms.[128] By 1980 Spanish-language media had spread across the Southwest and along the East Coast, and they now had sufficient capacity to broadcast mass advertising for the Census Bureau.

Race Analogies and the 1980 Hispanic Data

After several months of publicity, the 1980 census was launched and the data were compiled. The Census Bureau reported data on Hispanics mainly by comparing Spanish/Hispanic-origin respondents to two newly defined populations: non-Hispanic whites and non-Hispanic blacks. Even though the "Hispanic" category was technically a panethnic classification, the comparisons with whites and blacks made the idea of Hispanic panethnicity seem race-like. These racial analogies soon became a staple of most census reports. For example, a 1987 census report noted, "The educational attainment of Hispanic persons was considerably lower than that for persons of White or Black races."[129] Another report, published in 1990, stated:

The Hispanic share of the total population, and the share of all race groups except Whites, increased from July 1, 1980 to July 1, 1988. The proportion of Blacks grew from 11.8 percent in 1980 to 12.3 percent in 1988 . . . while the proportion [of] Hispanic[s] was 8.1 percent, up from 6.4 percent in 1980.[130]

In effect, by 1990 the Hispanic category had become institutionalized in all census surveys and was used in comparisons to highlight the characteristics of other racial groups in America.[131]

By interpreting the Hispanic data in comparison to racial data, the bureau made the notion of Hispanic panethnicity seem commensurate with, although not equal to, race. Moreover, the racial analogy served as a categorical filter: by describing Hispanics through racial comparisons, the bureau insinuated that a person might be Hispanic if he or she was neither white nor black. This was never a written policy, and the bureau did explain that Hispanics could be of any race, but its reports and charts insinuated that Hispanics constituted a distinct group that was commensurate with whites and blacks.

To be clear, the bureau did at times break down statistics to show differences among some of the larger Latin American subgroups.[132] These statistics were included only in special Hispanic population reports, however, not in the general reports issued by the bureau about, for example, housing, poverty, and education. In these broader national reports, the Hispanic data were simply presented as commensurate with racial data.[133]

Conclusion

The bureau continued to work closely with Hispanic community leaders throughout the 1980s, using this connection to try to popularize the Hispanic category and to convince other government agencies to also collect Hispanic data. For example, in the mid-1980s the bureau worked closely with community leaders to gain leverage with vital statistics agencies across the country. Even in the 1980s, these agencies often still classified persons of Latin American descent as white on birth and death certificates, thus weakening the bureau's ability to estimate a Hispanic undercount.[134] Officials in several states, especially those who believed that their state had a minuscule Latin American population, refused to implement a Hispanic category. Hispanic civic and media leaders helped the bureau by lobbying and meeting with these officials and imploring them to institute a separate Hispanic category. By 1992 all fifty states had instituted some kind of Hispanic category.

And by the time the 1990 census was administered, the Spanish/Hispanic-origin question had become institutionalized in all census surveys. For the most part, the bureau no longer entertained the notion that Mexican Americans, Puerto Ricans, and Cuban Americans were simply white, and self-identifying Hispanic leaders readily volunteered to serve on the SOAC. Some activist organizations even sent their members to the bureau's statistical training workshops to learn how to better analyze Hispanic data.[135]

Indeed, the emergence of the "Hispanic" census category between 1970 and 1990 was the product of ongoing negotiations among several sets of actors, each of whom had distinct interests and abided by distinct organizational logics. This history shows that the federal government is not necessarily an external force that simply imposes data categories on its population. It was through interactive relationships with others in the new field of Hispanic politics that the bureau came to construct new identity categories and to institute new forms of racial and ethnic classification.

The negotiation process, which began in the 1960s when activists started to demand that the census more accurately measure the Spanish-origin population, comprised five important moments. First, activists fomented a legitimacy crisis and enlisted important assistance from government officials. With the help of the IMAA and CCOSSP, activists brought their criticism to the attention of elected officials in the Southwest and officials within the Johnson and Nixon administrations who were interested in the Spanish-speaking vote. This coalition of activists and elected and appointed officials generated an environment that questioned the social consequences of government classification.

In the second phase, census officials addressed the mounting legitimacy crisis by forming a group—the SOAC—to negotiate with. The bureau's selection of members for the SOAC was strategic: the bureau chose to negotiate with those who had academic ties or ties to the federal or state governments. Census officials did not select activists who, for example, sought Chicano self-determination or Puerto Rican independence. While advisory council members like Samora, Martinez, and Creitoff often supported protest activities, they did not represent the more radical cultural nationalist factions within their communities. The bureau chose to negotiate with a more tempered group that, it believed, might appreciate the need for scientific rigor.

Third, these groups negotiated. The new Spanish-origin census question helped the bureau quell the growing legitimacy crisis that it faced. The structure of the question also allowed it to retain some historical racial statistics. Census officials could still categorize Hispanics as whites, but at the same time they could also create reports that distinguished between Hispanics and whites, blacks, and others. To do so, however, the bureau had to make a concession regarding the objectivity of its racial/ ethnic categories. Instead of relying on minutely defined characteristics such as language and surname to measure ethnicity, the bureau adopted self-identification questions and focused on measuring those labels that were reliable. Importantly, however, the idea of Hispanic panethnicity remained broad and ambiguous. Census officials only vaguely defined Hispanics as having some kind of ancestral origin, however subjectively interpreted, in Spain and Latin America. A person of mixed heritage with one great-grandparent from Cuba could be lumped into the same category as a first-generation immigrant from Mexico.

For SOAC members and activists, the new question provided local-level data that distinguished their communities from Anglo whites. It also provided an opportunity to expand their constituency inasmuch as the Spanish-origin category referred to a metagroup. The SOAC and activists, however, did have to give up the idea that Mexican Americans, Puerto Ricans, and Cuban Americans were a racially distinct group. Although many organizations, including NCLR, continued to describe Hispanics as a racial minority, "Hispanic" was officially designated an ethnic category. The new census question also pleased black, Asian, and Native American activists, because it ensured that their numbers would not diminish.

Fourth, census officials enlisted the help of activists and media executives to popularize the Hispanic category. Activists held town hall meetings across the country in which they reminded their communities to be counted and to identify themselves as Spanish/Hispanic-origin. Media executives generated commercials, documentaries, and special programming that introduced Spanish-language audiences to the new Hispanic question. In effect, political activists and media executives helped to legitimate the new category by endorsing the notion of a collective Hispanic identity—the category was not simply a label imposed by the government.

Fifth, scientists used analogies with race to articulate who Hispanics were and to place boundaries around the new category. In census reports, Hispanic data were now compared to "non-Hispanic white" and "non-Hispanic black" racial data. Hispanics were Hispanic because they chose to be, but also because they were statistically different from other racial groups. In other words, Hispanics made up a statistical group that was neither white nor black nor Asian. Although technically Hispanics could be of any race, the racial analogies made the Hispanic category seem race-like. The bureau made the notion of Hispanic panethnicity commensurate with, though not officially equal to, race.

The bureau's tendency to report Hispanic data in comparison to racial data helped to undergird activists' claims that Hispanics were a disadvantaged minority whose situation was comparable to that of blacks. Throughout the late 1970s and 1980s, NCLR and other activists used bureau reports that, for example, showed Hispanics had lower incomes than whites to pen grant applications and to support their broader claims about inequality. Bureau reports essentially helped to legitimate activists' claims about inequality and indirectly helped Hispanic activist groups like NCLR to grow into large, national advocacy organizations.

Ultimately, the "Hispanic" statistical category emerged from a negotiating process in which a variety of interest groups vied to assert their own interpretations of group identity. Census officials had to tend to the interests not simply of Mexican American, Puerto Rican, and some Cuban American leaders but also of black and Asian activists, as well as selected officials and government representatives. In the process, census officials abandoned the attempt to measure the Spanish-origin population objectively through questions about language, surname, and birth and focused instead on using their resources and networks to craft reliable categories. Activists and media executives helped to popularize the "Hispanic" category precisely because they had developed a vested interest in the notion of panethnicity. The next chapter zeroes in on media executives and reveals why and how they helped produce the idea of a Hispanic collective identity.

FOUR

Broadcasting Panethnicity: Univision and the Rise of Hispanic Television

By the 1980s Spanish-language television networks had created documentaries, variety shows, and news programming that advanced the notion of Hispanic panethnicity. Alongside commercials designed to promote the Hispanic census category were talk and entertainment programs that included Mexican, Cuban, and Puerto Rican personalities. News programs stitched together segments about different Latin American countries with reports on the cultural, political, and demographic profile of America's Hispanic population.

Spanish-language television, however, had not always embraced the idea of panethnicity. During the 1950s and early 1960s, the nascent industry was a disparate endeavor focused on providing individual immigrant groups with coethnic media. Mexican media entrepreneurs broadcast several hours of Mexican soap operas, movies, and variety shows to audiences in the Southwest, while Puerto Rican entrepreneurs broadcast programming from San Juan to audiences in New York. The shift for Spanish-language television would not come until the 1970s, when the leading network expanded and accommodated to the changes within its organizational field.

In effect, Spanish-language television evolved as it responded to advertisers' expectations, adjusted to Census Bureau policies, and forged networks with newly emerging

Hispanic activist groups like NCLR. Advertisers wanted Spanish-language television to mimic mainstream media's national, rather than regional, structure, and this persuaded Mexican American media pioneers to establish stations in Puerto Rican and Cuban barrios on the East Coast. As television expanded nationally, it forged a new identity and began to describe its audiences as a national Hispanic consumer market. At the same time, Spanish-language media executives learned to analyze and use Hispanic census data to create Hispanic marketing reports and concepts like Hispanic purchasing power. And by the mid-1980s, media executives had formed close links with Hispanic activists, who supported media expansion and became regular contributors on Spanish-language public affairs programming.

This chapter documents how these changes occurred by examining the rise and expansion of Univision, the nation's largest and best-established Spanish-language television network. The network's parent company, Univision Communications Corporation, began as a joint venture between Mexican and Mexican American executives in the early 1960s, and within thirty years it became one of the nation's foremost television corporations. Before I delve into how Univision became the nation's first Hispanic television network, however, it is important to first provide a brief history of the international origins of Spanish-language television. In fact, it was Mexican media executives who provided the funding, programming, and technological resources necessary to build and sustain the first Spanish-language television network in the United States. The story of Univision thus begins not in the impoverished immigrant barrios of the American Southwest, but in the high-powered elite circles of midcentury Mexico.

Emilio Azcárraga's Latin American Media Monopoly

In 1951 the Mexican government granted one of the country's first television licenses to Emilio Azcárraga Vidaurreta. A successful radio entrepreneur, Azcárraga had transformed Mexico into one of Latin America's leading exporters of Spanish-language radio programming in the 1940s. By establishing radio stations whose signal could reach as far south as Central America and by shipping programming to countries in the Caribbean and South America, Azcárraga had pushed Mexico to the forefront of Latin American broadcasting.[1]

Azcárraga came from an upper-class Mexican family that specialized in international trade. Educated in Texas boarding schools and universities, he married into the elite Milmo family, which had amassed a small fortune from its interests in North American banking and trade industries.[2] In 1930 the Radio Corporation of America (RCA) provided Azcárraga with the resources to establish the station XEW in Mexico City.[3] At the time, RCA was eager to expand its sale of American-made radio parts, phonographs, and records in Latin America, but it needed to first help develop the region's radio industry.[4] Specifically, RCA provided Azcárraga with capital, technology, and low-cost access to American radio programs that were produced by RCA's affiliate, the National Broadcasting Corporation (NBC).[5] Additionally, RCA provided Azcárraga with connections to US corporations seeking to sell their products in Latin America.[6]

Access to RCA resources, along with a revenue stream from US corporations, soon allowed Azcárraga to establish several more radio stations throughout Mexico in the 1930s.[7] During this period, Azcárraga also established a series of production studios where his staff created radio news and soap opera broadcasts that would be heard across the country. By the mid-1940s, almost half of all Mexican radio stations were either owned by Azcárraga or affiliated with his network.[8]

Azcárraga's aspirations, however, stretched beyond Mexico. XEW's tagline was "The Voice of Latin America," and its powerful radio wave frequency allowed its broadcasts to be heard as far south as Costa Rica.[9] Azcárraga also used his connections to RCA-affiliated executives in other countries to facilitate media trades between Mexico and nations like Argentina and Cuba.[10] To cater to this more diverse Latin American market, Azcárraga's production studios created soap operas that touched on themes that could resonate with broader Spanish-speaking audiences, such as religion, the extended family, and the urban-rural divide. The heart-wrenching storylines were usually set to the melodramatic beat of a bolero score, a genre that Azcárraga hoped would appeal to audiences beyond Mexico. The strategy seems to have worked. By 1942, just twelve years after establishing XEW, Azcárraga was exporting Mexican shows to eleven Spanish-speaking countries.[11]

Given his success in radio, it was no surprise that Azcárraga received one of Mexico's first television licenses. In 1951 he established XEW-TV in Mexico City and soon thereafter several more stations in the interior and northern regions of Mexico. Azcárraga's stations broadcast a combination of dubbed US programming provided by NBC and other networks as well as television programs produced in his Mexican studios. Other Mexican television networks formed in the early 1950s, but in 1955 they merged with Azcárraga's corporation to form Telesistema Mexicano SA, monopolizing the Mexican media industry.[12] From 1955 through 1967,

Azcárraga's corporation owned the *only* commercial broadcast television network in Mexico.[13]

During this period, Azcárraga also developed a corporation devoted solely to exporting Spanish-language television. Teleprogramas Acapulco, a Telesistema subsidiary established in 1960, produced soap operas for export to Latin America and, later, the United States.[14] As he had done with radio, Azcárraga focused on creating programs that could be understood and enjoyed by most persons in Latin America. To this end, Azcárraga hired actors from across Latin America to star in the Teleprogramas Acapulco programs. And to make the shows seem cohesive, Azcárraga's staff carefully edited out different nation-specific idioms and phrases to create a more generic Spanish.[15]

Such practices made Azcárraga the world's leading producer and exporter of Spanish-language television programming. Other countries, such as Argentina and Cuba, soon came under dictatorship rule, and they failed to provide the legal and market resources necessary to export television programs. In Brazil, where television had also developed extensively, access barriers, especially linguistic, inhibited trade.[16]

As the 1960s approached, Azcárraga set his sights on the Spanish-speaking population of the United States.[17] He believed that since his products had been successful in Mexico, Puerto Rico, and Cuba (before the revolution), they would also be popular in Mexican American, Puerto Rican, and Cuban American communities north of the US-Mexico border.

Early Spanish-Language Television in America

Azcárraga, though, was not the first producer of Spanish-language television in the United States. In 1955 Raúl Cortez and his son-in-law Emilio Nicolás, Mexican immigrants residing in San Antonio, established KCOR-TV, the nation's first full-time Spanish-language television station. KCOR-TV was an independent station, not connected to any network, and it broadcast on a local frequency. The station's programming lineup consisted of imported Mexican programming and shows produced in the KCOR-TV studio. For their in-house productions, Cortez and Nicolás frequently traveled to Mexico and hired actors who could cross the border to perform in their shows.[18]

Cortez and Nicolás financed KCOR-TV primarily through advertisements purchased by local Mexican immigrant business owners.[19] This provided enough revenue to produce some programming, but it offered little opportunity to expand beyond San Antonio. Over time, Cortez and

Nicolás found it increasingly difficult to meet operating costs, and after three years in business, KCOR-TV went bankrupt and shut down.[20]

Although there were no other full-time Spanish-language stations, immigrant media entrepreneurs did produce programs that aired on English-language television stations. In New York, Anibal Gonzalez-Irizarry produced a variety program that showcased Puerto Rican musical acts.[21] Similarly, in Corpus Christi, Texas, José Pérez "Pepe" del Río created a local program for Mexican Americans that aired on Sunday afternoons.[22]

By providing media products that reminded immigrants of their home country, and by limiting broadcasts to local audiences, early Spanish-language television helped to reinforce Latin American ethnonational identities in the United States. In other words, Mexican entrepreneurs created programming that reinforced Mexican culture in the Southwest. Puerto Rican entrepreneurs did the same for their coethnics in the Northeast. Although the technology was available and heavily used by the mainstream media, financial difficulties precluded early Spanish-language media entrepreneurs from diversifying their programming strategies and expanding outside of their local ethnic enclaves.

Azcárraga's US Debut

In 1960 Azcárraga approached NBC and offered to sell it exclusive rights to films, soap operas, and variety shows produced by Telesistema. Hoping to capitalize on the technology and market infrastructure created by NBC within the United States, Azcárraga expected the deal to create an export market for his Mexican programs. The trade agreement would potentially mirror the agreement he had already established with NBC to air American programs on Mexican stations; it would literally create a reverse flow (from south to north) of television programming.[23] Azcárraga was turned down by NBC and, later, by ABC and CBS.

Enraged, Azcárraga decided to establish his own network of full-time Spanish-language broadcast stations. Because the FCC stipulated that only US citizens could own American stations, Azcárraga organized a group of American partners and financed their purchase of two stations in the Southwest.[24] To lead this venture, Azcárraga recruited Reynold (Rene) Anselmo, an Italian American who had lived in Mexico for several years and had worked for Telesistema. Anselmo had no experience working in US media, but his degree from the University of Chicago, his history of working for Azcárraga in Mexican media, and his strong

Table 2 Structure of SICC and SIN, 1962–86

	Spanish International Communications Corporation (SICC, formerly SIBC [Spanish International Broadcasting Corporation])	Spanish International Network (SIN)
Ownership structure	Multiple shareholders, Azcárraga's share limited to 20%	Azcárraga sole shareholder until 1971, then 75% shareholder
Purpose	Official owner of Spanish-language television stations and licensee to affiliates	Provider of the network feed to SICC stations and affiliates

Spanish-language fluency made him a likely candidate.[25] Azcárraga also recruited Emilio Nicolás, a naturalized citizen and a co-owner of the short-lived KCOR-TV in San Antonio. From Los Angeles, Azcárraga enlisted Frank Fouce, a Mexican American theater owner who had made a personal fortune by screening Azcárraga's Telesistema films for Mexican Americans in Los Angeles.[26]

Azcárraga and his group formed the Spanish International Communications Corporation (SICC), which would hold the station licenses, and the Spanish International Network (SIN), which would provide the Mexican feed.[27] Because Azcárraga was not an American citizen, his share of SICC was limited to 20 percent, but because there were no foreign ownership restrictions on networks, Azcárraga became SIN's sole shareholder.[28]

Anselmo was named the president of SICC, and Azcárraga held the title of president of SIN. Nicolás served on the executive boards of both SICC and SIN, but his main duty was to manage the San Antonio station, the corporation's flagship outlet. Fouce was SICC's largest shareholder, but he did not hold shares in SIN and played a limited role in managing SICC's stations.[29]

SICC's first purchases were KWEX-TV in San Antonio in 1962 and KMEX in Los Angeles in 1964.[30] Since all the VHF channels had already been allocated to English-language stations, these stations broadcast in the UHF spectrum.[31] KWEX and KMEX were a natural choice for Azcárraga and his associates because they served the two largest Mexican American communities in the United States at that time. First-generation Mexican immigrants who were already familiar with Telesistema programming were probably the new network's most loyal American audience.

Before the end of the 1960s, Azcárraga and Anselmo also purchased stations in non–Mexican immigrant communities farther east. In 1968 SICC acquired WXTV in New Jersey to serve Spanish speakers in New York, who at the time were mainly Puerto Rican. Similarly, it acquired affiliate WCIU in Chicago and reached out to heavily Puerto Rican neighborhoods in the Midwest. SICC's 1971 purchase of WLTV in Miami allowed Anselmo and Azcárraga to broadcast Spanish-language media products to the newly established Cuban immigrant community.[32]

In 1972, shortly before he passed away, Azcárraga made Anselmo president of SIN. Azcárraga's son, Emilio Azcárraga Milmo, became head of Telesistema and inherited most of his father's shares of SIN.[33] Together, Anselmo and Azcárraga Milmo reorganized SIN and SICC and increased the network's reach. In 1979 they paid cable franchise operators across the country ten cents for every subscriber with a Spanish surname.[34] In exchange, cable franchises agreed to carry SIN's feed. By 1982 SIN's feed was being broadcast by twenty-nine cable franchises.[35]

Anselmo and Azcárraga Milmo were also among the first to employ satellite technology. In 1971 the duo developed SIN-West, which was the first US network to broadcast its programming via satellite. SIN-West connected five stations in the Southwest to stations in Mexico City and along the US-Mexico border.[36] The technology made real-time television possible—audiences in Los Angeles and Mexico City, for example, were able to see the same programs at the same time—and it facilitated the international exchange of television programs. By 1979 more than sixty-four hours of weekly programming were being distributed across the border to SICC's stations.[37]

By 1980 the list of SICC's stations and subsidiaries had grown to include stations in every major media market.[38] And by 1985 SIN was broadcasting to an estimated 90 percent of Spanish-speaking households

Table 3 Geographic dispersion of SICC stations, 1965–80

	1965		1970		1975		1980	
	Station	City	Station	City	Station	City	Station	City
Southwest	KWEX	San Antonio	KWEX	San Antonio	KWEX	San Antonio	KWEX	San Antonio
	KMEX	Los Angeles	KMEX	Los Angeles	KMEX	Los Angeles	KMEX	Los Angeles
			KFTV	Fresno	KFTV	Fresno	KFTV	Fresno
					KLOC	Modesto	KLOC	Modesto
							KCBA	Salinas
							KTVW	Phoenix
Northeast			WXTV	New York	WXTV	New York	WXTV	New York
Southeast			WLTV	Miami	WLTV	Miami	WLTV	Miami
Midwest					WCIU	Chicago	WCIU	Chicago

(about nine million people) and was carried on several cable systems throughout the United States and Puerto Rico.[39]

Financing SIN and Creating a Hispanic Market

Why did the Azcárragas and Anselmo decide to expand nationally? Given that SIN and SICC had ready, low-cost access to Telesistema's content from Mexico, and that Mexican immigrants represented at least 60 percent of the Latin American population in the United States,[40] why would media executives decide to expand beyond the Southwest? One might posit that the supranational structure of Latin American media influenced this decision. As mentioned earlier, Azcárraga profited handsomely from his international trade ventures, and it may have seemed logical for him to expand outside of Mexican immigrant communities.

Although Latin American trade practices certainly influenced how media executives perceived their audience, it is not clear that this was the only reason for network expansion.[41] Expansion beyond the Southwest entailed severe financial losses for SICC because its East Coast stations often operated in the red during the 1970s.[42] WXTV, in the New York City area, was the most problematic because of the higher cost of real estate and labor and, simply the higher cost of conducting business transactions in that area.[43] Given these losses, it would have been logical for the executives of SIN and SICC to remain in the Southwest and continue to provide Mexican Americans with Mexican programming.[44] So why did the company decide to expand to the East Coast?

The reason for the network's expansion becomes clear when we examine the relationship between the network and advertisers. In effect, SIN and corporate marketers had starkly different perceptions of Spanish-language audiences. SIN and SICC media executives perceived their audience as a captive market. Given that no other Spanish-language television networks existed at that time, they believed that the network's potential advertisers had a rare opportunity to sell their products to a virtually untapped market of Spanish-speaking consumers. Yet media marketers had a different perception of Mexicans and other subgroups. Unlike the network executives, they perceived Spanish speakers as part of the general mainstream market. In a press interview, Anselmo recalled that during the 1960s advertising agents would say:

Well, you know, these people aren't going to [watch television in] Spanish. They have all these English channels they've been looking at for 15 years. Why would they want to look at a Spanish station? And they're old, these people will be dying and the second generation doesn't speak Spanish.[45]

According to Anselmo, marketers at that time did not believe that Mexican immigrants would be interested in Mexican programming because they perceived them as an assimilating population that was disappearing under a white racial umbrella. The fact that SIN could provide shows that reminded them of their home country would soon be irrelevant because, like other white ethnic European groups, Mexican immigrants were, or would eventually become, Americanized and would thus prefer English-language programming. These ideas were reinforced by the Census Bureau and some other government agencies. As we saw in chapter 3, several data sets, such as the US census, lumped Mexican American data together with European American data under a simple "white" classification, thus creating the impression that Mexican immigrants were somehow similar to European immigrants.

Besides creating the impression of whiteness, Census Bureau practices also made it difficult for advertisers to estimate the size of SIN's southwestern audience. The Census Bureau's failure to provide Spanish speakers with Spanish-language census forms and to dispatch bilingual enumerators to southwestern neighborhoods for the 1960 census is one example.[46] To make matters worse, the bureau also used measures, such as the Spanish-surname question, that yielded overly conservative estimates of the Mexican American population.[47]

Under these conditions, SIN and SICC executives and researchers had to piece together regional and national data sets to prove to advertisers that the Mexican American population was a sizable one, and one that was continuously replenished by a stream of new immigrants. This method often led to confusion, however, because it produced different numbers for the same groups of people. One article in a 1962 issue of *Broadcast* highlighted how wide this variation could be when it quoted a top media researcher who quipped, "The Spanish population of the border states? I don't know. . . . [It] could be anywhere between one and four million."[48]

SIN and SICC executives also found it difficult to convince marketers that Mexican immigrants preferred Spanish-language programming. At the time there were no large surveys that provided data on Mexican immigrants' language abilities, much less their consumer behaviors and habits. As a result, the executives had no solid quantitative data on how much Spanish Mexicans spoke, what they purchased, or even whether they watched television.[49]

These difficulties were exacerbated by the fact that the viewership rating system used by Nielsen and Arbitron, the two largest US media research firms, did not accommodate SIN's audience. Like the Census Bureau, Nielsen and Arbitron used only English-language questionnaires, and they relied on a mail-based system for their distribution and return. Anselmo and other network executives informed the research firms that the English-language forms probably would not be understood by first-generation Mexican immigrants and that a significant percentage of their audience members lived in places without a formal postal address, but the firms refused to change their practices.[50] As a result, data on the viewing habits of the Mexican-origin population were incomplete, and the estimates reported for the number of SIN's viewers were overly conservative.[51]

Given this, it is not surprising that marketers had a hard time accepting the idea of a sizable and captive Mexican-origin media market. And this posed a major hurdle for SIN and SICC executives. Indeed, the network and stations could survive for a few years with Azcárraga's funding, but only advertising revenue from national corporations could generate a profit. Given the reluctance to see Mexican Americans as a viable market, the network's executives knew they had to create their own marketing division, which could produce market research and focus on selling airtime to national advertisers.[52] In the mid-1960s SIN established a sales office in Los Angeles. Company executives soon discovered, however, that they would have to move the office to New York City. As a former sales executive noted, "SIN needed to move to Madison Avenue [in New York City]. . . . [They] couldn't get the big advertising dollars if they were only in Los Angeles; all the decisions were made in New York."[53] In 1968 Anselmo hired Eduardo Caballero, then a thirty-year-old Cuban exile, and placed him in charge of a newly established network sales office in New York.[54]

Yet it was not enough to establish a sales office in New York City, for national corporations also expected networks to have a station in that market. Although this was never an official rule, Caballero claimed that it was extremely difficult to sell SIN programming to New York–based advertising firms if "they couldn't turn on the television set and see [the network's programming] in New York."[55] Anselmo and Azcárraga quickly realized the strategic importance of establishing a station in New York, and in late 1968 Anselmo launched WXTV for audiences in the Tri-state area. For Caballero the establishment of WXTV was a boon. Instead of having to claim that he represented a regional media venture focused on Mexican American communities, he could now claim that he represented a national television network that catered to Spanish speakers nationwide. With the move west, SIN and SICC were also well on their way to appearing more like a mainstream American corporation rather than simply a regional fringe one.

Promoting its audience as a national panethnic market bounded by the Spanish language soon became SIN's signature strategy. Caballero recalled that one of his favorite ways of opening a sales pitch to corporations was to play a tape recording of a news report in Greek. After a few minutes, and a few blank stares, Caballero would stop the tape and ask the corporate executives how much they had understood. When executives confessed to not understanding a word, Caballero would analogize their experience with that of Spanish speakers in the United States, arguing that if companies were not advertising on Spanish-language television, their products were not reaching the large number of Spanish speakers that stretched from California to New York.

In creating this strategy, SIN and SICC executives were essentially highlighting one cultural characteristic—the Spanish language—and using it as proof of a panethnic collective. For these executives, the Spanish language became the cultural characteristic that could transcend national—Puerto Rican, Cuban, and Mexican American—boundaries. This decision to elevate language was made despite the lack of social science data on Spanish-language skills, and despite the fact that bilingual second- and third-generation immigrants might not have preferred Spanish-language over English-language television.[56]

The arguments about the unifying effects of the Spanish language and panethnicity were restated continually during the 1970s and early 1980s in advertising and media marketing trade journals.[57] And over time, SIN salesmen attached these arguments to images of an upwardly mobile, national, Hispanic consumer market. For example, an advertisement printed in *Advertising Age* in 1981 claimed that "only SIN-TV has the kind of programming and the credibility to attract Mexicans, Puerto Ricans, Cubans and Hispanics from every country . . . uniting young, getting richer *Spanish* USA into a single national marketing opportunity."[58] Another advertisement, printed in 1980, noted that "Spanish eyes are on SIN 24 hours a day" and showed "Spanish USA" spread across the country, suggesting that Spanish-language audiences composed a national constituency (fig. 1).[59]

SIN and SICC executives also financed audience research to compensate for the lack of demographic data and consumer behavior research on

Spanish eyes are on SIN 24 hours a day.

The eyes of Spanish USA are on the SIN National Spanish Television Network, stretching coast to coast across the fifth-largest Spanish-speaking country in the world...the 20 million Hispanics in Spanish USA.

In 1980 SIN's 40 network affiliates are growing to more than 100, all served through the first and only satellite-interconnected commercial television network in the U.S.

Now in its 20th year, SIN takes another giant step. Beginning April 27, SIN will be on the satellite 24 hours a day, seven days a week with the best Spanish-language television in the world.

In the 1980's the SIN National Spanish Television Network provides programming that mirrors the rich cultural diversity of the Hispanic population of the U.S. As SIN grows, it continues to be, for the nation's top advertisers, the most efficient, effective and exciting medium to sell to America's fastest-growing market.

All-Spanish, all via satellite, all the time.

When Spanish eyes are on SIN, they like what they see.

SIN NATIONAL SPANISH TELEVISION NETWORK
250 Park Avenue, New York, New York 10017. (212) 557-9050

1   SIN advertisement in *Advertising Age*, April 7, 1980

the Spanish-speaking population. In the late 1960s they commissioned the Strategy Research Corporation (SRC) to conduct Spanish-language media market studies in Los Angeles, New York, and, later, Miami. SRC's reports incorporated the same panethnic language that SIN and SICC executives used. Reports from the 1970s thus detailed the income, age, and consumer habits of SIN's audiences, but SRC researchers did not necessarily describe these differences in terms of ethnonational identities.[60]

As 1980 approached, SIN and SICC executives took an active role in preparations for the census, working alongside Census Bureau officials and political leaders to help ensure an accurate count of the Spanish/Hispanic-origin population. In the weeks leading up to the census, SIN stations across the country ran television advertisements and documentaries that reminded audiences to fill out their census forms and to answer the bureau's newly instituted Spanish/Hispanic-origin question.[61] Activists were also invited onto SIN national and local news programs to speak about how to fill out the census form and what the new Hispanic category meant.[62] The 1980 census count was crucial for SIN and SICC because it could settle debates among marketers about the size of the potential audience for Spanish-language media.

The 1980 census, however, also served an important symbolic function by generating statistical proof that Hispanics really did exist. Caballero thus contends that the 1980 census results finally put the idea of a Hispanic market "on the map"—if only because SIN sales representatives could now point to the fact that census officials were also labeling and recognizing Mexican Americans, Puerto Ricans, and Cuban Americans as one national and panethnic Hispanic group.[63] Indeed, shortly after the count was tabulated, the SIN sales team used the census data on Hispanics to define the contours of what they and others in the newly emerging group of Spanish-language media marketers had termed the "Hispanic market."[64] Specifically, the SIN sales team aggregated the data on Latin American subgroups and created new statistics for concepts such as "Hispanic disposable income" and "Hispanic buying power."[65] SIN marketers also used the national data to show demographic trends, creating statistical descriptions of, for example, Hispanic women and Hispanic youth. In short, the 1980 census provided SIN executives with government-issued (read: legitimate) data to characterize Mexican Americans, Puerto Ricans, Cuban Americans, and others as Hispanics.

Ethnic Formulas for Panethnic Television

Given that SIN and SICC executives had ready access to Mexican programming, and that they argued that language united America's Spanish speakers, one might expect that SIN and SICC would simply provide Mexican programming to all of the corporation's stations. This was true in the network's first decade. During that time about 90 percent of SIN's programming came from Mexico. This was the case even on the East Coast, where on an average day five of the six hours of programming shown on SICC stations were reserved for Mexican shows.[66] Things changed dramatically throughout the 1970s, however, as media executives experimented with new ways of attracting larger segments of Puerto Rican and Cuban audiences.

Indeed, by 1980 SIN executives had developed two distinct regional programming strategies. A southwestern programming formula was used for Mexican immigrant communities and included mass quantities of Mexican films, soap operas, and variety shows. In contrast, the East Coast programming formula combined Mexican, Puerto Rican, and other Latin American shows with programs produced in the United States. Joaquin Blaya, a former SIN executive and station manager for WLTV in Miami, noted that Anselmo spearheaded the development of the formulas because he eventually came to believe in "ethnic matching,"[67] the notion that immigrants would be most apt to watch shows that reflected their home country.

The regional strategies become apparent when we compare station programming lineups in different areas. Figures 2 and 3 chart the prime-time programming trends for Los Angeles and New York stations. As expected, the Los Angeles station was heavily reliant on Mexican programming. Specifically, figure 2 shows that Mexican programming remained relatively stable between 1970 and 1985, fluctuating between 75 and 90 percent of prime-time shows. And although the chart provides data for only those shows that were aired in Los Angeles, this programming was distributed to a number of different stations in southwestern cities such as Fresno and San Antonio, and it is representative of the network's southwestern programming strategy.

In contrast, figure 3 shows that the New York station broadcast significantly less Mexican programming during prime time. Although New York station managers did provide audiences with some Mexican programming (mainly soap operas), they combined this programming with shows from Puerto Rico and other parts of Latin America. Additionally, WXTV aired a significant amount of US-produced programming. Essentially, by 1985 about five times more programming hours were dedicated to US-produced Spanish-language shows in New York than in Los Angeles. The programs broadcast in New York were shared with the Miami station and constituted SIN and SICC's East Coast formula.

Why did the programming formulas differ, and why did they lead to more US-based programming on the East Coast than on the West Coast? Regional factors explain much. In Los Angeles, the heavy concentration of Mexican American audiences allowed SIN and SICC executives to remain reliant on Mexican programming, while in New York competition from a new Puerto Rican-focused television station motivated station managers to diversify their programming. Last, in Miami, a vocal Cuban American constituency group prompted station managers there to create

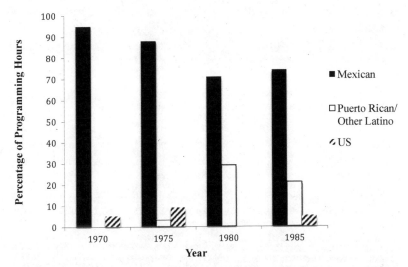

2   KMEX Los Angeles prime-time programming origin (7:00 p.m.–11:00 p.m.), 1970–85 (*Note*: Data were derived from *TV Guide*, 1970–85, by sampling the first week in February on every fifth year. The programming data were then coupled with origin information that was cross-checked on Alma Latina Television Data Base, Internet Movie Database, and Televisa Online Database.)

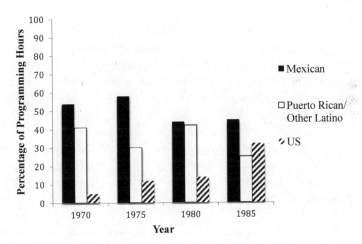

3   WXTV New York prime-time programming origin (7:00 p.m.–11:00 p.m.), 1970–85 (*Note*: Data were derived from *TV Guide*, 1970–85, by sampling the first week in February on every fifth year. The programming data were then coupled with origin information that was cross-checked on Alma Latina Television Data Base, Internet Movie Database, and Televisa Online Database.)

programs in Miami that could provide a platform for local Cuban American issues and talents.

Not everyone was content with the regional strategy, however. Daniel Villanueva, the station manager for KMEX in Los Angeles from 1971 to 1989, recalled that second-generation Chicanos often pressured him to produce fewer news segments about Mexico and Latin America and more about Mexican American issues in California, such as the Chicano student movement, the United Farm Workers movement, and the plight of East Los Angeles communities.[68] Villanueva was not unsympathetic to these concerns. In 1970 he made Rubén Salazar, a prominent Chicano activist and *Los Angeles Times* columnist, news director of KMEX.[69] As a result, KMEX news became more focused on community issues and even won the prestigious Peabody Award for its coverage of the Chicano experience in Vietnam.[70]

There is evidence that second-generation Mexican immigrants also craved entertainment programs that spoke to their experiences in the United States. In a letter to the *Los Angeles Times*, a Mexican American who had grown up watching KMEX wrote that English-language programs eventually drew him away from Spanish-language television because the US-produced shows best reflected his experiences. He ended the letter by urging KMEX to "stop depending on Mexico so much for its programming and to start producing programs that shed light on the real life [of its viewers]."[71]

While Villanueva did revamp his news programming, he stopped short of creating too many new entertainment programs that would appeal to the second generation because it was simply too expensive and unpopular with his general audience. Building production studios, hiring actors, and directing major Spanish-language entertainment programs was just not cost-effective, especially when programming from Mexico could be imported for much less. Additionally, Villanueva notes that first-generation Mexican immigrants often demanded Mexican programs. He states, "Every time I'd replace the [Mexican] soap operas with some other special news programming for Chicanos, I'd hear it from the [first-generation] Mexican immigrants calling my station and threatening me."[72]

The scope and scale of Chicano and Mexican American displeasure, however, are not certain. Aside from the occasional complaints to Villanueva and the *Los Angeles Times*, these groups did not really try to challenge SICC's programming formulas. For example, there is no evidence that there were any organized attempts between 1960 and 1985 to change

KMEX programming. And, in fact, there is evidence that national Chicano and Mexican American political groups enthusiastically endorsed the corporation. In 1976, for example, the National Council of La Raza (NCLR) printed a story in its newsletter about the advent of SIN-West (the satellite that connected southwestern SICC stations to Mexico City stations) as a "historic media step for Chicanos."[73]

The situation was much different on the East Coast, where audiences were less willing to watch continuous streams of Mexican programs. There, the network's New York station, WXTV, competed for viewers with WNJU, a Spanish-language station established by a US network that also owned a station in San Juan, Puerto Rico. Unlike WXTV, WNJU had ready access to large amounts of imported Puerto Rican programming. The largely Puerto Rican audiences in New York displayed their discontent not necessarily through complaints, but by flipping the channel.[74]

As a result, SICC's New York station was at an initial disadvantage because although Anselmo could purchase Puerto Rican programs, these were more expensive than simply airing SIN's Mexican shows. Ultimately, New York station managers decided on a tripartite strategy.[75] First, they would broadcast the Mexican programs that Azcárraga exported to Puerto Rico. At the time, these shows were doing well in San Juan, and WXTV executives reasoned that they would also do well in New York.[76] Second, station managers asked Anselmo to purchase programming from Puerto Rico and South American countries. Third, and perhaps most important, WXTV managers began investing in US-based programs. Initially these were low-cost entertainment programs that simply showcased New York Puerto Rican talent. Programs like the *Yomo Toro* show, which provided opportunities for audiences to view local Puerto Rican musical and dancing talent, were filmed on WXTV's small studio lot and broadcast throughout the 1970s. This three-part strategy allowed WXTV to remain somewhat competitive with WNJU.[77]

Just as KMEX in Los Angeles shared its programs with other southwestern stations, WXTV in New York shared its programming with WLTV in Miami. Miami station managers, however, operated within a different context than the New York station did. Although there was no major competing Spanish-language station in Miami, station managers there quickly realized that Mexican programs were rather unpopular among Cuban American audiences. More so than Chicanos in the Southwest and Puerto Ricans in New York, Miami Cuban Americans were vocal about their media preferences and took to calling WLTV on a regular basis, demanding media programs that discussed issues of relevance to the Cuban

American community.[78] These demands became more pressing as leaders in Mexico and Cuba developed international accords that angered Cuban exiles and made them suspicious of Mexican products.[79]

During the 1970s, these tensions culminated in violence as a small faction of radical Cuban exiles in Miami sought to pressure the city's Spanish-language media into taking certain stances on Cuban politics. In 1974 anti-Castro terrorists bombed the Miami headquarters of *Replica* magazine for allegedly publishing pro-Castro articles. Two years later, Miami radio station QBA-AM was bombed for the same reason.[80] The heightened tension haunted SIN and SICC personnel. Jorge Ramos, a Mexican journalist sent to Miami to anchor a SIN news program, remembers that he was often denigrated by Cuban Americans and labeled a "Castro sympathizer" simply for being Mexican.[81]

WLTV's general manager at the time, Joaquin Blaya, faced a conundrum. While station managers in New York could provide Puerto Ricans with programs from San Juan, and while southwestern stations could provide Mexicans with shows from Mexico City, Blaya could not simply purchase feed from Castro-controlled Havana. After several discussions with Anselmo, Blaya resolved this issue by investing in WLTV production studios and creating several Miami-based news and information shows.[82]

Specifically, Blaya's Miami programming consisted mainly of variety and talk shows, in large part because they were cheaper to produce than more elaborate shows like soap operas. Soap operas required a budget for a number of sets, actors, writers, and producers, but variety shows needed just one set and a host. Most of WLTV's first shows were initially used only for local programming, but over time, as the shows became more elaborate, the station shared this programming with SIN's New York station. As a result, what evolved were two different programming strategies—Mexican programming was aired for Mexican American audiences in the Southwest, and a combination of US-produced Puerto Rican and Cuban-focused programs was circulated in the East.

Figure 4 shows that considerably more non-Mexican variety shows were aired in New York than in Los Angeles. By 1985 close to half of the variety shows aired in New York were produced in the United States, in comparison to approximately 25 percent aired for Los Angeles audiences. Los Angeles stations did show non-Mexican variety programs, but station managers there tended to broadcast them during the late-night or early-morning hours.

By 1990, however, programming had also become standardized across all SICC stations. That is, by that time SICC had eliminated its two pro-

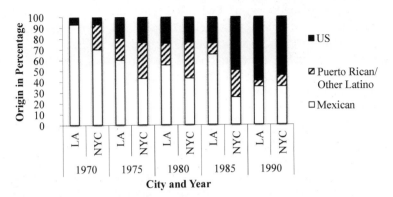

4 Origin of variety programs and talk shows by city, 1970–90 (*Note:* Data were derived from *TV Guide*, 1970–90, by sampling the first week in February on every fifth year in both cities. The programming data were then coupled with origin information that was cross-checked on Alma Latina Television Data Base, Internet Movie Database, and Televisa Online Database.)

gramming formulas and created one national formula. As such, by 1990 audiences in Los Angeles watched exactly the same network programming during the same time slots as audiences in New York did. The only programming differences occurred during local time slots. But what did these US-based programs look like?

Made-in-Miami Panethnic Programming

By the mid-1980s, Miami had become the hub of US-based Spanish-language programming. Although KMEX in Los Angeles remained the network's most profitable station, it was WLTV that had developed the best facilities to produce Spanish-language programming. Blaya's work in Miami soon gained the attention of SIN and SICC executives. And when Anselmo decided to establish a SIN news show in 1980, he eventually turned to Miami.

Villanueva recalled that there were strategic reasons for developing a network news show. One important consideration was that the newscast could make SIN seem more like a mainstream, instead of a fringe, network and thus generate more advertising revenue.[83] Villanueva contended that he fought hard to convince Anselmo to produce the news program in Los Angeles. Because KMEX drew the highest ratings and attracted the largest advertising accounts, Villanueva reasoned that KMEX had the right to produce the news.[84] Blaya disagreed. Since the Miami station had more experience creating shows in the United States, and because operating-costs were lower in Miami than in Los Angeles, Blaya reasoned that Miami was a natural site for SIN to produce a news program.[85] In the end, several other factors, including the time difference, swayed the decision. Anselmo did, however, make one important concession: at Villanueva's insistence, he agreed to reserve the main news anchor positions for Mexican American journalists.[86]

Created in the style of the nightly news that aired every evening at 6:30 on the mainstream English-language networks, *SIN Noticiero* went on the air in 1981.[87] In order to appeal to a broad panethnic audience, the Mexican newscasters had to go through phonetic and grammatical training to eliminate their Mexican colloquialisms and accents and produce what industry insiders labeled a "Walter Cronkite Spanish."[88] Gustavo Godoy, a Cuban American and former director of *SIN Noticiero*, recalled that he created the first "Spanish-language style manual" for the Mexican anchors back in 1981. Eliminating "Spanglish" was a major focus of the style manual, as Godoy noted: "Spanglish was detrimental for our newscast. . . . [I]f we were going to be taken seriously and seen as a professional newscast, we had to provide our viewers with a proper vocabulary that could preserve the Spanish language."[89] Godoy's manual thus included a long list of Spanglish words and phrases that newscasters were not, under any circumstances, to use in news reports.[90] In effect, Spanglish threatened not only SIN's appearance of legitimacy vis-à-vis other American and Latin American news programs but also the notion that Latin American subgroups were part of a larger panethnic group united by language.

In addition, Godoy's manual had a long list of ethnic-specific cultural idioms and words that newscasters and reporters were instructed to avoid lest they offend certain subgroups. Godoy recalled that during one early news report, a SIN news reporter used the Spanish-language word *bola* for "ball" in a story about President Reagan throwing a snowball. Within a few hours, the station was inundated with calls from angry Puerto Rican and Cuban American viewers who were offended by the word *bola* because in their home countries it was slang for male genitalia.[91]

Aside from the news, SIN also produced variety and talk shows that conveyed a Hispanic identity to panethnic audiences. These shows explored issues of adaptation, nostalgia, and other experiences associated with the migration and settlement process. They promoted the idea that Hispanic panethnicity was based on the experience of migration as well as on language. For example, SIN's most highly rated network talk show,

El Show de Cristina, appeared in an afternoon time slot and featured different topics about immigrant family life and settlement in the United States. Although the hosts and their guests did talk about Latin America, they often did so from a US perspective. Latin American experts were also frequently invited to comment on US immigrant issues.

Later, the network also produced game and variety shows. Its most important game show, *Sábado Gigante*, which filled a three-hour time slot, solicited game show contestants from the different Latin American subgroups across the country. By featuring a diverse array of contestants and showcasing the musical talents of Mexican, Puerto Rican, and Cuban entertainers, *Sábado Gigante* also helped solidify the idea that Hispanics were a distinct cultural group. And as these US-based shows became more popular, SIN used them to replace some imported Mexican, Puerto Rican, and South American shows. Eventually, the network's lineup would consist of imported soap operas and comedies and US-based variety, talk, and game shows.

SIN also began to develop more political programming during the 1980s. For the 1980 election, network stations launched *Destino 80*, a series of news programs and documentaries covering the 1980 census count as well as the elections and their impact on the Hispanic community. In addition, SIN translated political speeches made by presidential candidates and created news segments in which activists from groups like NCLR spoke about the importance of the Hispanic vote. In fact, SIN had long-established ties with activists if only because the number of organizational leaders who promoted the idea of Hispanic panethnicity was quite small. In an interview, Emilio Nicolás, a former SICC vice president, noted, "[W]e all came to know each other at that time; the world of Hispanic leaders was small. . . . [W]e would invite [a Hispanic activist] to come on our station and talk about community issues all of the time."[92] When the 1984 election came around, SIN once again broadcast a series of news segments and special programs about the importance of the Hispanic vote.[93] For the 1988 election, SIN's successor, Univision, maintained this practice.

By 1990 Univision had developed various strategies and programs designed to promote the idea of a Hispanic consumer market, a Hispanic vote, and—most important—a Hispanic community. The question of why SIN and then Univision switched programming strategies, however, remains unanswered. In other words, it is still unclear why SIN and SICC executives suddenly shifted to more US-based programs in the mid-1980s. Figure 5 provides greater programming detail for SICC's Los

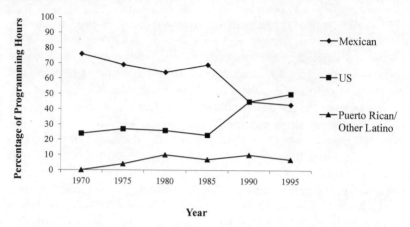

5   Origin of SIN and Univision programming for KMEX, 1970–95 (*Note*: Data were derived from *TV Guide*, 1970–95, by sampling the first week in February on every fifth year. The programming data were then coupled with origin information that was cross-checked on Alma Latina Television Data Base, Internet Movie Database, and Televisa Online Database.)

Angeles station and highlights a crucial timing element involved in the adoption of US-based programming. Specifically, the graph shows that between 1980 and 1985, the number of programming hours dedicated to US-based shows almost doubled.

At the same time that SIN executives were airing more US-based programs, they also began to standardize programming formulas. Thus, between 1985 and 1990, the Los Angeles station increased its US-based programming significantly, and so did the SICC stations in New York, Miami, and elsewhere. The question, then, becomes why US-based programming increased during this five-year period. The answer has to do with the federal government, which in 1986 oversaw the sale of SIN and SICC to Hallmark First Capital.

The FCC and the Expansion of SIN and SICC

The FCC had been closely involved with SIN and SICC since the corporation's inception, in part because Anselmo repeatedly petitioned the commission for assistance. Although the FCC denied most of Anselmo's requests, it did grant two important ones. In 1977 the commission granted SIN the right to sell spot advertisements for SICC stations. At the time network executives were barred from helping local stations acquire advertisements for nonnetwork programs. Network executives were expected to sell advertising time for network shows only, while local station managers were responsible for selling advertisements for local programming. Anselmo argued that this restriction placed an undue burden on SICC because of the difficulty of obtaining advertising revenue for Spanish-language television.[94] In an unprecedented ruling, the FCC agreed, noting that due to the corporation's unique structure—Anselmo was president of SICC and vice president of SIN—the network and the individual stations shared a "common viewpoint."[95]

In 1978 the FCC also granted Anselmo's petition to establish five new low-power translator stations that could operate on UHF wavelengths in smaller southwestern markets.[96] These were among the first low-power television licenses granted in the country. The FCC rulings allowed SICC to expand to cities like Denver and Albuquerque, leading to record profits as the cost of operations was reduced and advertising revenue increased. Indeed, in 1978 the two corporations netted ten million dollars in advertising revenue; just four years after the rulings, this figure doubled to twenty million dollars.[97]

The FCC granted Anselmo's requests in part because the agency considered the network to be a minority-serving media company. During the mid-1970s Chicano lobbying groups, especially NCLR, joined African American organizations in pressuring the FCC to establish special provisions for minority media owners.[98] NCLR members thus wrote letters to the FCC and organized a national lobbying campaign to urge the FCC to implement more provisions for increasing Hispanic media ownership.[99] From NCLR's perspective, more Hispanic media owners meant greater programming diversity on America's airwaves. In other words, NCLR argued that Hispanic media owners could best create programming that reflected Hispanic community issues.[100]

At the same time, other government agencies, such as the US Commission on Civil Rights, were promoting the notion that Spanish speakers, like blacks, were an underserved minority group whose rights deserved special protections.[101] The Voting Rights Act had been extended to Spanish-speaking communities in 1975, and by the late 1970s, President Jimmy Carter had instituted a series of Hispanic Town Hall meetings across the country.[102] There was a growing sense, then, that Mexican Americans, Puerto Ricans, and Cuban Americans were now being perceived as an aggrieved, underrepresented minority and not simply another immigrant group destined to assimilate into a broad white category.

Under the Carter administration, the FCC responded to activists' requests for minority ownership provisions by establishing a Minority Ownership Task Force, which ultimately recommended that the FCC create provisions such as tax breaks for minority-owned media stations and that it award favorable consideration to minority-owned corporations that applied for station licenses.[103] The FCC adopted these recommendations knowing that increased minority ownership would lead to increased media diversity.[104] The fact that the SICC executive board was mostly composed of Mexican Americans, and that the network catered to Spanish-speaking audiences, made the company eligible for this consideration. Moreover, the ruling allowed other Hispanic entrepreneurs to purchase their own stations and become SIN affiliates. Thus, in the late 1970s, Armando Rendon, an NCLR member and Census Bureau consultant, established his own media corporation and purchased a low-power SIN affiliate station in Washington, DC, by taking advantage of the FCC's special tax break and license preference rulings.[105]

By the late 1970s the FCC perceived SIN and SICC not simply as another American network but as an important political enterprise as well. In 1979, when an FCC judge approved another one of SICC's low-power translator television licenses, he stated:

[Granting] of [the SICC] applications would serve the public interest. It appears that in each of the proposed communities of license, in spite of large *Hispanic* populations, very little, if any off-the-air Spanish-language television programming is available. The Commission believes that your proposal is an efficient and desirable means of alleviating this problem and filling the gap in Spanish-language programming.[106]

Taken together, the FCC rulings effectively allowed SIN and SICC, and its affiliates, to expand beyond its established southwestern base to audiences nationwide. The FCC's perception of SIN and SICC, however, would shift dramatically by the early 1980s.

The Struggle over Spanish-Language Media

In 1980 the Spanish Radio Broadcasters of America (SRBA), a group composed mainly of Mexican American broadcasters in the Southwest, filed a formal complaint with the FCC alleging that SICC had violated the FCC's foreign control clause. The clause, which was established soon after World War I to protect America's airways from foreign enemies, especially in times of war, prohibits the issuance of broadcast licenses to aliens, to the representatives of aliens, or to corporations in which aliens control more than one-fifth of the stock.[107] In its complaint, the SRBA claimed that Rene Anselmo (by now president of both SIN and SICC) operated

SICC in the interest of the Azcárraga family, making him a representative of an alien Mexican investor.

In response, Anselmo filed several letters with the FCC arguing that Azcárraga's involvement in SICC operations was limited and did not constitute a form of foreign control over US media. Anselmo also pointed out that the FCC had already previously approved the financial relationship between SIN and SICC executives.[108] In fact, on several occasions over the span of more than two decades, SICC executives had disclosed the relationship between SICC and SIN to the FCC.[109] Anselmo claimed that the SRBA was upset because Spanish-language television was providing competition in markets previously monopolized by Spanish-language radio.[110]

SIN and SICC had weathered similar complaints in the past. In 1965 the Trans-Tel media corporation, in its bid for what would later become SICC's New York station, had sought a hearing to determine whether SICC was under foreign control. The FCC responded that while it was aware of the relationship between Azcárraga and SICC, there was no evidence that Azcárraga controlled or influenced the daily operations of SICC, or that any of SICC's shareholders were beholden to Azcárraga's (or Telesistema's) interests or were operating as his representatives. Trans-Tel's request was dismissed as "unsupported speculation."[111]

By 1980, however, the FCC would decide that there was enough suspicion to warrant an investigation into the issue of foreign control. What made the FCC change its mind? Two simultaneous events led to this investigation. First, in 1980 SIN and SICC were involved in a shareholder derivative lawsuit between Frank L. Fouce Jr., son of the then deceased Frank Fouce Sr., and other SICC executive board members. In the civil court lawsuit, Frank Fouce Jr. argued that Anselmo operated SICC in the economic interest of SIN, thus leading stations to bear large financial losses. Frank L. Fouce had inherited his father's SICC shares, but at the time he held no interest in SIN; thus, for him, any losses for SICC were not balanced by gains made by SIN. In 1981 a district court judge in Los Angeles ruled in favor of Fouce Jr.[112] Thus, by the time SRBA filed its complaint with the FCC, a district court judge had already suggested that the relationship between Anselmo and Azcárraga was problematic.[113]

Also important to the FCC was the fact that the SRBA was composed mainly of Mexican Americans who essentially argued that the unique relationship between Azcárraga and SICC hurt US Spanish-language media ventures. The SRBA, led by Edward Gomez of radio station KABQ in Albuquerque, filed a complaint that argued that SICC's foreign connections created an unfair competitive advantage. Low-cost access to Azcárraga's media programming, as well as loans from Azcárraga, the SRBA argued, essentially undercut the Spanish-language radio stations' ability to compete for advertising revenue.[114] In effect, the SRBA complaint implied that foreign connections to Mexico would drive Mexican American broadcast ventures into bankruptcy.[115] This, of course, undermined the FCC's goals of increasing minority representation in media ownership.[116]

The FCC began its investigation shortly after the ruling in the civil suit. In 1986 an FCC administrative law judge ruled that even though the commission had known about the nature of the relationship between SIN and SICC for decades, the new evidence provided in the Fouce lawsuit and the FCC's subsequent investigations proved that SICC was in violation of Section 310(b) of the Federal Communications Act.[117] The judge denied the renewal of SICC's applications, but he encouraged the parties to use the review process to seek a "less drastic remedial solution, such as corporate restructuring."[118] SICC first appealed the ruling to the FCC's review board, then, before a decision was reached, the corporation proposed a settlement in which its licenses would be transferred to an unrelated buyer.

Yet, despite its decision, the FCC did acknowledge the valuable contribution that Azcárraga had made toward advancing Spanish-language television. In one deciding opinion, the commission noted:

There can be no serious refutal of the proposition that SICC's and SIN's prodigious two-decade effort to implant a functional Spanish-language network of stations in this country has served the public's interest—and the Commission's interest in promoting special programming for minority groups.

Additionally, it stated that Rene Anselmo was a "talented individual" who had overcome

enormous obstacles, not least of which were a number of UHF-handicapped television stations, and a skeptical, resistant advertising community . . . [to] pioneer and perfect Spanish Language programming in the United States.[119]

In 1987, in accordance with the provisions of the settlement, Hallmark Cards Inc. and First Chicago Venture Capital purchased several SICC station licenses and named the new corporation Univision Communications Corporation. According to insiders, Hallmark had become interested in Spanish-language television soon after the 1980 census had established Hispanics as a sizable constituency.[120] Hallmark undoubtedly saw Univision as an early opportunity to establish itself in the Hispanic market.

Although there was some protest from Mexican American and even Cuban American activists, the FCC approved the license transfers in part because Hallmark had sufficient capital to keep the corporation afloat. Other bids from Mexican American groups were turned down because the groups lacked sufficient capital to maintain the venture.[121] Moreover, Hallmark had gained support among important advocacy organizations such as NCLR and the Mexican American Legal Defense and Education Fund,[122] and it had promised the FCC that it would exert a serious effort to develop more US-produced "Hispanic" programming.[123]

Univision and the Further Development of Hispanic Programming

The sale of SIN and SICC had two primary effects on Spanish-language television. The first concerned staffing. After the Hallmark takeover, many of the founding members of SIN and SICC either left the corporations or were not hired by Hallmark. Anselmo retired from the television industry and devoted his time to developing satellite technology. Villanueva and Nicolás also left shortly after the sale.[124]

Among those who remained was Blaya, the manager of SIN's Miami station, who was elevated to president of the new company in 1988. Blaya was Chilean and had vast experience producing US-based Spanish-language programs. As the manager of WLTV, he had solved the conundrum of how to provide Cuban media for Cuban immigrants by creating local news and variety shows. As Miami became more diverse, Blaya had accommodated immigrants from Central and South America by creating more panethnic, Hispanic shows.

Soon after Blaya stepped into his new role, others who had worked with him in Miami were promoted. Guillermo Martinez and Tony Ordonez, both Cuban Americans from Miami, were appointed to vice presidential positions. Hallmark also hired a few media executives from English-language firms. Most notably, Bill Grimes, an Anglo businessman who had previously worked for CBS and ESPN, was hired as Univision Communication Corporation's CEO.[125] These staffing choices made Univision seem less "Mexican" than SICC had been by filling key positions with Anglos or non-Mexican Latin Americans.

It would not be a stretch to say that Hallmark executives were concerned with appearing too foreign. Hallmark had to revamp Univision to lessen the network's dependence on Azcárraga Milmo's Mexican programming. In 1989 Blaya granted media interviews and proclaimed that

Univision would now become an "American network in Spanish."[126] What Blaya meant was that Univision would imitate many of the strategies that mainstream networks used to run their national operations. By looking more like the mainstream networks, Univision hoped to appear more American and less foreign (read: less Mexican) to investors and regulators.

Univision executives thus began to package the network's programming as Hispanic versions of English-language shows. *El Show de Cristina*, which was based in Miami, was described by Univision executives as the "Spanish Oprah."[127] Similarly, *Sábado Gigante*, the game show, was presented as the Spanish version of *The Price Is Right*, and Univision's *Desde Hollywood* was touted as similar to *Entertainment Tonight*.[128] At the same time that these shows were being promoted by Univision, the network was also beginning to standardize its programming formula across its media markets. For the first time, Spanish-language audiences in Los Angeles were watching the same shows, during the same time slots, as audiences in New York, Miami, and Chicago. By 1990 Univision's lineup not only was standardized, as English-language networks' lineups were, but it also resembled them: children's programming was aired in the morning, followed by talk shows and US-produced soap operas in the afternoon, and the early evening was reserved for the nightly network newscast. In a press interview, Blaya described the strategy:

Our main concern in the past three years was to do what I define as "American television in Spanish." In other words, we are not a Latin American television network in the United States. We are an American television network that speaks Spanish. With shows like *Cristina*, for example, which is an American format, dealing with issues and subjects that for centuries have been taboo in our community. We do it through shows like *Portada*, a news magazine that addressed the needs and concerns of U.S. Hispanics. We do this by striking a balance between U.S.-produced television shows and the product that comes from Latin America.[129]

To be sure, it was not simply that Blaya took control of Univision and changed the programming formula. Important moves toward more US-based programming had already been under way during the mid-1980s as SICC was being investigated by the FCC. In fact, three news and/or information shows were being aired even before the FCC ruling: *SIN Noticiero*, *Temas y Debates*, and *Mundo Latino*. By 1990, however, the number of US-based programs had increased by 50 percent under the aegis of Joaquin Blaya.[130] The increase in US-based shows meant that the network's producers now focused on themes and issues relevant to the US immigrant population and created shows that highlighted the experience of immigration as well as the cultural diversity of Hispanics.

And although Univision strove to become an "American network in Spanish," it still used a few distinctively Mexican programming strategies. Most notably, prime-time slots continued to be dominated by Mexican soap operas. Unlike the mainstream networks' soap operas, which were scheduled in daytime slots, Univision's soap operas also aired in the evening, garnering high viewership ratings. What evolved was a system in which Mexican soap operas were used as a staple during prime time, but US-produced shows filled most of the daily lineup.

Yet becoming more mainstream was expensive for Hallmark. The high cost of producing so many new US-based shows began to deplete the organization's resources. Within two years after taking over, Hallmark was recording severe losses even though Univision's US-based shows generated export profits in Latin America. In 1991, just four years after stepping into the venture, Hallmark sold Univision to A. Jerrold Perenchio and a group of Venezuelan and Mexican investors that included Diego Cisneros from Venevision and Emilio Azcárraga Milmo and his son Emilio Azcárraga Jean.[131]

By the late 1980s, Univision had reinvented itself as an "American network" that catered to a panethnic, Hispanic immigrant audience. The US-based shows allowed the network to claim that it created programs that underscored the experience of US immigrant communities; at the same time they granted the network legitimacy because it now operated more like the mainstream networks. Although this move was initially costly for owners, the model of mixing US-based programs with Latin American imports would soon be solidified as new Spanish-language networks such as Telemundo entered the field.

Telemundo and the Diversification of Hispanic Television

Until the early 1980s, SIN had been the country's sole Spanish-language television network. The only significant competition that emerged was WNJU in New York, but this station did not belong to a Spanish-language network at the time. Perhaps one of the main reasons that other Spanish-language networks did not emerge was the lack of start-up capital. Early on, SIN and SICC relied on Azcárraga's money and programming in order to survive, in part because investors remained skeptical of Spanish-language media. Without a connection to low-cost Spanish-language programming or access to credit and start-up capital, it would have been virtually impossible for lone immigrant entrepreneurs to construct a competing Spanish-language television network.

This had changed by the mid-1980s. Hallmark's bid for SICC's stations was one of the first signs that mainstream media corporations were beginning to perceive Spanish-language audiences as a profitable niche market. By the mid-1980s several national marketing firms portrayed Spanish-language audiences as members of a common Hispanic consumer market.[132] In an interview with the *Los Angeles Times*, a representative of a leading market research firm stated that "Hispanics share characteristics more commercially significant than the language and culture that distinguishes them from Anglo consumers."[133] Other studies noted that Hispanics' strong family values and attention to extended kin could explain why they, more than any other racial group, spent more of their disposable income on household goods. Additionally, by the late 1980s, other firms claimed that Hispanics' strong sense of loyalty to the family explained why they were among the most brand-loyal consumer groups in the country.[134]

Corporations also took notice. During the 1980s Procter & Gamble, Philip Morris, and Coors Brewing Company increased the number of advertising dollars that they spent on Spanish-language media. The *Los Angeles Times* noted that between 1982 and 1986, the amount of money spent on Spanish-language advertising more than doubled, rising from $172 million to nearly $400 million.[135] As advertising expenditures grew, so did the Spanish-language radio, print, and television industries. Between 1975 and 1985, the number of Spanish-language radio stations nearly tripled.[136] The number of Spanish-language and Hispanic-oriented periodicals (like the English-language *Hispanic Business* magazine) also increased by more than 25 percent.[137] And the number of full-power Spanish-language television stations increased by 20 percent.[138]

The buzz about Spanish-language media soon caught the attention of Saul Steinberg. Steinberg was an American business magnate who had not previously dabbled in Spanish-language media but became interested after reading several marketing reports on Hispanic consumers. He recalled that "everyone was talking about Hispanics and the Hispanic market [back then]. Hallmark's interest in Univision was a big signal that this was going to be a huge industry."[139]

In 1987 Steinberg and a group of investors purchased stations in Puerto Rico, New York, Miami, and Chicago and created a new Spanish-language network called Telemundo, the primary asset of Telemundo Group Inc. Steinberg recalled that his impetus for creating the network was his belief that Univision was overly reliant on Mexican programming and had neglected other Latin American subgroups. He believed that a new network could be competitive if it catered more adequately to all subgroups. In an interview he recalled:

SIN was just Mexican programming. . . . [They] were ignoring Cubans and Puerto Ricans that lived on the East Coast. . . . [They] provided them with Mexican soap operas. . . . We thought we could do something different. We planned to have a more diverse programming schedule with shows from Puerto Rico and South America. We also tried to have high-quality soap operas produced in some of the world's best outdoor filming sets like Italy and Miami with famous Latino actors from across Latin America. . . . [You] know, we wanted to bring variety to Spanish-language television.[140]

Instead of simply combining Mexican products with some US-based programs, Steinberg planned to mix programs imported from across Latin America with shows created to represent Latin American diversity.

Steinberg's group first purchased WNJU, a full-time Spanish-language station in New York run by Carlos Barba. Barba was a Cuban exile who had worked for several years in Puerto Rican and Venezuelan television before joining WNJU in the mid-1970s.[141] Throughout that time Barba had maintained WNJU's competitiveness with SIN's New York station by providing audiences with imported programs from Puerto Rico and South America. With Barba's help, Steinberg quickly purchased stations in Miami and Los Angeles and developed a programming lineup that helped distinguish the new network from the Univision monolith. Specifically, Steinberg purchased feeds from Mexican, Brazilian, Argentine, Spanish, Venezuelan, and Puerto Rican broadcasting corporations, and he created a Telemundo studio for the production of US-based programs.[142] Like the US-based programs shown on Univision, the US-produced Telemundo talk shows, soap operas, and variety shows focused on Latin Americans' common experience of immigration and highlighted their cultural diversity. For instance, Telemundo's *Angelica, Mi Vida* was the first US-produced Spanish-language soap opera; its plot centered on immigrant families adjusting to living in the United States, and the cast included an array of Mexican, Puerto Rican, and Cuban actors.[143]

Soon after launching *Angelica, Mi Vida*, Telemundo introduced another soap opera called *Viento del Norte*. Half of the shooting for this show was done in the United States, and the other half was done in Puerto Rico. A majority of the actors on the program were Latin American; some were recent immigrants, and others were US born. When asked during a press interview why Telemundo was investing so much in US-based soap operas, Barba noted:

We have to produce a segment of our programming in the United States because we'd like to give to the Hispanic community a product that has more identification with their lives. . . . [We] need to give them a product that they can identify with and feel proud of.[144]

Telemundo would keep creating US-based shows, he said, as long as they spoke to the experience of US Hispanics.[145] With time, Telemundo would follow with other US-based soap operas, such as *Marielena, Guadalupe*, and *Tres Destinos*, all of which were produced in Telemundo's Miami studios.

Additionally, Telemundo structured its news programming around subgroup diversity. In 1991 it joined with CNN to form *Noticiero Telemundo CNN*, the country's first transcontinental Spanish-language newscast. This program was produced in Telemundo's Miami studios using content produced by local journalists at CNN's Havana, Buenos Aires, Mexico City, and Managua affiliates. The broadcast was a montage of news and feature clips produced in each country. Unlike *SIN Noticiero* (later *Noticiero Univision*), which had initially focused on muting subgroup differences by creating a generic Hispanic depiction, *Noticiero Telemundo CNN* invested in making these differences more pronounced.[146]

Telemundo also partnered with MTV to create *MTV Internacional*, a music video program that Telemundo hoped would attract young second-generation Hispanics. *MTV Internacional* featured Spanish-language music videos from across Latin America as well as popular English-language music videos. The video DJ for the show was Daisy Fuentes, a US-born Cuban American who hosted the show in Spanglish, slipping between English and Spanish.[147]

When Univision was sold in 1992, Steinberg lured Blaya away and provided him with the resources to develop US-based programs on Telemundo. In a press interview shortly after being hired by Telemundo, Blaya noted the difference between Telemundo and Univision by pointing to Univision's purchasers, which included Azcárraga Milmo:

I have no doubt, and my judgment has proven me correct, that if [Azcárraga Milmo] acquired Univision, Univision would be required to devote most of its daily lineup to Mexican produced programming. This is a recipe for disaster. To achieve success in the United States in Spanish-language television, it is absolutely essential to broadcast large segments of US-produced programming.[148]

By 1995 Telemundo was producing several US-based soap operas and had worked on a US-based comedy and drama series. Nevertheless, its ratings lagged far behind Univision's throughout the 1990s. Telemundo stations fared better on the East Coast, especially in Miami, but Univision still dominated Spanish-language television ratings at a national level. Steinberg blamed this on Telemundo's inability to comprehend just how popular Mexican programming would become among all subgroups. Steinberg recalls that even though his soap operas were of purportedly higher quality and were often directed by top Latin American and European creative directors, audiences on the East Coast eventually preferred Mexican soap operas. As a result, Telemundo could not compete seriously with Univision.[149]

In 1998, after being purchased by Liberty Media, Telemundo began to produce a variety of Spanish-language shows based loosely on American programs. *Los Angeles de Charlie* replicated *Charlie's Angels*, and *Rey y Reyes*, which included a Mexican immigrant and a Mexican American law enforcement tag team, replicated *Starsky and Hutch*. These shows never achieved the ratings enjoyed by Univision, but they did provide Spanish-language audiences with alternatives to Univision's programming formula. At the turn of the twenty-first century, Telemundo began to replace its unsuccessful US-based comedies and drama series with comedies, movies, and soap operas imported from Latin America.[150]

For its part, Univision slowly began to include more US-based programming. The "more American" shows that were introduced shortly after the Hallmark sale survived the 1991 sale, and in the mid-1990s the network created more talk shows and variety programs to fill its weekend and late-night time slots. In 1997 Univision launched ¡*Despierta América!*, a Spanish-language version of the morning news shows that were being produced by the mainstream networks. With a cast of Mexican, Puerto Rican, and South American anchors, ¡*Despierta América!* provided news from Latin America and highlighted issues unique to Latin American immigrants in the United States.[151]

Univision also further developed the notion of Hispanic politics and the Latino vote. In 1988 Univision created its first Spanish-language poll to survey viewers about their political attitudes. Like the other networks, Univision asked its viewers whom they favored for the presidency and what they thought about national issues.[152] Univision invited Hispanic activists, including many from the National Council of La Raza, to appear on news segments to comment on election results and to share their insights on Hispanic political issues. While on television, activists often argued that the Hispanic vote was critical for elections. And this sentiment about the importance of the Hispanic or Latino vote would later become a stable part of Univision's political commentary. Thus, one reporter quipped early on during the 1988 election:

From all of this growth of the Hispanic vote, one could conclude that for the first time in the history of this country Hispanics can decide who will be the future president of the United States.[153]

Univision's election coverage became even more comprehensive in the 1990s. Throughout this period, the network created more political news segments and developed more national and local political polls, and it even hired activists to serve as Hispanic political analysts and comment on the role of the Hispanic vote in state and national elections.[154] This attention to Latino voters was not one-sided. By 2000 both Democratic and Republican presidential contenders had amped up the practice started by Richard Nixon and the CCOSSP and were spending an unprecedented amount of money on Spanish-language political ads during election seasons.[155] For instance, one of George W. Bush's 2000 presidential primary ads promised Hispanics that his administration would usher in a "new day" for them and concluded with Bush noting in his heavily accented Spanish that "the American dream is for all who live in this country."[156]

As the second millennium approached, Univision had become not only the nation's largest and most well-established Spanish-language television network but also one of the nation's foremost Hispanic institutions, delivering cultural and political messages about the size, scope, and character of the Hispanic community.

Conclusion

Between 1960 and 1990, SIN and Univision expanded by developing the idea that Mexican Americans, Cuban Americans, and Puerto Ricans were part of a common Hispanic consumer market. To gain national advertising accounts, the network had to connect Puerto Rican and Cuban markets on the East Coast with Mexican markets in the Southwest. To accomplish this, Univision executives endorsed the idea that Spanish-language audiences were united by a common consumer culture and shared similar media tastes and purchasing behaviors.

In effect, this could not have been accomplished without the resources and networks provided by federal bureaucrats and civic groups. Census officials, especially, created census data that Univision executives, in turn, could use to describe their market. Activists supported Univision's efforts vis-à-vis federal regulators, but they also helped to authenticate the notion of panethnicity by appearing on Univision news segments and speaking about the political needs of the Hispanic community. What emerged was an interconnected field of relationships with bureaucrats and activists, a field which media executives used to market the idea that Mexican Americans, Puerto Ricans, and Cuban Americans composed a national, panethnic community.

Moreover, Univision grew by developing two distinct strategies for communicating the notion of panethnicity. The first entailed crafting a Hispanic image, which required the network to develop a Hispanic look, sound, and vocabulary. Univision's marketers and programming directors hired actors and personalities who had dark eyes and olive-colored skin—the ideal "Hispanic" look. The skin tone, hair color, and eye color, however, could not be too identifiably Mexican, Puerto Rican, or Cuban. Instead, this Hispanic look had to resemble aspects of all these nationalities so that the actor could pass as a member of any Latin American subgroup.[157]

Even more important were Univision's efforts to create a Hispanic sound and to teach its personalities, especially those in the newsroom, how to speak a Spanish that could be understood and accepted by most subgroups. The programming team also developed an on-air vocabulary that avoided regional idioms and helped promote a generic Hispanic vocabulary.

Yet even as Univision executives attempted to create an ideal Hispanic image, they also had to recognize the diversity within the Hispanic population. Denying Latin American subgroup distinctions, and thus suggesting that panethnicity and nationality were mutually exclusive, would have been disastrous if only because much of Univision's audience was composed of first-generation immigrants. Therefore, Univision's second major strategy was to define the Hispanic population as a diverse group with distinct national roots. Univision created programming that focused on specific groups, generating segments or advertisements that acknowledged, for example, Mexican or Puerto Rican holidays. Some of its news and entertainment shows were also directed toward specific subgroups. A show might spotlight Latin American culture by airing segments about Cuban, Mexican, and Puerto Rican music. In addition, individual station managers often supplemented Univision news programs with local coethnic programming.

The two strategies needed to be balanced, and Univision executives spent much of their time assessing and revising how the ideal Hispanic as well as Latin American subgroups were represented. This was perhaps most visible in the nightly network news, where anchors were trained to look, sound, and speak like ideal Hispanics, but the stories that were reported were mainly about country-specific events. The balancing of these two goals helped media executives buffer criticism about the artificiality of the Hispanic image and, conversely, about bias toward one subgroup or another. When Univision executives were accused of being too Mexican, or too Cuban, they could point to their "American Hispanic" shows and claim that their programming transcended national differences. And when the network was accused of being too insensitive to subgroup distinctions, it could defend itself by pointing to its local programming and stressing the diversity represented by its shows.

Above all, Univision executives claimed that Hispanics were united by a common culture. This idea of an American Hispanic culture was linked to the notion of Hispanic panethnicity, which some activist groups, such as the NCLR, endorsed to claim that Hispanics represented a distinct minority community and which government statisticians employed to show that Cuban Americans, Puerto Ricans, Mexican Americans, and select others comprised a statistically bounded group.

The Hispanic Category and the Development of a New Identity Politics in America

In the late 1960s, activists, government bureaucrats, and media executives each embarked on separate projects to develop the notion of panethnicity. Mexican American activists, eager to recast their movement as a national, Hispanic one, reached out to Puerto Rican and Cuban communities alike. Bureaucrats from the Cabinet Committee on Opportunities for Spanish-Speaking People (CCOSSP) and the Census Bureau began recasting Latin American origin groups panethnically and creating reports on the conditions of Hispanics in the United States. Finally, media executives, eager to grow the market for their Spanish-language programming, expanded nationally, forging a television network that would bring together Mexican American, Puerto Rican, and Cuban audiences across the country.

Throughout the 1970s and 1980s, however, the efforts of these stakeholders would become intertwined. Activists took part in census hearings and supported state officials' work to institutionalize panethnicity. In turn, the Census Bureau sponsored regular workshops to teach activists more sophisticated ways of analyzing Hispanic census data. Media executives also became plugged into these networks by helping the bureau and activists promote panethnicity on their Spanish-language television programming. Indeed, by 1990 a viewer could tune into Spanish-language television, brimming with various panethnic entertainment and public affairs programs, to watch census spokespersons and activists comment on the future of the Hispanic community.

In effect, Hispanic panethnicity became institutionalized over time as activists, bureaucrats, and media executives forged a new field centered around the new category. Within this field, stakeholders developed networks, shared resources, and worked together to advance the notion that Mexican Americans, Puerto Ricans, Cuban Americans, and others constituted a single, national community. As one media executive recalled, "We all came to know each other . . . [the] world of Hispanic leaders was small . . . we could call one another up easily."[1]

Ambiguity was a critical element of this new Hispanic field. Activists, media executives, and census officials never really defined who Hispanics were, nor did they argue definitively that characteristics like language, place of birth, or surname made Hispanics Hispanic. Instead, they reiterated that, above all, Hispanics were Hispanic because they shared a common set of values and a common culture. The stakeholders used descriptors like *hardworking*, *religious*, and *family-oriented*—adjectives that could be applied to any group—to describe the unique characteristics uniting Hispanics.

This ambiguity allowed stakeholders to reduce any potential resistance to the idea of panethnicity. By pointing toward a vague cultural definition of panethnicity, stakeholders could position the category as broad and as complementary to, rather than in conflict with, national identity. One did not have to speak Spanish or have a Spanish surname to be Hispanic because panethnicity was predicated on a set of historically based cultural values. More important, stakeholders suggested that one did not have to choose between nationality and panethnicity because one could be both Hispanic *and* Mexican, or Hispanic *and* Puerto Rican. The nationality issue remained open because panethnicity was not about being descended from a specific set of countries, or even about harboring certain feelings (nostalgic or loyal) toward Latin America or Spain. Instead, stakeholders framed panethnicity as a shared if hazily defined set of cultural values and experiences. As a result, an immigrant with close connections to his or her homeland could claim to be as Hispanic as a fourth-generation individual with little or no connection to Latin America.

Equally important, the ambiguous narrative about panethnicity allowed stakeholders to bend the notion in ways that helped them attain their organizational goals. Activists framed Hispanics as an underrepresented minority group that suffered from discrimination, poverty, and other forms of disadvantage. They claimed that Hispanics wanted to contribute to the nation but were held back by an unequal playing field. This framing allowed activists to position Hispanics as a national constituency that merited federal, and not only state, attention. Media executives framed the issue differently. In order to attract advertising revenue from corporations, they described Hispanics as a young national consumer market that was "getting richer" and "growing larger."[2] Their marketing manuals thus combined Hispanic census data with their own claims about Hispanic consumption habits and brand loyalty. For their part, bureaucrats in CCOSSP and the Census Bureau framed Hispanics as a sizable demographic group identifiable through a unique set of economic, family, and cultural patterns.

Over time, as the networks between bureaucrats, activists, and media executives became more extensive, stakeholders learned to appropriate frames from one another. Activists developed Hispanic advocacy organizations and used the "Hispanic market" frame to attract corporate sponsors; contributions to Hispanic causes, they argued, could translate into positive publicity among Hispanic consumers. For their part, media executives employed the activists' frame of an underserved, Hispanic minority to reap special concessions from regulators. For example, the Federal Communications Commission granted special licensing preferences to Spanish-language station owners because it came to consider Hispanics as an underserved population.

Indeed, by 1990 shareholders created a new field undergirded by what sociologist Peter Berger has called a "plausibility structure": a sociocultural web of agreed-upon meanings and accepted roles. In these structures, roles become institutionalized and connected to one another through a broader set of shared meanings.[3] Thus, activists developed Hispanic political agendas and reports and soon called themselves experts on Hispanic politics. The Census Bureau created positions for "Hispanic data analysts," and media executives began calling themselves Hispanic marketing consultants. In their new roles, these stakeholders helped to legitimate one another's work. To give one telling example, by 1990 Hispanic data analysts from the Census Bureau were regularly featured speakers at national Hispanic activist conventions, which were covered annually on Spanish-language television.

Ultimately, the history of the Hispanic category invites scholars to revisit understandings of how racial and ethnic classifications are institutionalized. Much of the available research stresses the workings of the state, or the agendas of ethnic political and market leaders, without paying much attention to *how* categories are negotiated and developed through forging networks and relationships. This has obscured the way that processes of co-optation, negotiation, and marketing play a role in determining when new categories emerge and how they will be defined. These processes are interactive; new categories can emerge when conflicts and struggles force stakeholders to cooperate and find areas of mutual interest with their fellow actors.

Again, ambiguity facilitates this cooperation. Categories that are defined narrowly, such as those based on surname or language, make it difficult for stakeholders to develop mutual interests and work together. For example, activists would have had a difficult time supporting a definition of Hispanics as those who spoke Spanish because many second-plus-generation Mexican Americans, including many activist leaders themselves, were monolingual English speakers. By defining the Hispanic category in a cultural manner, however, stakeholders could insinuate that the category was much broader and they could develop their own frames about panethnicity.

Moreover, ambiguity allows for a broad definition that can help to absorb resistance. Ambiguous categories can be combined with others, since their broad definition makes it difficult to discern who lies outside of the group. This allows stakeholders to include those individuals who might have felt shut out of a classification, or to preempt resistance from those who feel that they must give up one identity in order to be part of a new category. The idea that Hispanic panethnicity was complementary to national identity was incredibly important for overcoming resistance.

Ambiguity, however, works in tandem with analogy. Stakeholders recognize that a thoroughly ambiguous category is in danger of becoming irrelevant; as such, they make analogous comparisons between new classifications and existing ones in the hopes of delimiting the category. In effect, analogies allow stakeholders to make a new category seem more familiar by connecting it to an already established category.[4] Thus, when activists claim that Hispanics are like blacks, they want listeners to understand that, like blacks, Hispanics are a distinct, bounded minority group with a long history of disadvantage. And when census officials make comparisons between Hispanic and black communities, they want to convey that, like blacks, Hispanics are a sizable, bounded American demographic community.

At the same time, analogies also allow stakeholders to construct a barrier between categories. When stakeholders use analogies, they are suggesting similarities, but they are also asserting the existence of two distinct categories. The claim that Hispanics are like blacks suggests that while the communities share similarities, the Hispanic category is separate and distinct from the black one. The analogy thus places a boundary around the Hispanic category by suggesting that those who are Hispanic are not black. This distinction of course becomes problematic when we consider the population of individuals who straddle two categories, such as Afro-Latinos.

Nonetheless, as a field forms around a new classification, the origins of a new category become obscured. The web of interconnected positions, resources, and frames makes it difficult to say that one particular interest (political, economic, social) exclusively produced a given category. Stakeholders further obscure their individual interests and actions by drawing on history to persuade people that the new category has deep historical roots. In the Hispanic case, census officials wrote reports contending that Hispanics were united by their "common heritage from Spain," which stretched back to more than five centuries in the Americas.[5] Activists also historicized the notion of panethnicity in the United States by, for example, pointing to the Mexican American soldiers who had fought in the Civil War and contending that "Hispanics," not simply Mexican Americans, had played a key role in shaping American military history.[6]

Over time, the ambiguous category becomes more popular as more actors enter the field and use the new classification to achieve their organizational goals. A sort of collective amnesia[7] sets in as organizations begin to refer to the new category's long history and develop narratives about the rich cultural basis of the classification. By then, the category is completely institutionalized, and the new classification is, like other classifications, assumed to have always existed.

The Organizational Diffusion of the Hispanic Category

This book has mainly focused on outlining the efforts of the pioneering organizations that helped to institutionalize the notion of panethnicity. However, there were certainly other vital processes that emerged later as a result of these pioneering efforts. Beginning in the mid-1970s, for example, NCLR activists, former CCOSSP officials, and congressmen like Edward Roybal placed pressure on the Office of Management and Budget to issue Statistical Policy Directive 15, which it did in 1977. The directive required that all federal data collection agencies institute a Hispanic category, and this was instrumental in further institutionalizing the notion of panethnicity within the federal government.

Yet, while federal agencies could be directed to collect Hispanic data through a federal mandate, state agencies were under no obligation to follow suit. This was challenging for the Census Bureau because officials relied on the states' vital statistics to estimate undercounts. The resistance was particularly acute in places like New Hampshire and Vermont, where vital statistics offices claimed that there were too few Mexican Americans, Puerto Ricans, or Cuban Americans to justify adding the Hispanic category on birth and death certificate forms.

To resolve the issue, officials turned to their activists and ethnic leaders for help. Activists eagerly complied, understanding that more accurate data could aid them in their lobbying and grant-writing efforts. For example, throughout the 1980s, groups like NCLR wrote to vital statistics agencies across the country to argue that Hispanics were a separate community and should not simply be labeled as racially white or black. By 1993, all fifty states had included some kind of Hispanic category on birth and death certificates.[8]

Post-Nixon executive administrations also helped institutionalize pan-ethnicity by creating offices that expanded on work done by CCOSSP. Gerald Ford created the Office of Hispanic Affairs in 1974.[9] Run by Fernando De Baca, the group continued efforts to lobby federal agencies to funnel resources and grants to Hispanic communities. Subsequently, Jimmy Carter established his own Hispanic affairs office, which instituted a series of Hispanic town hall meetings in the late 1970s.[10] The Reagan and Bush administrations also continued the trend by appointing special assistants to advise them on Hispanic affairs.[11]

Throughout the late 1970s and 1980s, activists met with the staffs of these Hispanic affairs offices regularly, seeking opportunities to both garner resources and increase the executive office's awareness of Hispanic issues. NCLR, for example, appealed to these new offices for resources to fund community projects across the country. Moreover, Spanish-language television often interviewed the members of these agencies for news segments about Hispanic political and social affairs.[12]

In addition, by the mid-1970s, the Republican and Democratic Parties had also continued CCOSSP's work by formally instituting plans to secure more Hispanic votes. Both parties created Hispanic advisory groups, whose function it would be to advise their national committees on the needs and political goals of the Hispanic community. Furthermore, both political parties began working closely with marketers to create Spanish-language advertising that would appeal to Hispanic voters. These efforts became more pronounced after a group of Hispanics who had worked with CCOSSP and for the Nixon administration established their own political marketing agencies.[13] Over time, candidates solidified their links to these Hispanic marketing firms and spent an increasingly larger share of their budgets on courting the Hispanic vote.[14]

In addition, important political figures began attending Hispanic activist conventions, bringing even more national attention to the idea of the Hispanic vote. George H.W. Bush attended NCLR's national convention when he was vice president, and he became the first sitting president to attend the convention in 1990.[15] President Bill Clinton also attended the 1994 convention and spoke about issues like immigration and healthcare policy.[16]

During the 1980s, the idea of Hispanic panethnicity also spread rapidly through academia, especially in the social sciences. Soon after 1980 census data were released, social scientists used those and other data to write the first compendiums on the United States' Hispanic population. Notable early works include Joan Moore and Harry Pachon's *Hispanics in the United States* (1985) and Frank Bean and Marta Tienda's seminal text, *The Hispanic Population of the United States* (1987).[17]

Additionally, the influx of Hispanic data spurred the creation of new social science journals. The *Hispanic Journal of Behavioral Science* was established in late 1979, and the *Harvard Journal of Hispanic Policy* was founded in 1986.[18] These journals published articles that focused on specific subgroups alongside articles that analyzed the characteristics of the national, Hispanic community. A single volume on Hispanic education might, for example, deal with the specific challenges facing Mexican Americans while also considering how Hispanic education rates compared with those of non-Hispanic blacks and whites. In bringing together these different areas of research, these journals showcased the diversity within the Hispanic community *and* suggested that Latin American subgroups composed a single, national panethnic group.

Indeed, it was only after the idea of Hispanic panethnicity had been institutionalized as a data category that the Hispanic identity became the object of scientific scrutiny. In 1989, Rodolfo de la Garza and his collaborators developed the Latino National Political Survey, which asked individuals to rank identity labels such as "Mexican," "Hispanic," and "Latino."[19] Others soon began to code panethnic identification within their data sets.[20] Important qualitative studies about panethnicity emerged soon after the 1980 census as well. After interviewing Mexican and Puerto Rican community leaders in Chicago, sociologist Felix Padilla argued that a "Latino panethnic consciousness" was a viable element of a personal, albeit situational, identity that was often employed instrumentally.[21] More critical were researchers like Earl Shorris and Shirley Croucher, who pointed to interethnic antagonisms and the importance of national identity as a way to discredit the new category.[22] Still other

academics argued that panethnicity fostered a sense of solidarity arising from a common experience of discrimination and marginality in the
United States.[23]

Taken together, these Hispanic/Latino studies helped map out new
academic domains. Disciplines ranging from sociology to political science created Latino subfields. Research on Hispanic/Latino panethnicity,
as well as works on single ethnic groups, became categorized as "Latino
studies," a classification that also became institutionalized in academic
programs and departments. By 2000, a typical Latino studies program
included courses not only on subgroups such as Chicanos or Puerto Ricans but also on panethnic topics such as Latino literature and Latino
migration.[24]

Outside of academia, other civic organizations, including several with
ties to NCLR and the Forum of National Hispanic Organizations, had also
adopted the notion of panethnicity by the mid-1980s. Bodies that had
initially focused on representing specific ethnic groups, like the Mexican
American–focused League of United Latin American Citizens (LULAC)
and the American GI Forum, eventually changed their mission statements to include panethnic language and began recruiting a panethnic
constituency.[25] Some organizations even changed their names to reflect
their new panethnic status. For example, in 1994, the Mexican American
National Association changed its name to MANA—A National Latina Organization,[26] and in 2008, the Puerto Rican Legal Defense and Education
Fund changed its name to Latino Justice PRLDEF.[27] Many of these activist
groups eventually helped institutionalize panethnicity within the legal
system as well by filing court cases on behalf of Hispanics/Latinos.

Following the trail blazed by NCLR and state agencies, panethnic professional and nonprofit civic organizations began to emerge during the
late 1970s and the 1980s. Examples include the United States Hispanic
Chamber of Commerce (established in 1979), the Committee for Hispanic Children and Families (established in 1982), and the National Hispanic Bar Association (renamed and reestablished in 1985).

For its part, the media adopted an international strategy to promote
panethnicity throughout the 1990s. Univision began exporting its news
and entertainment shows to Latin America, where they gained popularity. Univision's *El Show de Cristina* and *Noticiero Univision*, for example,
were highly rated in about twenty Latin American countries by 1998.[28]
By broadcasting stories about Hispanic families, Hispanic politics, and
Hispanic current events, these shows provided Latin Americans with insights into the panethnic world of Latin American immigrants in the
United States.[29]

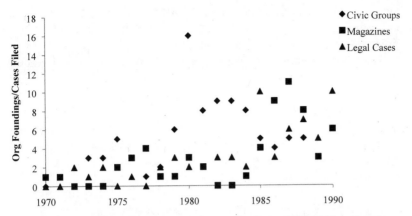

6   Rise of Hispanic civic organizations, magazines, and legal cases, 1970–90 (*Note*: Organizations were codèd as panethnic if their names included the terms *Hispanic, Latino,* or *Spanish
Speaking,* or if they signaled more than one ethnic group in their description. Organizations using the term *Hispanic* to signal persons of Spanish descent [second-plus-generation
Spaniards], academic institutes, and government organizations were excluded. All listed,
nationally circulating Spanish-language magazines were included in this count, unless the
periodical's description or title specifically mentioned a single ethnic group. And finally, all
federal and state legal cases that included "Hispanic," "Latino," or "Spanish-speaking" panethnic descriptors were included. Civic organizations data [excluding religious organizations]
collected from the *Encyclopedia of Associations, National Organizations* [Detroit: Gale Research
Corporation, 1970–90]; magazine data collected from *Standard Periodical Directory* [New
York: Oxbridge Communications, 1965–90]; and legal data collected from LexisNexis.)

The notion of panethnicity also spread through other forms of mass
media. Eduardo Caballero, who had worked for Univision during its initial phase, was an early Spanish-language radio pioneer who brought
together stations in the Southwest with those in Miami and New York
by shipping songs across the nation. His and other radio stations promoted what the industry eventually labeled the "International" or "Espa-
nol Continental" format, which mixed together music from across Latin
America and Spain.[30]

Media entrepreneurs also established magazines with titles like *Hispanic Business* (established in 1979) and *Hispanic Magazine* (established
in 1986).[31] The magazines served to further popularize the notion of panethnicity by telling compelling stories about the political, business, and
social aspects of the Hispanic community. A typical issue in *Hispanic Magazine*, for example, would include an interview with a Mexican American
celebrity, a recipe for a Cuban dish, and an article about Hispanic politics
or marketing.[32] Trade magazines like *Hispanic Business* served as syner-
gistic mediums by covering the activities of Spanish-language television

and radio as well as the current trends within Hispanic marketing. Such publications thus provided executives with an opportunity to monitor the developments within the broader Hispanic media field.

The accompanying figure examines the founding of Hispanic panethnic civic organizations and the establishment of panethnic magazines. It illustrates how Hispanic magazines and civic organizations grew over time. Moreover, the graph depicts the rise of legal cases filed on behalf of "Hispanic(s)/Latino(s)," demonstrating how the panethnic category expanded to broader discourses. To be sure, there are a considerable number of variables that account for the rise of civic organizations, magazines, and court cases related to Hispanic panethnicity. Nonetheless, the parallel increases in the trends are striking and suggest that the Hispanic panethnic category grew steadily more popular over time.

The rise of panethnicity, however, did not mean that *all* civic organizations and media entities accepted the notion. Some groups, such as the Mexican American Political Association (MAPA) and select Spanish-language radio stations, argued that panethnicity was contrived, an identity imposed on Mexican Americans, Puerto Ricans, Cuban Americans, and others by government bureaucrats and ethnic elites. Some academics supported this argument, noting that individuals overwhelmingly preferred national to panethnic labels. For the most part, though, these were faint voices easily overwhelmed by the growing chorus of organizations that hailed the notion of panethnicity. Indeed, by the 1990s, it was not only the large national political advocacy groups and media organizations that were promoting the idea of a Hispanic culture; an increasing number of small civic and local media organizations were also calling themselves Hispanic. Like the national groups before them, the local civic organizations sought grants and resources to aid the "Hispanic community," and the media organizations developed marketing manuals about Hispanic consumers. Hispanic panethnicity had become a strong narrative that could overpower criticisms precisely because diverse stakeholders bought into its unifying message.

Another category of protesters vigorously disapproved of the "Hispanic" label even though they agreed with the notion of panethnicity more generally. Public commentators and academics argued that the term *Hispanic* was conservative because it seemed to prioritize a cultural attachment to a white, European, specifically Spanish past and thus glossed over the important contributions of indigenous and African peoples within Latin America.[33] Many preferred *Latino* as an alternative way to signify panethnicity.[34] While it was not an ideal term, some argued that *Latino* was the best referent for panethnicity because it less overtly connoted Spain (though I should observe here that the meaning of the *Latino* label itself has remained ambiguous).[35]

Several organizations—including NCLR, the Census Bureau, and Univision—paid attention to the growing debate. The issue of which label and which definition to use had always been a thorny one because narrow categorizations threatened the stability of the relationships among civic and media organizations and federal agencies. Moreover, one label—be it *Spanish-speaking, Raza, Hispanic,* or *Latino*—never seemed to please everyone. Civic organizations responded to the debate not by taking a firm stance but by referring to a "Hispanic/Latino" panethnicity. Indeed, that *Hispanic* and *Latino* would eventually come to be used interchangeably speaks to the inherent ambiguity of panethnicity itself. The practice of using both terms continues today, although cross-sectional research shows that most persons of Latin American descent have a slight preference for the term *Hispanic.*[36]

Demography and Panethnicity

To be sure, the diffusion of Hispanic panethnicity that occurred in the 1980s was also made possible by Latin American population growth. While national organizations like the Census Bureau, Univision, and NCLR pioneered the effort to define and promote panethnicity in the 1970s, these efforts could have fizzled out were it not for three important demographic processes: the growth of the Hispanic population, the rise of panethnic communities, and the increase in panethnic marriages.

Throughout the 1970s and 1980s, the Hispanic population increased, prompting government, civic, and market organizations to direct more attention to these communities. High fertility rates among Hispanics and an increase in Latin American migration, especially from Mexico, allowed the population to grow substantially during that period. This population increase caught the attention of federal and state agencies, which turned to census reports to make sense of the demographic changes and forge new social policies. Population growth also gave rise to new civic groups, especially professional and political organizations, as well as to commercial media and retail firms that were eager to cater to the burgeoning Hispanic community.

Initially, population growth followed the same historical demographic patterns: Mexicans migrated to the Southwest, while Puerto Ricans and Cubans settled on the East Coast.[37] These two regions became increasingly panethnic as Central and South American migration increased throughout the 1980s.[38] Cities like Miami became home not only to Cuban Americans but also to newly arriving Nicaraguans, Venezuelans, and Argentines.[39] Los Angeles developed vibrant Central American business districts that helped revitalize what were once almost exclusively Mexican American barrios.[40] Also, Puerto Rican mainstays like "Spanish Harlem" became the new home for an increasing number of Dominican immigrants.[41]

The new Latin American migration of the 1980s created panethnic spaces that provided opportunities for subgroups to not only live, shop, and work together,[42] but also to fall in love. Intermarriages between Puerto Ricans and Dominicans in New York and Central Americans and Mexicans in Los Angeles increased significantly, if unevenly, throughout the 1980s.[43] Puerto Ricans and Cuban Americans were much more likely than other Hispanics to marry Latin Americans outside of their subgroup, while Mexican Americans were the least likely. Second-generation immigrants were also more likely to intermarry than were first-generation immigrants.[44]

As panethnic spaces and unions grew, so too did the number of local-level, panethnic civic and market organizations. Community studies on panethnic neighborhoods show that "Latino" and "Hispanic" newspapers, neighborhood groups, religious organizations, and markets emerged in these spaces and catered to the diverse array of Latin American subgroups. Hispanic bodegas in New York, for example, included items from Puerto Rico as well as delicacies from the Dominican Republic and South America.[45] Churches also hosted religious events and services that brought different Latin American subgroups together.[46]

More research is certainly needed to untangle the relationship between demography and the rise of local-level panethnic organizations. Were these organizations significantly more likely to emerge in panethnic spaces? What role did local labor market trends and connections to national panethnic bodies play in facilitating the emergence of these organizations? Were these local-level panethnic organizations more likely to emerge in places where Latin American subgroups experienced occupational segregation?[47] Regardless, what is certain is that the panethnic claims advanced by national market and political organizations provided a Hispanic category that could subsequently be adopted by those in panethnic neighborhoods during the 1980s.

In effect, the developments throughout the 1970s and 1980s created a completely new context for the Latin American diaspora, which continues today. A young Mexican American currently has several panethnic options that were unavailable to her three decades ago. She can join a variety of Hispanic-labeled civic clubs and organizations, tune in and watch Hispanic television programming, listen to bands on Hispanic/Latino radio stations, visit panethnic neighborhoods, and take part in Hispanic marketing and social science surveys. Her birth certificate, school forms, and driver's license will likely identify her as Hispanic. If she chooses to go to college, she can apply for Hispanic scholarships, take courses in Latino studies, and, eventually, she can be hired as a Hispanic marketing specialist, a Hispanic data analyst, or a Hispanic political analyst.[48] Now more than ever, the idea of Hispanic panethnicity has become part of the American cultural fabric.

Hispanic Categorization, Identification, and Politics

As this book went to press, the US Census Bureau announced that it would consider revamping its race question to include Hispanic as an option alongside race categories. The new question would read: "What is your Origin or Race?" Respondents would then be able to choose from options including Black, Hispanic/Latino, White, Indian, and several Asian nationalities. In a press conference about the proposed new question, the bureau's spokespersons noted that the agency was considering the change because it needed a better way to classify the vast number of Hispanic respondents who had rejected the conventional white, black, and Asian race categories on the last enumeration. These respondents had instead simply checked the "Some Other Race" box and had written in a Latin American country of origin or "Hispanic" or "Latino" on the race question.[49] A final decision will not be made for some time, giving the bureau several years to test different versions of a new racial category.

The decision on whether to change the race question will be consequential for the way that Latino identities are perceived. The two-question format used in the 2010 decennial census asked individuals first to identify if they were of Hispanic/Latino origin and then to choose a race option from categories that included white, black, Asian, and Native American. This formulation implies that persons of Latin American descent can somehow be sorted out among the established race categories. By not providing a Hispanic/Latino racial option, the formulation dismisses the Latino "racialization" thesis, which contends that Latino identities are durable and shape life chances because they signal a nonwhite, racial minority status in the United States.[50] Instead, the census formulation seems to imply that persons of Latin American descent are in fact racially white (or in some cases black or Native American) and that Latino identities, whether they be panethnic or national, are, like European American identities, ephemeral, lasting only a generation or so.[51]

A new combined question would not only help lend credence to the idea that Latinidad/Hispanidad is a durable racial identity that shapes an individual's life chances in meaningful and lasting ways, but it would also better accord with more recent studies on the issue. Indeed, census researchers have found that a significant number of persons of Latin American descent (sometimes more than half) believe that the traditional census categories of white, black, Native American, and Asian do not apply to them,[52] and most recently, in 2006, a national, comprehensive survey on Latino attitudes found that over 50 percent of persons of Latin American descent answered "yes" to a query about whether Hispanics/Latinos composed a distinct racial group.[53] With a combined question, these individuals could simply check the Hispanic/Latino box and move on without having to stumble over a separate race query.

The idea that Hispanics/Latinos might compose a race points as much to the larger issue of racial inequality as to the preference for a particular identity. When we see Hispanics/Latinos as a racial group, we can understand them as a distinct minority yet to reach socioeconomic parity with whites. This perception is not without supporting evidence. Overall, Latinos/Hispanics suffer high poverty rates and low educational attainment rates, they experience high rates of racial profiling, and they are disproportionately represented in the American penal population. Moreover, there is no question that many persons of Latin American descent, whether they are immigrants or not, continue to be stigmatized by a discourse that depicts them as "alien" foreigners in the American landscape.[54]

At the same time, any move toward a racial understanding of Hispanic/Latino identity should proceed with caution because it could lead to incorrectly framing Hispanics as a homogenous community with little internal variation. Many, though certainly not all, Cuban Americans consider themselves white, have higher levels of social mobility than other groups, and intermarry with whites more frequently. This contrasts starkly with the experiences of, to take one group, Mexican Americans, who are poorer, less educated, and less likely than other subgroups to marry whites.[55] The issue becomes more complicated when we consider research that finds that Afro-Latinos have a particularly different experience of Latinidad from that of their lighter-skinned counterparts.[56]

The uncertainty and caution surrounding the Hispanic/Latino race issue is ultimately a reflection of how ambiguity upholds the notion of panethnicity in the first place. In attempting to bring such a diverse array of peoples together, the Hispanic category by design resists tight definition. Its broadness gives it strength because it refers to a wide variety of understandings and can thus be molded to conform to different organizational goals and to encompass an assortment of different groups. However, this very flexibility also makes the category's contours difficult to discern at times. Policy makers, census officials, and ethnic leaders would be wise to balance issues of internal diversity with the impulse to cast the category too broadly.

In conclusion, it is important to consider what the history related in this book means for identity politics. That my study reveals the web of interests and organizations that helped to institutionalize the Hispanic category over time does not necessarily mean that panethnicity is somehow untrue or false. All identities are social constructs, and none are completely accepted by every member of a given group. Nation-states had to forge national identities at one point, just as ethnic and racial group leaders have had to do for ethnicity and race, respectively. There are no true or false identities, for each is the product of a sociohistorical process.

In fact, the idea of Hispanic panethnicity is much more popular now than it ever has been. Survey research tells us that Mexican Americans, Puerto Ricans, and Cuban Americans, not to mention Central and South Americans, are more apt to identify with Hispanic and Latino labels today.[57] Whether or not this identity category was widespread in the late 1960s is inconsequential to many who feel that it adequately represents their community now.

Ultimately, Hispanic panethnicity has become a salient form of collective identification in America. This is true despite the fact that organizations frame Hispanic/Latino panethnicity in various ways, and despite the fact that the category still seems ambiguous to many. We should be cautious of any statements that depict Hispanics as a homogenous community with little internal variation. At the same time, however, we should not dismiss the social currents that are attempting to unify subgroups and the potential impact that Latino/Hispanic solidarity can have on American institutions. The challenge for Hispanic/Latino organizations will be to honor their community's differences while emphasizing that community's similarities. The task will be delicate and difficult, but the outcome will certainly affect the American political landscape and change our discussion about race and ethnicity for generations to come.

Notes

INTRODUCTION

1. "El presidente Barack Obama fue a Naleo en Florida en busca del voto hispano," Univision Network News website, June 26, 2012 (my translation), accessed July 15, 2012, http://noticias.univision.com/noticiero-univision/videos /video/2012-06-22/barack-obama-en-naleo-florida.
2. See US Census Bureau, "Most Children Younger than Age 1 Are Minorities," US Census Bureau Public Information Office website, May 17, 2012, accessed July 20, 2012, http://www .census.gov/newsroom/releases/archives/population/cb12 -90.html. See also Daniel Borunda and Zahira Torres, "Hispanic Students Attain Majority in Texas Schools," *El Paso Times* online, March 23, 2011, http://www.elpasotimes .com/news/ci_17677779; and Jim Carlton, "Hispanics Surge in California," *Wall Street Journal* online, March 9, 2011, http://online.wsj.com/article/SB10001424052748703662804 576189031330152462.html.
3. "El poder del voto latino en 2012," Univision Network News website, February 9, 2012, accessed July 17, 2012, http:// univision65.univision.com/destino-2012/videos/video/2012 -02-09/el-poder-del-voto-latino.
4. "Univision impulsa la campaña libera tu voz," Primer Impacto website, April 24, 2012, accessed July 20, 2012, http:// noticias.univision.com/primer-impacto/videos/video/2012 -04-24/univision-impulsa-la-campana-libera.
5. Julia Preston and Fernanda Santo, "A Record Latino Turnout, Solidly Backing Obama," *New York Times*, November 8, 2012, 13; and Donna St. George and Brady Dennis, "Growing Share of Hispanic Voters Helped Push Obama to Victory," *Washington Post* online, November 7, 2012, http://www

.washingtonpost.com/politics/decision2012/growing-share-of-hispanic
-voters-helped-push-obama-to-victory/2012/11/07/b4087d0a-28ff-11e2
-b4e0-346287b7e56c_story_1.html. But see also Tyche Hendricks, "Exit
Interviews on the Exit Polls," KQED website, November 12, 2012, accessed
December 2, 2012, http://blogs.kqed.org/election2012/2012/11/12/exit
-interviews-on-the-exit-poll/#more-6195.

6. See quote by Chuck Todd in "Obama's Demographic Edge," NBCNews.com,
November 7, 2012, accessed November 7, 2012, http://firstread.nbcnews
.com/_news/2012/11/07/14993875-first-thoughts-obamas-demographic
-edge?lite. See also Cindy Rodriguez, "Latino Vote Key to Obama's Reelection," CNN Politics website, November 9, 2012, accessed December 2,
2012, http://www.cnn.com/2012/11/09/politics/latino-vote-key-election
/index.html; and Molly Hennenberg, "Republicans Losing Ground among
Hispanic Voters," FoxNews.com, November 9, 2012, accessed December 2,
2012, http://www.foxnews.com/politics/2012/11/09/republicans-losing
-ground-among-hispanic-voters.

7. I use *Mexican American* throughout to refer to first-, second-, and third-plus-
generation persons of Mexican descent living in the United States. In those
places where immigrants need to be distinguished from their American-
born counterparts, I use *Mexican immigrants* and *second-plus-generation
Mexican Americans.* I use the term *Cuban American* in the same fashion.

8. Jack Rosenthal, "The Goal among the Spanish-Speaking: 'Unidos,'" *New
York Times*, October 31, 1971, E9.

9. Thomas J. Foley, "Latin Conference Votes to Set Up Political Power Base in
Capital," *Los Angeles Times*, October 25, 1971, A4.

10. In an interview following a 1971 conference between Mexican Americans
and Puerto Ricans, Puerto Rican delegate Herman Badillo stated that panethnicity was an idea "whose time had not yet come." Quoted in Rosenthal, "Goal among the Spanish-Speaking," E9. See also Herman Badillo
(cofounder of PRLDEF [Puerto Rican Legal Defense and Education Fund],
1972), interview by G. Cristina Mora, March 25, 2010. Badillo helped
convene the Spanish Speaking Unity Summit, and he was a former member
of the US House of Representatives (D-NY) and a former executive board
member of the Puerto Rican Legal Defense and Education Fund.

11. Nampeo McKenney (employee at the US Census Bureau, Ethnic Origins
Statistics Branch, 1960–2000), interview by G. Cristina Mora, May 16, 2012.

12. Daniel Villanueva (former SICC executive and station manager of KMEX,
1971–89), interview by G. Cristina Mora, December 12, 2007.

13. Jorge Ramos, *The Other Face of America: Chronicles of Immigrants Shaping Our
Future* (New York: Harper Books, 2003); and Jorge Ramos, *The Latino Wave:
How Hispanics Are Transforming Politics in America* (New York: Harper Books,
2005).

14. Frank D. Bean and Marta Tienda, *The Hispanic Population of the United States*
(New York: Russell Sage Foundation, 1987); and Joan Moore and Harry

Pachon, *Hispanics in the United States* (Englewood Cliffs, NJ: Prentice-Hall, 1985).

15. Felix Padilla, *Latino Ethnic Consciousness: The Case of Mexican Americans and Puerto Ricans in Chicago* (South Bend, IN: Notre Dame Press, 1985); and Roberto Villareal and Norma G. Hernandez, *Latinos and Political Coalitions: Political Empowerment for the 1990s* (New York: Praeger, 1991).

16. Mirabal Greenbaum, *More Than Black: Afro-Cubans in Tampa* (Gainesville: University of Florida Press, 2002); Lisandro Perez, "Racialization among Cubans and Cuban Americans," in *How the United States Racializes Latinos: White Hegemony and Its Consequences*, ed. Jose A. Cobas, Jorge Duany, and Joe R. Fagin, 134–48 (Boulder, CO: Paradigm Press, 2009); and Maria de Los Angeles Torres, *In the Land of Mirrors: Cuban Exile Politics in the United States* (Ann Arbor: University of Michigan Press, 2001). The trend continues today with Cuban immigrants being significantly more likely than any other Latin American immigrant group to state that they are racially white. See Sonya Tafoya, *Shades of Belonging* (Washington, DC: Pew Hispanic Research Center, 2004).

17. Juan Gómez-Quiñones, *Chicano Politics: Reality and Promise, 1940–1990* (Albuquerque: University of New Mexico Press, 1990); Carlos Muñoz Jr., *Youth, Identity and Power: The Chicano Movement* (London: Verso, 1989); and Rodolfo Acuña, *Occupied America: A History of Chicanos*, 6th ed. (New York: Longman Publishing, 2006).

18. Basilio Serrano, "Rifle, Canon y Escopeta!' A Chronicle of the Puerto Rican Student Forum," in *The Puerto Rican Movement: Voices from the Diaspora*, ed. Andrés Torres and José E. Velázquez, 124–43 (Philadelphia: Temple University Press, 1998); Andrés Torres and José E. Velázquez, preface to *The Puerto Rican Movement: Voices from the Diaspora*, xi–xiii (Philadelphia: Temple University Press, 1998); and Jose Sanchez, *Boricua Power: A Political History of Puerto Ricans in the United States* (New York: New York University Press, 2006).

19. Eduardo Caballero (former SIN executive, 1967–72, founder of Caballero Spanish Media), interview by G. Cristina Mora, November 14, 2007. The account of these commercials was also mentioned in Armando Rendon (founder of Los Cerezos Media, SIN affiliate, and former member of the Census Bureau's Office of Public Relations, 1979–88), interview by G. Cristina Mora, May 20, 2012.

20. By institutionalization, I mean the process by which ideas, in this case the notion of Hispanic panethnicity, become attached to organizational resources, forms, and practices. See Elisabeth S. Clemens, *The People's Lobby: Organizational Innovation and the Rise of Interest Group Politics in the United States, 1890–1925* (Chicago: University of Chicago Press, 1997).

21. Latin American independence leaders like Simón Bolívar and José Martí advocated for a "Pan-American" unity based on the notion that Latin American states had commonly shed the yoke of Spanish imperialism. Bolivarian and Martian writings exhorted Latin Americans to band together

in order to best protect their sovereignty and gain true self-determination. See Simon Collier, "Nationality, Nationalism, and Supranationalism in the Writings of Simon Bolivar," *Hispanic American Historical Review* 63, no. 1 (1983): 37–64; and Laura Lomas, *Translating Empire: José Martí, Migrant Latino Subjects, and American Modernities* (Durham, NC: Duke University Press, 2008).

22. Spanish politicians and philosophers advocated a Hispanic unity, which they argued indicated a shared history and culture between Latin America and Spain. For politicians, the notion was steeped in political interests as state officials anticipated that it would help Spain to maintain allies in the Western Hemisphere. Frederick Pike, *Hispanismo, 1898–1936: Spanish Conservatives and Liberals and Their Relations with Spanish America* (South Bend, IN: University of Notre Dame Press, 1971).

23. Whether the term *Spanish* referred to the Spanish language, to Spanish descent, or to both is not clear. What we do know is that established American media institutions used the term in reference to both Puerto Rican and Mexican American communities. In addition, leaders from both communities write in their memoirs that Anglo and African American groups would use the term regularly. See, for example, "Deportation Talk Revised," *New York Times*, February 16, 1936, E11; and Charles Grutzner, "City Puerto Ricans Found Ill-Housed: Crowded Conditions, Race Bias Are Seen as Reasons for the Social Problem; Homes Are Kept Clean Despite Ugly Surroundings, Social Worker Says Women Are Instinctively Tidy," *New York Times*, October 4, 1949, 3. See also Ernesto Galarza, *Barrio Boy* (South Bend, IN: University of Notre Dame Press, 1991); and Antonia Pantoja, *Memoir of a Visionary: Antonia Pantoja* (Houston: Arte Público Press, 2002).

24. See Laura E. Gómez, "The Birth of the 'Hispanic' Generation: Attitudes of Mexican American Political Elite towards the Hispanic Label," *Latin American Perspectives* 19, no. 4 (1992): 48.

25. Bean and Tienda, *Hispanic Population of the United States*; Suzanne Oboler, *Ethnic Labels, Latino Lives: Identity and the Politics of (Re)Presentation in the United States* (Minneapolis: University of Minnesota Press, 1995); Juan Flores and George Yudice, *Divided Borders: Essays in Puerto Rican Identity* (Houston: Arte Público Press, 1993); and Marcelo M. Suarez-Orozco and Mariela M. Paez, "Introduction: The Research Agenda," in *Latinos: Remaking America*, ed. Marcelo M. Suarez-Orozco and Mariela M. Paez, 1–38 (Berkeley: University of California Press, 2002).

26. Alejandro Portes and Robert L. Bach, *Latin Journey: Cuban and Mexican Immigrants in the United States* (Berkeley: University of California Press, 1985); Bean and Tienda, *Hispanic Population of the United States*; and Marta Tienda and Faith Mitchel, *Hispanics and the Future of America* (Washington, DC: National Academies Press, 2006).

27. John A. Garcia, *Latino Politics in America: Community, Culture and Interests* (Lanham, MD: Rowman and Littlefield, 2003); and Chris Garcia and

Gabriel Sanchez, *Hispanics and the U.S. Political System: Moving towards the Mainstream* (New York: Prentice Hall, 2008).

28. J. A. Garcia, *Latino Politics in America*; and C. Garcia and G. Sanchez, *Hispanics and the U.S. Political System*.

29. Richard Alba and Victor Nee, *Remaking the American Mainstream: Assimilation and Contemporary Immigration* (Cambridge, MA: Harvard University Press, 2003); and Ruben Rumbaut, Douglas Massey, and Frank Bean, "Linguistic Life Expectancies: Immigrant Language Retention in Southern California," *Population and Development Review* 32, no. 3 (2006): 447–60.

30. Bean and Tienda, *Hispanic Population of the United States*.

31. Anthony Stevens-Arroyo and Andres Perez y Mena, *Enigmatic Powers: Syncretism with African and Indigenous Peoples' Religions among Latinos* (New York: Bildner Center Series on Religion, PARAL, 1995); Anthony Stevens-Arroyo and Gilbert Cardenas, *Old Masks, New Faces: Religion and Latino Identities* (New York: Bildner Center Series on Religion, PARAL, 1995); and Juan Francisco Martinez, *Los Protestantes: An Introduction to Latino Protestantism in the United States* (Santa Barbara, CA: BC-CLIO, 2011).

32. Alejandro Portes and Dag MacLeod, "What Shall I Call Myself? Hispanic Identity Formation in the Second Generation," *Ethnic and Racial Studies* 19 (1996): 523–47; Pew Hispanic Center, *2002 National Survey of Latinos: Summary of Findings* (Washington, DC: Pew Hispanic Center, 2002); Luis Ricardo Fraga, John A. Garcia, Rodney E. Hero, Michael Jones-Correa, Valerie Martinez-Ebers, and Gary M. Segura, *Latino Lives in America: Making It Home* (Philadelphia: Temple University Press, 2009). For recent analysis that indicates that the second generation is now more likely to identify nationally rather than panethnically, see Luis R. Fraga, John A. Garcia, Rodney E. Hero, Michael Jones-Correa, Valerie Martinez-Ebers, and Gary M. Segura, *Latinos in the New Millennium: An Almanac of Opinion, Behavior and Policy Preferences* (New York: Cambridge University Press, 2012).

33. Sheila L. Croucher, *Imagining Miami: Ethnic Politics in a Postmodern World* (Charlottesville: University of Virginia Press, 1997), 55.

34. Michael Jones-Correa and David Leal, "Becoming 'Hispanic': Secondary Panethnic Identification among Latin American Origin Groups," *Hispanic Journal of Behavioral and Social Sciences* 18, no. 2 (1996): 214–54.

35. See Paul Taylor, Mark Hugo Lopez, Jessica Hamar Martinez, and Gabriel Valasco, *When Labels Don't Fit: Hispanics and Their Views of Identity* (Washington, DC: Pew Hispanic Research Center, 2012), 10.

36. Oboler, *Ethnic Labels, Latino Lives*; see also Nicholas De Genova and Ana Y. Ramos-Zayas, *Latino Crossings: Mexicans, Puerto Ricans and the Politics of Race and Citizenship* (New York: Routledge, 2003).

37. Some historical accounts simply point to Directive 15, which was issued by the Office of Management and Budget in 1977, to argue that the Hispanic category emerged that year. See Jorge Idler, *Officially Hispanic: Classification Policy and Identity* (Lanham, MD: Lexington Books, 2007); Victoria Hattam,

In the Shadow of Race: Jews, Latinos and Immigrant Politics in the United States (Chicago: University of Chicago Press, 2007); and Dvora Yanov, *Constructing "Race" and "Ethnicity" in America: Category-Making in Public Policy Administration* (Armonk, NY: M.E. Sharpe, 2003). Other works either focus mainly on the Census Bureau or point out that the Census Bureau had created a "Spanish Origin" category in 1970, which was well before OMB's directive. See Martha E. Gimenez, "Latino/Hispanic—Who Needs a Name? The Case against a Standardized Terminology," *International Journal of Health Services* 19 (1989): 557–71; Martha E. Gimenez, "U.S. Ethnic Politics: Implications for Latin Americans," *Latin American Perspectives* 19, no. 4 (1992): 7–17; David Goldberg, *Racial Subjects: Writing on Race in America* (New York: Routledge, 1997); and Clara Rodriguez, *Changing Race: Latinos, the Census, and the History of Race in the United States* (New York: New York University Press, 2000).

38. Harvey Choldin's classic piece on the Hispanic category was largely written in conversation with political scientists who denounced the politicization of the Census Bureau. As such, his piece focuses not on the question of how the Hispanic category was developed and defined, but rather on the effect that activists had on enumeration procedures and strategies. Harvey Choldin, "Statistics and Politics: The 'Hispanic Issue' in the 1980 Census," *Demography* 23, no. 3 (1986): 403–18. See also William Petersen, "Politics and the Measurement of Ethnicity," in *The Politics of Numbers*, ed. William Alonso and Paul Starr, 207–34 (New York: Russell Sage Foundation, 1987).

39. Some have labeled the "political entrepreneur" interpretation as an "ethnic elite" interpretation, although the definition of *elite* has varied. See Max Weber, "Ethnic Groups," in *Economy and Society: An Outline of Interpretive Sociology*, ed. Guenther Ross and Claus Wittich, 385–98 (Berkeley: University of California Press, 1978); Cynthia Enloe, *Ethnic Conflict and Political Development* (New York: University Press of America, 1986); and Donald Horowitz, *Ethnic Groups in Conflict* (Berkeley: University of California Press, 2000). For collaborations between Mexican American and Puerto Rican civic leaders, as well as their congressional allies, see J. A. Garcia, *Latino Politics in America*; José Calderón, " 'Hispanic' and 'Latino': The Viability of Categories for Panethnic Unity," *Latin American Perspectives* 19, no. 4 (1992): 37–44; Fraga et al., *Latino Lives in America*; and Padilla, *Latino Ethnic Consciousness*.

40. See chap. 2.

41. America Rodriguez, *Making Latino News: Race, Language, Class* (Thousand Oaks, CA: Sage Publications, 1999).

42. Arlene Davila, *Latinos Inc.: The Marketing and Making of a People* (Berkeley: University of California Press, 2001). See also America Rodriguez, "Commercial Ethnicity: Language, Class and Race in the Marketing of the Hispanic Audience," *Communication Review* 2, no. 3 (1997): 283–309.

43. See Pierre Bourdieu, "The Social Space and the Genesis of Groups," *Theory and Society* 14, no. 6 (1985): 726–44. See also Pierre Bourdieu, *The Logic of*

Practice, trans. Richard Nice (1980; repr., Stanford, CA: Stanford University Press, 1990).

44. A field is a central concept in institutional analysis, and Bourdieu's concept of it is akin to, although not identical with, the way that it is used by organizational scholars. Specifically, scholars use the idea of an organizational field to describe a crowded landscape comprised of organizations and their regulators, suppliers, competitors, and constituents. Within these fields, organizations jockey for status, which carries with it the ability to impose certain legitimate definitions and frames on one another. See Paul Dimaggio and Walter Powell, introduction to *The New Institutionalism in Organizational Analysis*, ed. Walter Powell and Paul Dimaggio, 1–41 (Chicago: University of Chicago Press, 1991). See also Neil Fligstein and Doug McAdam, *A Theory of Fields* (Oxford: Oxford University Press, 2012).

45. Wimmer presents the notion of an "ethnic consensus" to argue that ethnic leaders and state bureaucrats can often negotiate a compromise on a mutual understanding of a new ethnic category. See Andreas Wimmer, "Elementary Strategies of Ethnic Boundary Making," *Ethnic and Racial Studies* 31, no. 6 (2008): 1025–55; and Andreas Wimmer, "The Making and Unmaking of Ethnic Boundaries: A Multilevel Process," *American Journal of Sociology* 113, no. 4 (2008): 970–1022.

46. See Peter L. Berger, *The Sacred Canopy: Elements of a Sociological Theory of Religion* (Garden City, NY: Doubleday, 1967).

CHAPTER ONE

1. Hugh Graham, *The Civil Rights Era: Origins and Development of National Policy* (Oxford: Oxford University Press, 1990).

2. Lyndon Johnson to Martin Luther King Jr. (telephone call), January 15, 1965 (emphasis added), American Radio Workswebsite, accessed February 26, 2011, http://americanradioworks.publicradio.org/features/prestapes /c1.html.

3. John David Skrentny also shows the way that foreign politics and the cold war context helped to spur civil rights policy. Countries like Nazi Germany and, later, the Soviet Union criticized the United States for purporting to spread democracy while supporting an unequal system that differentially affected blacks. Conscious of these criticisms, Presidents Roosevelt, Eisenhower, Truman, and Kennedy lent cautious attention to the issue of black civil rights. John David Skrentny, *The Minority Rights Revolution* (Cambridge, MA: Harvard University Press, 2003).

4. See Graham, *Civil Rights Era*; and Skrentny, *Minority Rights Revolution*. See also Dean Kotlowski, *Nixon's Civil Rights: Politics, Principle and Policy* (Cambridge, MA: Harvard University Press, 2002).

5. Graham, *Civil Rights Era*; and Skrentny, *Minority Rights Revolution*.

6. The issue of just how much assistance these policies actually provided to

African Americans is dubious. See John Andrews, *Lyndon Johnson and the Great Society* (Chicago: Ivan R. Dee, 1998).

7. See, for example, Johnson's historic address at Howard University, in which he stated that "nothing is more freighted with meaning for our own destiny than the revolution of the Negro American." *Public Papers of the Presidents of the United States: Lyndon B. Johnson, 1965*, vol. 2 (Washington, DC: Government Printing Office, 1966), 635.

8. See Ford Foundation, "Civil Rights, Social Justice, and Black America: A Review of Past and Current Ford Foundation Efforts to Promote Racial Justice for Black Americans in Employment, Education, Housing, Political Participation and Other Areas: A Working Paper" (Ford Foundation, New York, 1984).

9. Comments made by McGeorge Bundy in a 1966 speech at the annual banquet for the National Urban League. This sentiment was reiterated in "The President's Review," in Ford Foundation, *Annual Report* (New York: Ford Foundation, 1967), 2–14.

10. Christine M. Sierra, "The Political Transformation of a Minority Organization: The National Council of La Raza, 1965–1980" (PhD diss., Stanford University, 1983).

11. Gunnar Myrdal, *An American Dilemma: The Negro Problem and Modern Democracy* (New York: Harper and Row, 1944).

12. Daniel P. Moynihan, *The Negro Family: The Case for National Action* (Washington, DC: Government Printing Office, 1965).

13. Ibid. See also Anthony Quiroz, *Claiming Citizenship: Mexican Americans in Victoria, Texas* (College Station: Texas A&M University Press, 2005).

14. As it did with African Americans, the type and severity of racism shifted over time. Between 1860 and 1930, for example, Mexican Americans were hunted and lynched by nativist mobs. William Carrigan and Clive Webb estimate that the rate of Mexican American lynching only slightly lagged behind the rate of black lynching throughout the South and the Southwest between 1860 and 1930. William D. Carrigan and Clive Webb, "Lynching of Persons of Mexican Origin or Descent: 1828–1928," *Journal of Social History* 37, no. 2 (2003): 411–38.

15. See Martha Menchaca, *The Mexican Outsiders: A Community History of Marginalization and Discrimination in California* (Austin: University of Texas Press, 1995). By 1947, rulings in three court cases had found that Mexican students had been systematically relegated to "all Mexican" schools. See Inhabitants of Del Rio Independent School District v. Jesus Salvatierra, 33 S.W.2d 790 (Tex. Civ. App. 1930); Roberto Alvarez v. Board of Trustees of the Lemon School District, Superior Court, San Diego County, No. 66625 (1931); and Mendez et al. v. Westminster School District, 64 F Supp. 544 (S. D. Cal. 1946). See also Ruben Donato, *The Other Struggle for Equal Schools: Mexican Americans during the Civil Rights Era* (Albany: State University of New York, 1997).

16. Skrentny notes the important role that foreign policy had on the establishment of protected minority status for African Americans and Asians, especially Chinese; see Skrentny, *Minority Rights Revolution*. There is evidence that Latin American foreign policy, especially federal officials' desire to uphold Franklin Roosevelt's "Good Neighbor" policy, contributed to the establishment of a "Mexican American/Spanish American" protected minority category in the 1940s. See Roy Luján, "Dennis Chávez and the Roosevelt Era, 1933–1945" (PhD diss., University of New Mexico, 1987); Louis Rachames, *Race, Jobs, and Politics: The Story of FEPC* (New York: Columbia University Press, 1953); and Skrentny, *Minority Rights Revolution*.

17. Mario Garcia, *Mexican Americans: Leadership, Ideology and Identity, 1930–1960* (New Haven, CT: Yale University Press, 1989). See also Armando Navarro, *Mexicano Political Experience in Occupied Aztlán: Struggles and Change* (Walnut Creek, CA: Altamira Press, 2005).

18. Benjamin Marquez, *LULAC: The Evolution of a Mexican American Political Organization* (Austin: University of Texas Press, 1993); Craig A. Kaplowitz, *LULAC, Mexican Americans, and National Policy* (College Station: Texas A&M University Press, 2005); and Juan Gómez-Quiñones, *Chicano Politics: Reality and Promise, 1940–1990* (Albuquerque: University of New Mexico Press, 1990).

19. Gonzalez deftly traces how the meaning of these terms changed over time. He argues that between 1850 and roughly 1930, they were used by some to assert a level of class assimilation and thus distance themselves from poor and working-class Mexicans, by others to stress a connection to Spain and thus seem more culturally assimilable in an anti–Mexican American context, and by still others as synonyms for *Mexican American*. Thus, Gonzalez notes that individuals would often call themselves "Spanish American" while speaking in English (often because it seemed less threatening to European Americans) but "*Mexicano*" when speaking in Spanish. By the late 1930s and through the 1960s, however, the idea of a racialized Spanish American experience synonymous to the Mexican American experience had emerged, and it became increasingly common to use terms like *Spanish surnamed* and *Mexican* interchangeably. See Phillip Gonzalez, "The Political Construction of Latino Nomenclatures in Twentieth Century New Mexico," *Journal of the Southwest* 35, no. 2 (1993): 158–85; see also Laura E. Gómez, *Manifest Destinies: The Making of the Mexican American Race* (New York: New York University Press, 2007).

20. Despite their emphasis on cultural nationalism, Chicano leaders in the late 1960s struggled to define who Chicanos were. Some contended that Chicanos were people of Mexican descent. Others provided a broader definition of Chicanismo based on indigenous descent. Rather than being simply semantic variations, these issues had real consequences for how organizations would expend resources and recruit new members. See Navarro, *Mexicano Political Experience*; and Gómez-Quiñones, *Chicano Politics*.

See also Carlos Muñoz Jr., *Youth, Identity and Power: The Chicano Movement* (London: Verso, 1989); and Rodolfo Acuña, *Occupied America: A History of Chicanos*, 6th ed. (New York: Longman Publishing, 2006).

21. Navarro, *Mexicano Political Experience*; and Gómez-Quiñones, *Chicano Politics*. See also Muñoz, *Youth, Identity and Power*; and Acuña, *Occupied America*.

22. Jacques Levy, *César Chávez: Autobiography of La Causa* (St. Paul: University of Minnesota Press, 2007).

23. *Economic and Social Statistics for Americans of Spanish Origin: Hearing before the Subcommittee on Census and Population of the Committee on Post Office and Civil Service*, House of Representatives, 94th Cong. 51 (1975). See also chap. 2.

24. Many of these arguments emerged in the mid-1960s as Mexican Americans lobbied for but were unsuccessful at securing follow-through on civil rights commitments in the Southwest. See Navarro, *Mexicano Political Experience*.

25. Helen Rowan, "The Mexican American: A Paper for U.S. Commission on Civil Rights"(Washington, DC: US Commission on Civil Rights, 1968), 2.

26. Other government and press reports also commented on the "invisibility" of Mexican Americans vis-à-vis blacks. For example, see National Education Association, *The Invisible Minority: Report of the NEA-Tucson Survey on the Teaching of Spanish to the Spanish Speaking* (Washington, DC: National Education Association, 1966). See also "The Minority Nobody Knows," *Atlantic Monthly*, June 1967, 47–52; cited in Kaplowitz, *LULAC*.

27. Skrentny, *Minority Rights Revolution*.

28. Marta Tienda and Lief Jenson, "Poverty and Minorities: A Quarter-Century Profile of Color and Socioeconomic Disadvantage," in *Divided Opportunities: Minorities, Poverty and Social Policy*, ed. Gary Sandefur and Marta Tienda, 23–62 (New York: Plenum Press, 1988).

29. Sonia Nieto, "Puerto Rican Students in U.S. Schools: A Brief History," in *Puerto Rican Students in U.S. Schools*, ed. Sonia Nieto, 5–38 (New York: Taylor and Francis, 2000).

30. Clara Rodriguez posits that skin color variation among Puerto Ricans has historically correlated with experienced racism. Drawing from the memoirs of Puerto Ricans in New York, she suggests that the darker a Puerto Rican was, the more likely he was to be subjected to employment and housing discrimination. See Clara Rodriguez, *Puerto Ricans: Born in the U.S.A.* (Boulder, CO: Westview Press, 1991).

31. See Antonia Pantoja, *Memoir of a Visionary: Antonia Pantoja* (Houston: Arte Público Press, 2002).

32. Basilio Serrano, "Rifle, Canon y Escopeta!' A Chronicle of the Puerto Rican Student Forum," in *The Puerto Rican Movement: Voices from the Diaspora*, ed. Andrés Torres and José E. Velázquez, 124–43 (Philadelphia: Temple University Press, 1998).

33. This was likely because of the lack of Puerto Rican elected officials in the 1960s. See Andrés Torres and José E. Velázquez, preface to *The Puerto Rican*

Movement: Voices from the Diaspora, xi–xiii (Philadelphia: Temple University Press, 1998); Jose Sanchez, *Boricua Power: A Political History of Puerto Ricans in the United States* (New York: New York University Press, 2006); and Sherrie Baver, "Puerto Rican Politics in New York City: Post WWII Era," in *Puerto Rican Politics in Urban America*, ed. James Jennings and Monte Rivera, 43–61 (Westport, CT: Greenwood Press, 1984).

34. Lorrin Thomas, *Puerto Rican Citizen: History and Political Identity in Twentieth Century New York City* (Chicago: University of Chicago Press, 2010).

35. Gómez-Quiñones, *Chicano Politics*. For information on the Viva Kennedy and Viva Johnson campaigns, see Ignacio Garcia, *Viva Kennedy: Mexican Americans in Search of Camelot* (College Station: Texas A&M University Press, 2000); and Julie Pycior, *LBJ and the Mexican Americans: The Paradox of Power* (Austin: University of Texas Press, 1997).

36. See Kaplowitz, *LULAC*, 104.

37. Navarro, *Mexicano Political Experience*.

38. Gómez-Quiñones, *Chicano Politics*.

39. There is some disagreement about how many Mexican American leaders attended and walked out of the event. Navarro contends that fifty Mexican American leaders attended the EEOC conference. Beck also notes that fifty attended and claims that all fifty walked out, while Evans and Novak state that forty Mexican American leaders walked out. See Navarro, *Mexicano Political Experience*; Paul Beck, "Mexican American Walkout Mars U.S. Job Conference," *Los Angeles Times*, March 29, 1966, 3; and Rowland Evans and Robert Novak, "Inside Report: The Mexican Revolt," *Washington Post*, March 31, 1966, A21.

40. See Herman Gallegos, "History of the Southwest Council and the National Council of La Raza," Minutes of Board Meeting, April 22–24, 1977, Tucson, Records of the National Council of La Raza (hereafter NCLR Records), record group 1, box 1, folder 15, Department of Special Collections, Stanford University Libraries, Stanford, CA; and Julian Samora, *La Raza: Forgotten Americans*, ed. Julian Samora (South Bend, IN: University of Notre Dame Press, 1966).

41. Pycior, *LBJ and the Mexican Americans*, 188; and Skrentny, *Minority Rights Revolution*, 199.

42. Tony Castro, *Chicano Power: The Emergence of Mexican America* (New York: E. P. Dutton, 1974).

43. Pycior, *LBJ and the Mexican Americans*.

44. See Bruce Altschuler, "Lyndon Johnson in the Public Polls," *Public Opinion Quarterly* 50 (1986): 285–99.

45. Pycior, *LBJ and the Mexican Americans*, 188.

46. Ibid.

47. During the 1960s other groups—such as the Polish, the Italians, and, later, women—also demanded meetings about their civil rights. See Skrentny, *Minority Rights Revolution*.

48. See Mario Garcia, *Memories of Chicano History: The Life and Narrative of Bert Corona* (Berkeley: University of California Press, 1995).

49. Pycior, *LBJ and the Mexican Americans*.

50. Lyndon Johnson, "Memorandum from the President," June 9, 1967, reprinted in Inter-Agency Committee on Mexican American Affairs, *The Mexican Americans: A New Focus on Opportunity, Interagency Committee on Mexican American Affairs, 1967–1969* (Washington, DC: Government Printing Office, 1968), p. 1, White House Central Files, file group 145, Staff Member and Office of Files, Robert H. Finch CCOSSP File (hereafter Finch CCOSSP File), box 21, "Research Data" folder, Richard M. Nixon Presidential Library, San Clemente, CA (hereafter Nixon Library).

51. Although the event was labeled a hearing, it was essentially organized as a conference with a series of different workshops.

52. Pycior, *LBJ and the Mexican Americans*.

53. Reies López Tijerina, *They Called Me "King Tiger": My Struggle for the Land and Our Rights*, trans. José Angel Gutiérrez (Houston: Arte Público Press, 2000); and Rudy Busto, *King Tiger: The Religious Visions of Reies López Tijerina* (Albuquerque: University of New Mexico Press, 2005).

54. Rodolfo Gonzáles and Antonio Esquibel, *Message to Aztlán: Select Writings from Rodolfo "Corky" Gonzáles* (Houston: Arte Público Press, 2001); and Gómez-Quiñones, *Chicano Politics*.

55. Inter-Agency Committee on Mexican American Affairs, *The Mexican Americans: A New Focus on Opportunity, Inter-Agency Committee on Mexican American Affairs, 1967–1969* (Washington, DC: Government Printing Office, 1968), Finch CCOSSP File, box 21, "Research Data" folder.

56. Ibid.

57. Ibid.

58. Pycior, *LBJ and the Mexican Americans*.

59. Ibid.

60. Ibid., 211.

61. Ibid., 212.

62. See "Latins Organize Southwest Council," *Los Angeles Times*, October 10, 1967, A1; "Mexican American Unit Boycotts Conference," *Los Angeles Times*, October 17, 1967, OC12; Rubén Salazar, "Humphrey Asks Action by Mexican Americans," *Los Angeles Times*, October 28, 1967, 12; "Fair Share of Property Urged for Mexican Americans by HH," *Washington Post*, October 28, 1967, A2; and "Mexican Americans Boo Texas Governor," *Los Angeles Times*, October 29, 1967, E6.

63. Inter-Agency Committee on Mexican American Affairs, *Mexican Americans*, Finch CCOSSP File, box 21, "Research Data" folder.

64. Ibid.

65. Kotlowski, *Nixon's Civil Rights*. See also Ward Just, "Nixon Urges Program to Aid 'Black Capitalism,'" *Washington Post*, August 26, 1969, A1; and "Black Capitalism: Road to Pride," *Los Angeles Times*, June 2, 1969, K7.

66. Don Irwin, "Nixon Ready to Name Members of His Cabinet," *Los Angeles Times*, December 10, 1968, A1.

67. Pycior, *LBJ and the Mexican Americans*.

68. See Kaplowitz, *LULAC*.

69. See Inter-Agency Committee on Mexican American Affairs, *Mexican Americans*, Finch CCOSSP File, box 21, "Research Data" folder; and Rowan, "Mexican American."

70. Memorandum to Robert Finch from Martin Castillo and Henry Quevedo, "The Mexican-American and the New Administration," November 26, 1968, White House Central Files, file group 145, Staff Member and Office of Files, Daniel Patrick Moynihan Files, box 63, "Ethnic and Socio-Economic Groups: Mexican Americans" folder.

71. Rowan, "Mexican American," 69.

72. Burt Talcott to "Harry," July 1, 1969, White House Central Files, file group 145, Subject Files—Cabinet Committee on Opportunities for Spanish Speaking People (hereafter CCOSSP files), box 7, "FG 145—Inter-Agency Committee on Mexican American Affairs / Cabinet Committee on Opportunities for Spanish Speaking Americans" folder, Nixon Library.

73. See Memorandum to Daniel Patrick Moynihan from David. S. North, "The Nixon Administration and the Mexican Americans," February 4, 1969, Moynihan Files, box 63, "Ethnic and Socio-Economic Groups: Mexican Americans" folder, Nixon Library.

74. Jose de la Isla, *The Rise of Hispanic Political Power* (Santa Maria, CA: Archer Books, 2003).

75. See "List of Appointees," White House Central Files, Staff Member Office Files of Anne Armstrong (hereafter Armstrong Files), box 10, "Spanish Speaking Americans" folder, Nixon Library; and "Appointees under Johnson," Public Liaison Office, Theodore C. Marrs Files, 1974–1976 (hereafter Marrs Files), "Hispanic Presidential Appointees" file, box 9, Gerald R. Ford Presidential Library, Ann Arbor, MI (hereafter Ford Library).

76. See Peter Kihss, "'Benign Neglect' on Race Is Proposed by Moynihan," *New York Times*, March 1, 1970, 1.

77. See Memorandum for the president from Charles Wilkinson, "The Proposed Mexican American White House Conference," February 19, 1969, p. 1, Moynihan Files, box 63, "Ethnic and Socio-Economic Groups: Mexican Americans" folder.

78. See Memorandum to Edward Morgan from Story Zartman, "Legislation Concerning the Interagency on Mexican American Affairs," May 16, 1969, Moynihan Files, box 63, "Ethnic and Socio Economic Groups: Mexican Americans" folder.

79. See "Nixon Makes TV Film," *New York Times*, July 21, 1968, 38; and Don Irwin, "Nixon 5,000 Fans Override Hecklers at LA Area Rally: Nixon Campaigns in LA Area; Supporters Drown Out Hecklers," *Los Angeles Times*, October 10, 1968, A1.

80. Richard Phalon, "Javits's Backers Open Office Here," *New York Times*, September 10, 1968, 32.

81. See *Establish an Inter-Agency Committee on Mexican-American Affairs: Hearings before the Subcommittee on Executive Reorganization of the Committee on Government Operations*, United States Senate, 91st Cong. 740 (1969).

82. Ibid., 1.

83. Ibid., 92–100.

84. Ibid., 194.

85. Ibid., 195.

86. Ibid., 209.

87. Ibid., 204.

88. The issue of the extent to which civil rights policy had institutionalized a panethnic Spanish American minority category is difficult to settle because the category "Spanish American" was often used synonymously with "Mexican American" in the Southwest. It was not uncommon for members of the Fair Employment Practices Committee to write letters to one another that equated "Spanish Speakers" or "Spanish Americans" to Mexican Americans in the Southwest (as mentioned, this was not uncommon even among Mexican American leaders themselves). See Louis Kesselman, *The Social Politics of FEPC: A Study in Reform Pressure Movements* (Chapel Hill: University of North Carolina Press, 1948). See also Lujan, "Dennis Chávez and the Roosevelt Era"; and P. Gonzalez, "Political Construction of Latino Nomenclatures."

89. Puerto Rican community leaders had some experience with panethnic organizational structures. Although Puerto Ricans represented the overwhelming majority of Spanish-speaking Americans in the Northeast, large cities such as New York had attracted other Latin American groups, especially Cubans and some South American groups, that sometimes joined local Puerto Rican cultural clubs and civic associations. However, these organizations, such as Federación de Sociedades Hispanas, were short lived, few in number, and mainly run by and comprised of Puerto Ricans. See Thomas, *Puerto Rican Citizen*.

90. See P. Gonzalez, "Political Construction of Latino Nomenclatures."

91. Inter-Agency Committee on Mexican American Affairs, *Mexican Americans*, Finch CCOSSP File, p. 1, box 21, "Research Data" folder.

92. *Establish an Inter-Agency Committee on Mexican-American Affairs*, 91st Cong. 219 (1969).

93. Ibid.

94. *Departments of Labor, and Health, Education, and Welfare and Related Agencies Appropriation Bills 1970*, House of Representatives, 91st Cong. 1113 (1969) (H.R. Report No. 91-391).

95. Ibid., 1113.

96. See Joseph Novitski, "Demands Heard in East Village," *New York Times*, July 26, 1968, 39; James Clarity, "Puerto Ricans Hold City Official Captive in

Protest," *New York Times*, July 2, 1968, 18; and Murray Schumach, "CCNY Shut Down after a Blockade by 150 Students," *New York Times*, April 23, 1969, 1.

97. *Hearings before a Subcommittee on Departments of Labor, and Health, Education, and Welfare and Related Agencies Appropriations, 1970*, 91st Cong. 1117 (1969) (H.R. Report No. 91-391).

98. Ibid., 1113.

99. *Establishing the Cabinet Committee on Opportunities for Spanish Speaking People: Hearings before a Subcommittee of the Committee on Government Operations*, House of Representatives, 91st Cong. 18 (1969).

100. Ibid., 21.

101. Ibid.

102. See Memorandum from Leonard Garment to the president, February 5, 1971, Finch CCOSSP File, box 15, "Cabinet Committee on Opportunities for the Spanish Speaking" folder.

103. See Richard Nixon, "Statement on Signing the Bill Establishing the Cabinet Committee on Opportunities for Spanish Speaking People," December 31, 1969, *The American Presidency Project website*, accessed March 22, 2011, http://www.presidency.ucsb.edu/ws/?pid=2392.

104. Luis Ferrer to the president, January 29, 1970, Finch CCOSSP File, box 18.

105. Nelson Rockefeller to the president, July 30, 1970, CCOSSP Files, box 8, "FG 145" folder.

106. *New Era*, report by Cabinet Committee on Opportunities for Spanish Speaking People, 1970, p. 3, Finch CCOSSP File, box 21, "Spanish Speaking" folder.

107. See *Establish an Inter-Agency Committee on Mexican-American Affairs*, 91st Cong. 740 (1969).

108. See chap. 3 in this book.

109. *New Era*, p. 3, Finch CCOSSP File, box 21, "Spanish Speaking" folder.

110. See Memorandum from John Ehrlichman for the president, April 20, 1970, Finch CCOSSP File, box 15, "Correspondence Urging the President's Meeting with the Spanish Speaking" folder.

111. Memorandum from Daniel P. Moynihan to staff secretary, "Mexican American Conference," August 11, 1969, Finch CCOSSP File, box 16.

112. See Memorandum from John Ehrlichman for the president, April 20, 1970, Finch CCOSSP File, box 15, "Correspondence Urging the President's Meeting with the Spanish Speaking" folder.

113. For Nixon's refusal to meet with CCOSSP, see Memorandum from Dwight Chapin to Hugh Sloan and Stephen Bull, January 7, 1970, CCOSSP Files, box 7, "FG 145 Cabinet Committee on Opportunities for the Spanish Speaking People" folder. For Nixon's failure to appoint an advisory committee, see Memorandum from John Ehrlichman for the president, April 20, 1970, Finch CCOSSP File, box 15, "Correspondence Urging the President's Meeting with the Spanish Speaking" folder.

114. Memorandum from Leonard Garment for the president, p. 2, February 5, 1971, Finch CCOSSP File, box 15,"Cabinet Committee on Opportunities for the Spanish Speaking" folder.

115. Ibid., 3.

116. Edward Roybal and Herman Badillo to the president, August 9, 1971, Finch CCOSSP File, box 16, "Grassmuck, George" folder.

117. Jose Altero to the president, September 22, 1971, Finch CCOSSP File, box 16.

118. Salvador Ramos to the president, December 8, 1970, Finch CCOSSP File, box 16.

119. Memorandum from George Grassmuck for Clark MacGregor and George Shultz, "Concern of Spanish Speaking People for Results of Black Caucus Demands," May 10, 1971, Finch CCOSSP File, box 15, "Cabinet Committee on Opportunities for the Spanish Speaking" folder.

120. Minutes of the Cabinet Committee Meeting on Spanish Speaking, August 4, 1971, CCOSSP Files, box 15, "FG 145—Cabinet Committee on Opportunities for the Spanish Speaking" folder.

121. The President's Cabinet Committee on Opportunities for Spanish Speaking People—Press Release, August 5, 1971, Finch CCOSSP File, box 18, "Press Releases" folder.

122. See Establish an Inter-Agency Committee on Mexican-American Affairs, 91st Cong. 220 (1969).

123. Subcommittee on Departments of Labor, and Health, Education, and Welfare and Related Agencies Appropriations, 1970, 91st Cong. 1114 (1969) (H.R. Report No. 91-391).

124. For an excellent comparison of Mexican American and Cuban demographics, see Alejandro Portes and Robert L. Bach, Latin Journey: Cuban and Mexican Immigrants in the United States (Berkeley: University of California Press, 1985).

125. Edgardo Buttari to Robert Finch, December 15, 1971, Finch CCOSSP File, box 15, "Advisory Council" folder.

126. Report of Activities by Manuel Giberga on Activities for the Cabinet Committee and Reaction of Cuban Americans to the President's Appointment, undated, Finch CCOSSP File, box 15, "Advisory Council" folder.

127. Luisa Quintero, "In Spite of Ramirez, Aponte Still on Job," El Diario/La Prensa, December 30, 1971, p. 2, Finch CCOSSP File, box 21, "Spanish Speaking" folder.

128. "U.S. Panel Scorned by Puerto Ricans," New York Times, August 11, 1971, White House Central Files, file group 145, Staff Member and Office Files, Robert H. Finch, Rayburn Hanzlik File (hereafter Finch Hanzlik File), box 46, "Cabinet Committee on Opportunities for the Spanish Speaking" folder, Nixon Library.

129. Clifford Case to Robert Finch, July 30, 1971, CCOSSP File, box 15, "FG 145—Cabinet Committee on Opportunities for Spanish Speaking" folder.

130. "New Cabinet Aide to Help Latin Minority," Los Angeles Times, April 11, 1973, 19.

131. Notes on the Organization of the Cabinet Committee on Opportunities for Spanish Speaking, undated, Finch Hanzlik File, box 46, "Cabinet Committee on Opportunities for the Spanish Speaking" folder.

132. Memorandum from Bill Rhatican to Len Garment, "Briefings for Minority Groups," May 11, 1971, Finch Hanzlik File, box 46, "Cabinet Committee on Opportunities for the Spanish Speaking" folder.

133. Jerome Watson, "Stormy Sessions of US Officials with Latinos Here Told," *Chicago Sun Times*, October 21, 1971, p. 20, Finch CCOSSP File, box 21, "Spanish Speaking" folder.

134. Memorandum from Alfred J. Solano to Patricia Reilly Hitt, "Feedback on Chicago Regional Conference," October 18, 1971, Finch CCOSSP File, box 21, "Spanish Speaking" folder.

135. "New York Meeting Scheduled to Discuss Needs of Spanish Speaking Community," undated press release, Finch Hanzlik File, box 46, "Cabinet Committee on Opportunities for the Spanish Speaking" folder.

136. Cabinet Committee on Opportunities for Spanish Speaking People, *Annual Report of the Cabinet Committee on Opportunities for Spanish Speaking People* (Washington, DC: Cabinet Committee on Opportunities for Spanish Speaking People, 1971).

137. Ibid.

138. Ibid.

139. *Research Report: Spanish Speaking Americans*, undated, Finch CCOSSP File, box 21, "Research Data" folder.

140. Memorandum from Alex Armendariz to Frederic Malek, "Spanish Speaking Study," June 26, 1972, Committee for the Re-election of the President Collection, Frederic Malek Papers, Spanish Speaking Task Force (hereafter Malek Papers), box 36, "Citizen Groups: Spanish Speaking" folder, Nixon Library.

141. Cuban American CCOSSP advisory board members as well as important Cuban American media personalities supported Armendariz's efforts to obtain the Cuban American vote in Miami. For advisory board members, see US House of Representatives, *Stenographic Transcript of Hearings before the Committee on Rules, U.S. House of Representatives, October 16, 1973: H.R. 10397, H.R. 3927, Conference Report, H.R. 10586, H.R. 1071* (Washington, DC: Reynolds Reporting Associates, 1973). For media personalities, see Memorandum from Carlos Conde to Ken Clawson, "Cuban Rally," May 12, 1972, Malek Papers, box 36, "Citizen Groups: Spanish Speaking" folder.

142. "Spanish Speaking Campaign" newsletter, October 2, 1972, Malek Papers, box 36, "Citizen Groups: Spanish Speaking" folder.

143. Ibid.

144. Memorandum from Carlos Conde to Herbert Klein, "Spanish Speaking Media Program," May 1, 1972, Malek Papers, box 36, "Citizen Groups: Spanish Speaking" folder.

145. Memorandum from Carlos Conde to Herbert Klein, "Spanish Speaking Task

Force Media Team," May 31, 1972, Malek Papers, box 36, "Citizen Groups: Spanish Speaking" folder.

146. Ibid.

147. US House of Representatives, *Stenographic Transcript of Hearings before the Committee on Rules*. See also Edward Roybal and Herman Badillo to Henry Ramirez, November 29, 1972, Finch Hanzlik File, box 46, "Cabinet Committee on Opportunities for the Spanish Speaking" folder.

148. *The Record-Spanish*, videotapes, compilation tape 3, file ID 156, Committee to Re-elect the President record group, Nixon Library.

149. I examined every issue of *La Opinión*, the country's oldest and largest circulating Spanish-language newspaper,in the two weeks prior to the 1969 and 1972 elections. I coded the ethnic labels used in Nixon's campaign ads (there were none for Humphrey or McGovern) for these two election cycles. There was a total of four ads—two in 1968 and two in 1972—suggesting that Spanish-language print media were only one, and not a primary, source of publicity for the Nixon campaign.

150. "Nixon para presidente," *La Opinión*, November 3, 1968, 2 (my translation).

151. "Necesitamos al presidente Nixon!," *La Opinión*, November 1, 1972, 3 (my translation).

152. "Background Paper," Cabinet Committee on Opportunities for Spanish Speaking People, undated, Armstrong Files, box 10, "Spanish Speaking Americans" folder.

153. Cabinet Committee on Opportunities for Spanish Speaking People, *Annual Report*, 1973 (Washington, DC: Cabinet Committee on Opportunities for Spanish Speaking People).

154. *Equal Opportunities for Spanish Speaking People: Hearings before the Civil Rights and Constitutional Rights Subcommittee of the Committee on the Judiciary*, House of Representatives, 93rd Cong. (1973).

155. US House of Representatives, *Stenographic Transcript of Hearings before the Committee on Rules*, 5.

156. *Equal Opportunities for Spanish Speaking People*, 93rd Cong. (1973), 65.

157. Ibid.

158. "Nixon Loses Top Asian American," *Pasadena Star News*, September 2, 1973, CCOSSP Files, box 8, "FG 145—Cabinet Committee on Opportunities for the Spanish Speaking People" folder.

159. *Activities of the Cabinet Committee on Opportunities for Spanish Speaking People: Hearings before a Subcommittee of the Committee on Government Operations*, House of Representatives, 93rd Cong. 50, 64 (1973).

160. See "Agency for Spanish Speaking Under Fire on Watergate Ties," *Los Angeles Times*, July 1, 1974, 2.

161. Memorandum from Robert Shaw to Rey Maduro, "Henry Ramirez' Termination Date," September 19, 1974, White House Central Files, file group 145, box 159, Cabinet Committee on Opportunities for Spanish Speaking People, Ford Library.

162. "Cabinet Committee to Close Doors December 30, 1974: Ends Five Years of Service to Spanish Speaking," news release, December 27, 1974, Public Liaison Office, Fernando E.C. De Baca Files, 1974–1975, box 7, "Cabinet Committee on Opportunities for Spanish Speaking People" folder, Ford Library.
163. Ibid.
164. *Activities of the Cabinet Committee on Opportunities for Spanish Speaking People*, 93rd Cong. 71 (1973).
165. See chap. 3.
166. "Briefing Outline," Office of Hispanic Affairs, May 15, 1975, Marrs Files, "Spanish Speaking People" folder, box 26, Gerald R. Ford Presidential Library. See also chap. 3.
167. Republican National Committee, "GOP Spanish Speaking Effort Expanded with Plans for Organizational Conference of Republican National Hispanic Assembly Scheduled for July 11–13 in Washington D.C.," press release, undated, from Ford Vice Presidential Papers, Office of Deputy Assistant for Non-governmental Affairs Files, 1974, box 117, "Hispanic Americans" folder, Ford Library.
168. Republican National Hispanic Assembly of the United States, June 1976, President Ford Committee Records, 1975–1976, People for Ford Office, box F26, "Republican National Hispanic Assembly" folder, Ford Library.
169. See "Cuban American Newspaper Ad, Mexican American Ad, Puerto Rican Ad," memorandum, October 6, 1976, President Ford Committee Records, 1975–1976, box 3, "Campaign 76 Communications" folder, Ford Library.
170. For Carter, see Helen Dewar, "Carter Scours West for Support," *Washington Post*, July 2, 1976, Public Liaison Office, Thomas Aranda Files, 1976–1977, box 2, Ford Library. For Regan, see "Reagan Recognizes Our Era," *La Opinión*, October 26, 1980, 12.
171. Memorandum by Fernando De Baca, December 20, 1974, White House Central Files, file group 145, box 159, "Cabinet Committee on Opportunities for Spanish Speaking People" folder, Ford Library.
172. Memorandum from the special assistant to the assistant secretary for community and field services to Patricia Reilly Hill, "Highlights of National Spanish Speaking Coalition Conference," November 2, 1971, Finch CCOSSP File, box 23, "Task Force Reports" folder.
173. See Richard Santillan, "Politics of Cultural Nationalism: El Partido de la Raza Unida in Southern California, 1969–1978," government diss., Claremont Graduate School, 1978.
174. See James Tucker, *The Battle over Bilingual Ballots: Language Minorities and Political Access under the Voting Rights Act* (Burlington, VT: Ashgate, 2009).

CHAPTER TWO

1. These local groups were often focused on local civic issues and cultural and literary activities; some of those in New York eventually transformed into

Puerto Rican organizations. See Lorrin Thomas, *Puerto Rican Citizen: History and Political Identity in Twentieth-Century New York City* (Chicago: University of Chicago Press, 2010).

2. LULAC eventually expanded, but it formed Puerto Rican and Cuban American chapters only *after* NCLR had established itself as the nation's foremost Hispanic civil rights organization. See Benjamin Marquez, *LULAC: The Evolution of a Mexican American Political Organization* (Austin: University of Texas Press, 1993); and Craig A. Kaplowitz, *LULAC, Mexican Americans, and National Policy* (College Station: Texas A&M University Press, 2005).

3. Juan Gómez-Quiñones, *Chicano Politics: Reality and Promise, 1940–1990* (Albuquerque: University of New Mexico Press, 1990); Carlos Muñoz Jr., *Youth, Identity, and Power: The Chicano Movement* (London: Verso, 1989); and Rodolfo Acuña, *Occupied America: A History of Chicanos*, 6th ed. (New York: Longman Publishing, 2006).

4. Herman Gallegos, "History of the Southwest Council and the National Council of La Raza," 1977, in Minutes of Board Meeting, April 22–24, 1977, pp. 2–3, Tucson, Records of the National Council of La Raza (hereafter NCLR Records), record group 1, series 1, box 1, folder 15, Department of Special Collections, Stanford University Libraries, Stanford, CA.

5. Ibid. See also Christine M. Sierra, "The Political Transformation of a Minority Organization: The National Council of La Raza, 1965–1980" (PhD diss., Stanford University, 1983).

6. It should be clear, however, that the money that the Ford Foundation gave to Mexican American causes paled in comparison to that which they gave to African American ones. See Ford Foundation, *Annual Report* (New York: Ford Foundation, 1968).

7. See Leo Grebler, Joan W. Moore, and Ralph C. Guzman, *The Mexican-American People: The Nation's Second Largest Minority* (New York: Free Press, 1970).

8. Julian Samora, *La Raza: Forgotten Americans*, ed. Julian Samora (South Bend, IN: University of Notre Dame Press, 1966).

9. Minutes of the Board of Directors Meeting, June 16, 1968, El Paso, NCLR Records, record group 1, series 1, box 1, folder 1.

10. Ibid.

11. Gallegos, "History of the Southwest Council and the National Council of La Raza," NCLR Records, record group 1, series 1, box 1, folder 15.

12. Samora, *La Raza*.

13. Mario Garcia, *Memories of Chicano History: The Life and Narrative of Bert Corona* (Berkeley: University of California Press, 1995).

14. Ibid., 229.

15. Southwest Council of La Raza, Addendum to Progress Report, 1969, NCLR Records, record group 1, series 1, box 1, folder 3.

16. Minutes of the Board of Directors Meeting, November 9, 1968, San Francisco, NCLR Records, record group 1, series 1, box 1, folder 2.

17. Henry Santiestevan, "A Movement Is Born: National Emergence of La

Raza," *Agenda* 3, no. 5 (1973): pp. 4–5, NCLR Records, record group 6, series 4, box 24, folder 6.

18. See *Hearings before a Subcommittee on Departments of Labor, and Health, Education, and Welfare and Related Agencies*, House of Representatives, 91st Cong. 1117 (1969) (H.R. Report No. 91-391).

19. Mitchell Svirdoff to Herman Gallegos, April 30, 1969, "Attachment Three," Minutes of the Board of Directors Meeting, May 3, 1969, Phoenix, NCLR Records, record group 1, series 1, box 1, folder 3.

20. See Kai Bird, *The Color of Truth: McGeorge Bundy and William Bundy, Brothers in Arms* (New York: Simon and Schuster, 1998); and Fabio Rojas, *From Black Power to Black Studies: How a Radical Social Movement Became an Academic Discipline* (Baltimore: Johns Hopkins University Press, 2007).

21. Minutes of the Board of Directors Meeting, November 3, 1973, Scottsdale, AZ, NCLR Records, record group 1, series 1, box 1, folder 4.

22. See "National Council of La Raza: The First 25 Years," unpublished paper, provided to the author by Charles Kamasaki, vice president of the NCLR.

23. Other organizations funded by the Ford Foundation also moved to Washington, DC. For example, in 1973 MALDEF stated that "[it] moved to DC because [it] needed to have quick access to data collected by a number of federal agencies." This "information on minority needs," MALDEF argued, would be important for its lobbying and grant-writing efforts. "MALDEF Opens Office in Washington DC," *Agenda* 3, no. 5 (1973), NCLR Records, record group 6, series 4, box 23, folder 16.

24. See "National Council of La Raza: First 25 Years."

25. See "Raul Yzaguirre Biographical Narrative and Resume," September 1979, NCLR Records, record group 6, series 2, box 11, folder 35.

26. Sierra, "Political Transformation of a Minority Organization."

27. Minutes of the Board of Directors Meeting, April 22–24, 1977, Tucson, NCLR Records, record group 1, series 1, box 1, folder 13.

28. Ibid.

29. See Patricia Sullivan, *Lift Every Voice: The NAACP and the Making of the Civil Rights Movement* (New York: New Press, 2009).

30. In 1975, for example, there were seventeen African Americans in Congress compared to only five Mexican Americans.

31. *Economic and Social Statistics for Americans of Spanish Origin: Hearing before the Subcommittee on Census and Population of the Committee on Post Office and Civil Service*, House of Representatives, 94th Cong. 51 (1975).

32. Ibid.

33. Minutes of the Board of Directors Meeting, April 22–24, 1977, Tucson, p. 34, NCLR Records, record group 1, series 1, box 1, folder 13.

34. Ibid. (emphasis added).

35. Raul Yzaguirre, "Mex America," *Washington Post*, April 5, 1978, A14.

36. *Agenda* 5, no. 6 (1975): p. 1, NCLR Records, record group 6, series 4, box 23, folder 38.

37. See *Economic and Social Statistics for Americans of Spanish Origin*, 94th Cong. (1975).

38. Ibid.

39. See, for example, US Office of Management and Budget, *Social Indicators 1973* (Washington, DC: Government Printing Office, 1974). See also NCLR's reaction to the *Social Indicators* report wherein it argues that OMB reproduces inequality by obscuring the conditions of "Spanish Speakers." *Economic and Social Statistics for Spanish-Speaking Americans:Hearings before the Subcommittee on Census and Statistics of the Committee on Post Office and Civil Service*, House of Representatives, 93rd Cong. 174 (1974).

40. *Economic and Social Statistics for Spanish-Speaking Americans*, 93rd Cong. 43 (1974), 43.

41. Ibid.

42. Maria de Los Angeles Torres, *In the Land of Mirrors: Cuban Exile Politics in the United States* (Ann Arbor: University of Michigan Press, 2001); and Susan Eckstein, *The Immigrant Divide: How Cubans Changed the U.S. and Their Homeland* (New York: Routledge, 2009).

43. See Jorge Ramos, *No Borders: A Journalist's Search for Home* (New York: Harper Collins, 2003).

44. Muñoz, *Youth, Identity, and Power*; and Miguel Melendez, *We Took to the Streets: Fighting for Latino Rights with the Young Lords* (New York: St. Martin's Press, 2003).

45. See chap. 1.

46. Minutes of the Board of Directors Meeting, February 1979, San Diego, NCLR Records, record group 1, series 1, box 10, folder 2.

47. Ibid.

48. "Hispanics in the Arts," *Agenda* 7, no. 3 (1977): pp. 4–15, NCLR Records, record group 6, series 4, box 25, folder 10.

49. Raul Yzaguirre, "Investigating Our Identity," *Agenda* (Fall 1974): p. 22, NCLR Records, record group 6, series 4, box 24, folder 11.

50. NCLR to Jim Early, National Endowment for the Humanities, October 4, 1979, NCLR Records, record group 1, series 1, box 4, folder 4.

51. Ibid.

52. Arturo Morales-Carrion, "Reflecting on Common Hispanic Roots," *Agenda: A Journal of Hispanic Issues* (March–April 1980): pp. 28–31, NCLR Records, record group 6, series 4, box 25, folder 13.

53. José Speilberg Benitez, "The 'Little' Cultural Traditions of the Hispanics," *Agenda: A Journal of Hispanic Issues* (May–June 1980): pp. 30–37, NCLR Records, record group 6, series 4, box 25, folder 14.

54. Anthony Lozano, "Tracing the Spanish Language," *Agenda: A Journal of Hispanic Issues* (March–April 1980): pp. 32–38, NCLR Records, record group 6, series 4, box 25, folder 13.

55. Estelle Irizarry, "Reflecting on Culture," *Agenda: A Journal of Hispanic Issues*

(July–August 1980): p. 38, NCLR Records, record group 6, series 4, box 25, folder 15.

56. Morales-Carrion, "Reflecting on Common Hispanic Roots."

57. Ibid. See also Spielberg Benitez, "'Little' Cultural Traditions of Hispanics"; and José Olivera, "Hispanic American Literature: Preserving the Old Language, Blending with the New," *Agenda: A Journal of Hispanic Issues* (November–December 1980): pp. 16–17, NCLR Records, record group 6, series 4, box 25, folder 16.

58. See Frank Pino, "The 'Great' Cultural Traditions of the Hispanics," *Agenda: A Journal of Hispanic Issues* (May–June 1980): pp. 38–40, NCLR Records, record group 6, series 4, box 25, folder 14; Irizarry, "Reflecting on Culture"; and Tomas Atencio and Consuelo Pacheco, "The Concept of La Resolana," *Agenda: A Journal of Hispanic Issues* (January–February 1980): pp. 14–16, NCLR Records, record group 6, series 4, box 25, folder 12.

59. Spielberg Benitez, "'Little' Cultural Traditions of Hispanics," 34.

60. Irizarry, "Reflecting on Culture," 38.

61. "NCLR Historical Overview," in Minutes of the Board of Directors Meeting, October 13–14, 1980, Washington, DC, NCLR Records, record group 1, box 4, folder 4.

62. Forum of National Hispanic Organizations, "Revised List July," 1978, NCLR Records, record group 2, section 2, box 29, folder 9.

63. For a short description of the convention and those present, see William E. Nelson and Winston Van Horne, "Black Elected Administrators: The Trials of Office," *Public Administration Review* 34, no. 6 (1974): 526–33.

64. Ibid. See also Ronald Walters and Robert C. Smith, *African American Leadership* (Albany: State University of New York Press, 1999); and Manning Marable, *Black Leadership* (New York: Columbia University Press, 1999).

65. See, for example, Miguel Sandoval's statement in Minutes of the Forum of National Hispanic Organizations Meeting, April 27, 1979, NCLR Records, record group 2, section 2, box 29, folder 9.

66. "Media Panel Recommendations," in Testimony of the National Hispanic Leadership Conference before the Democratic National Committee, Platform Committee Hearings, 1984, NCLR Records, group 2, series 2, box 46, folder 4.

67. See Testimony of the National Hispanic Leadership Conference before the Democratic National Committee, Platform Committee Hearings, 1984, NCLR Records, group 2, series 2, box 46, folder 4.

68. Ibid.

69. Minutes of the Forum of National Hispanic Organizations Meeting, April 27, 1979, NCLR Records, record group 2, section 2, box 29, folder 9.

70. Ibid.

71. "National Hispanic Leadership Conference, Second Phase 'Executive Summary,'" NCLR Records, record group 2, series 2, box 46, folder 1.

72. Ibid.
73. Ibid.
74. "National Council of La Raza: First 25 Years."
75. Ibid.
76. Minutes of the Board of Directors Meeting, April 10, 1987, Washington, DC, NCLR Records, record group 1, series 1, box 9, folder 6.
77. "National Council of La Raza: First 25 Years," 23.
78. *Endowment/Reserve Fund Report*, February 1981, Minutes of the Board of Directors Meeting, Corpus Christi, February 19–21, 1981, NCLR Records, record group 1, box 4, folder 6.
79. See Gilbert Jonas, *Freedom's Sword: The NAACP and the Struggle against Racism in America, 1909–1969* (New York: Routledge, 2004).
80. See "Raul Yzaguirre: Biographical Narrative and Resume," NCLR Records, record group 6, series 2, box 11, folder 35.
81. Indeed, 75 percent of the costs for the 1985 NCLR annual convention were covered by corporate and corporate foundation sponsors. See Minutes of the Board of Directors Meeting, October 1988, Detroit, NCLR Records, record group 1, series 1, box 10.1, folders 8–10.
82. Letter to Raul Yzaguirre from Alex Armendariz, September 1977, NCLR Records, record group 1, box 1, folder 18. See also *Communications Report*, October 7–8, 1977, Report to the Board of Directors, NCLR Records, record group 1, series 1, box 1, folder 19.
83. *Endowment/Reserve Fund Report*, February 1981.
84. Ibid., 5.
85. "Bringing Together Two Communities: A Proposal Prepared for the National Council of La Raza by Yardang Consultant Services," p. 6, Minutes of the Board of Directors Meeting, February 19–21, 1981, Corpus Christi, NCLR Records, record group 1, box 4, folder 6.
86. Ibid.
87. "National Council of La Raza: First 25 Years."
88. Ibid.
89. See "Corporate and Philanthropic Responsibility Panel," May 1984, NCLR Records, record group 2, series 1, box 7, folder 4.
90. NCLR did vacillate back and forth between definitions. At times the organization referred to its group as the largest minority because it included Puerto Ricans on the island, and at times it restricted its definition to Hispanics on the mainland. For summaries of press interviews given in 1979, see Minutes of the Board of Directors Meeting, Dearborn, MI, November 9–10, 1979, NCLR Records, record group 1, series 1, box 3, folder 5. See also "NCLR Slide Show," Minutes of the Board of Directors Meeting, Corpus Christi, February 19–21, 1981, NCLR Records, record group 1, series 1, box 4, folder 6.
91. NCLR to Terry Patch, Frito-Lay, January 3, 1983, NCLR Records, record group 2, series 1, box 6, folder 8.

92. NCLR to Goldie Dietel, vice president of Equitable Life Insurance Society, May 12, 1980, NCLR Records, record group 2, series 1, box 5, folder 5.

93. "Hispanic Corporate Partnerships: Some Observations and Examples," speech delivered by Raul Yzaguirre to the First Corporate/Hispanic Partnership Summit, October 23, 1982, Sheraton Place, San Francisco, NCLR Records, record group 6, series 2, box 11, folder 38.

94. "Corporate and Philanthropic Responsibility Panel," May 1984 (emphasis added).

95. See "Coors Officials Say Union-Led Boycott Has Hurt Beer Sales: Brewer Was Struck in April, Volume Is Off About 5 Percent; Labor Is Accused of 'Lies,'" *Wall Street Journal*, October 26, 1977, 20; Larry Pryor, "Labor World Watching Coors: Brewery Strike Centers on Fight for Dominance," *Los Angeles Times*, November 21, 1977, A3; Molly Ivis, "Union at Coors May be Broken but It Hasn't Halted Its Boycott," *New York Times*, May 28, 1979, A7.

96. Janet Simons, "Coors Turns Boycotters into Buyers," *Advertising Age*, February 27, 1986, 46–47.

97. LULAC was part of the HACER coalition, but it refused to sign off on the pact, stating that Coors's promises would not go far enough to address Hispanic hiring concerns. See Laurie Beckland, "Coors Pact with Six Latino Groups Comes Under Fire," *Los Angles Times*, November 13, 1984, C1; and Matt Moffett, "LULAC, Hispanic Advocacy Group, Turns Away from Liberal Traditions under New Leadership," *Wall Street Journal*, March 19, 1986, 62.

98. Simons, "Coors Turns Boycotters into Buyers," 46–47.

99. Ibid.

100. Ibid.

101. Ibid., 46.

102. See Minutes of the Board of Directors Meeting, April 10, 1987, Washington DC, NCLR Records, record group 1, series 1, box 9, folder 6.

103. Roberto Cruz to Raul Yzaguirre, March 27, 1985, NCLR Records, record group 2, series 1, box 9, folder 1.

104. Minutes of the Board of Directors Meeting, February 16–17, 1990, San Diego, NCLR Records, record group 1, series 1, box 10.2, folder 7.

105. Memorandum from Charles Kamasaki to Raul Yzaguirre, March 19, 1985, NCLR Records, record group 2, series 1, box 9, folder 1.

106. See "Latin Temp: A Single Voice," undated press release [1985], NCLR Records, record group 6, series 2, box 3, folder 3.

107. See "Show Description 11/16/1984," NCLR Records, record group 6, series 2, box 3, folder 123.

108. Minutes of the Board of Directors Meeting, October 4–5, 1982, New York, NCLR Records, record group 1, series 1, box 8, folder 7.

109. Minutes of the National Hispanic Quincentennial Commission Organizing Board of Directors Meeting, February 26, 1985, NCLR Records, record group 2, series 2, box 47, folder 1. See also "'Attachment B,' Proposed Guidelines of the National Hispanic Quincentennial Commission," NCLR Records,

record group 2, series 2, box 47, folder 3; and "General Support Proposal for the National Hispanic Quincentennial Commission," April 1989, NCLR records, record group 14, box 3, folder 12.

110. "'Attachment B,' Proposed Guidelines of the National Hispanic Quincentennial Commission."

111. "Hispanic Trivial Pursuit," National Hispanic Quincentennial Commission, November 1990, NCLR Records, record group 14, box 3, folder 17.

112. Margaret Holland to NHQC Staff, July 21, 1991, NCLR Records, record group 14, box 5, folder 5.

113. Sally Norton to NHQC Staff, July 2, 1991, NCLR Records, record group 14, box 5, folder 5.

114. Patricia King to NHQC Staff, July 10, 1990, NCLR Records, record group 14, box 5, folder 4.

115. John Gueguen to NCLR, May 31, 1986, NCLR Records, record group 2, series 2, box 11.3, folder 3.

116. "Hispanic Corporate Partnerships: Some Observations and Examples," 4.

117. See, for example, David E. Hayes-Bautista, "Identifying Hispanic Populations: The Influence of Research Methodology on Public Policy," *American Journal of Public Health* 70, no. 4 (1980): 353–56; and Martha E. Gimenez, "Latino/Hispanic—Who Needs a Name? The Case against a Standardized Terminology," *International Journal of Health Services* 19 (1989): 557–71.

118. Gimenez, "Latino/Hispanic—Who Needs a Name?"; Martha E. Gimenez, "U.S. Ethnic Politics: Implications for Latin Americans," *Latin American Perspectives* 19, no. 4 (1992): 7–17; and José Calderón, "Hispanic' and 'Latino': The Viability of Categories for Panethnic Unity," *Latin American Perspectives* 19, no. 4 (1992): 37–44.

119. Rodolfo de la Garza, "From Rhetoric to Reality: Latinos and the 1988 Election in Review," in *From Rhetoric to Reality: Latino Politics in the 1988 Elections*, ed. Rodolfo de la Garza and Louis DeSipio, 171–81 (Boulder, CO: Westview Press, 1992).

120. See the conclusion in this book.

121. Antonio Bernal, "The Importance of Distinguishing between the Words Hispanic and Latino," *Los Angeles Times*, September 9, 1990, 103; and "The Hispanic/Latino Debate: The Language Is Still Searching for a Term That Satisfies Everyone," letter to the editor, *Los Angeles Times*, September 30, 1990, 91.

122. See Nicolás Kanellos, "Overview of Hispanic Literature," in *Herencia: The Anthology of Hispanic Literature in the United States*, ed. Nicolas Kanellos, 1–33 (Oxford: Oxford University Press, 2003).

123. Leobardo Estrada (former special assistant to the chief of the Population Division, 1975–77, and staff assistant to the deputy director, 1979–80, US Census Bureau), interview by G. Cristina Mora, March 12, 2009.

124. "Mexican American Help Groups Face Cubans' Opposition," *Miami Herald*, November 22, 1981, p. 7B, NCLR Records, record group 7, series 23, box 160, folder 10.

CHAPTER THREE

1. For a review of these programs, see US Commission on Civil Rights, *Counting the Forgotten: The 1970 Census Count of Persons of Spanish Speaking Background in the United States* (Washington, DC: Government Printing Office, 1974).
2. Harvey Choldin, "Statistics and Politics: The 'Hispanic Issue' in the 1980 Census," *Demography* 23, no. 3 (1986): 403–18.
3. Vincent Barraba (director of the Census Bureau, 1973–80), interview by G. Cristina Mora, January 24, 2012.
4. See Inter-Agency for Mexican American Affairs, *The Mexican Americans: A New Focus on Opportunity, Inter-Agency Committee on Mexican American Affairs, 1967–1969* (Washington, DC: Government Printing Office, 1968), Finch CCOSSP File, box 21, "Research Data" folder. See also Cabinet Committee on Opportunities for Spanish Speaking People, *Education Task Force, June 21–25* (Washington, DC: Cabinet Committee on Opportunities for Spanish Speaking People, 1971), 3.
5. Clara Rodriguez, *Changing Race: Latinos, the Census, and the History of Race in the United States* (New York: New York University Press, 2000); and Victoria Hattam, *In the Shadow of Race: Jews, Latinos and Immigrant Politics in the United States* (Chicago: University of Chicago Press, 2007). See also Paul Schor, "Mobilizing for Pure Prestige? Challenging Federal Census Categories in the U.S.A., 1850–1940," *International Social Science Journal* 57, no. 183 (2005): 89–101.
6. For a brief explanation of how LULAC leaders protested a nonwhite designation category, see Craig A. Kaplowitz, *LULAC, Mexican Americans, and National Policy* (College Station: Texas A&M University Press, 2005).
7. Francisco Balderrama and Raymond Rodriguez, *Decade of Betrayal: Mexican Repatriation in the 1930s* (Albuquerque: University of New Mexico Press, 1995).
8. Winnie White, "The Spanish Surname Criterion for Identifying Hispanos in the Southwestern United States: A Preliminary Evaluation," *Social Forces* 38, no. 4 (1959): 363–66; and Robert Buechley, "A Reproducible Method of Counting Persons of Spanish Surname," *Journal of the American Statistical Association* 56, no. 293 (1961): 88–97.
9. White, "Spanish Surname Criterion for Identifying Hispanos"; and Buechley, "Reproducible Method of Counting Persons of Spanish Surname." See also Julian Samora, *La Raza: Forgotten Americans*, ed. Julian Samora (South Bend, IN: University of Notre Dame Press, 1966); and Leo Grebler, Joan W. Moore, and Ralph C. Guzman, *The Mexican-American People: The Nation's Second Largest Minority* (New York: Free Press, 1970).
10. See Inter-Agency Committee on Mexican-American Affairs, *Mexican-Americans*.
11. *Hearings before the Subcommittee on the Census and Statistics of the Committee*

*on Post Office and Civil Service,*House of Representatives, 91st Cong. (1969) (Serial No. 91-9).

12. Ibid.
13. For the 1970 census, the bureau created two long forms. One was mailed to 15 percent of the population; a second, considerably longer, form was mailed to 5 percent of the population.
14. Choldin, "Statistics and Politics."
15. Ibid.; and Harvey Choldin, *Looking for the Last Percent: The Controversy over Census Undercounts* (New Brunswick, NJ: Rutgers University Press, 1994).
16. Daryl Lembke, "New Spanish Speaking Census Urged," *Los Angeles Times*, November 30, 1971, B6; Edward Burks, "Puerto Ricans Say Census Cuts Political Power Here," *New York Times*, October 2, 1972, 1; and Edward Burks, "Puerto Rican Totals Given for Boroughs," *New York Times*, October 2, 1972, 32.
17. US Commission on Civil Rights, *Counting the Forgotten.*
18. Mexican-American Population Commission of California, "Mexican-American Population in California as of April, 1973," MexicanAmerican Legal Defense and Education Fund Records (hereafter MALDEF Records), record group 6, box 50, folder 5, Department of Special Collections, Stanford University Libraries, Stanford University.
19. US Commission on Civil Rights, *Counting the Forgotten*, 99.
20. MALDEF had been established with a large grant by the Ford Foundation in 1968. See Armando Navarro, *Mexicano Political Experience in Occupied Aztlán: Struggles and Change* (Walnut Creek, CA: Alta Mira Press, 2005). For the lawsuit, see Confederación de La Raza Unida v. George H. Brown,"Complaint for Injunctive and Declaratory Relief," p. 1, U.S. District Court, San Francisco, Harvey M. Choldin Collection (hereafter Choldin Collection), box 8, "Confederacion de La Raza v. Brown" folder, University of Illinois Archives, University of Illinois at Urbana-Champaign.
21. See US Commission on Civil Rights, *Counting the Forgotten.*
22. La Confederación de La Raza Unida v. George H. Brown, 345 F.Supp. 909 (1972).
23. "Deposition of Conrad Taeuber," Confederación de La Raza Unida v. George H. Brown, December 16, 1971, p. 47, Choldin Collection, box 8, "Confederacion de La Raza v. Brown" folder.
24. Ibid., 48.
25. Ibid.
26. Conrad Taeuber, oral history conducted by Robert Voight, US Census Bureau, Office of the Historian, accessed July 1, 2009, https://www.census.gov/history/www/reference/oral_histories/conrad_taeuber_1.html.
27. "Deposition of Conrad Taeuber."
28. Ibid.
29. Mexican-American Population Commission of California to George Hay Brown, October 27, 1971, MALDEF Records, record group 6, box 50, folder 5;

and Mexican-American Population Commission of California, "Mexican-American Population in California as of April, 1973."

30. "Deposition of Conrad Taeuber."
31. Ibid., 31.
32. Ibid., 7 (emphasis added).
33. Ibid., 67.
34. US Commission on Civil Rights, *Counting the Forgotten*.
35. See Peter Kihss, "Those of Spanish Origin Are Put at 15 Percent by 1970 Census," *New York Times*, July 9, 1972, 45; Burks, "Puerto Ricans Say Census Cuts Political Power Here," 1; and "Final Count of Puerto Ricans Is Due: Census Bureau to Announce Figures in Early 1973," *New York Times*, October 3, 1972, 49.
36. US Commission on Civil Rights, *Counting the Forgotten*, iii.
37. Ibid., 99.
38. The letter was published in *Economic and Social Statistics for Spanish-Speaking Americans: Hearings before the Subcommittee on Census and Statistics of the Committee on Post Office and Civil Service*, House of Representatives, 93rd Cong. 92–95 (1974).
39. Vincent P. Barabba, oral history conducted by Barbara Milton and David Pemberton, August 7, 1989, US Census Bureau, Office of the Historian, accessed June 1, 2007, https://www.census.gov/history/www/reference/oral_histories/conrad_taeuber_1.html.
40. Vincent Barabba to Robert Gnaizda, January 31, 1974, Records of the Bureau of the Census, E.385, record group 29, Office of the Director, Census Advisory Committees, Management Files, 1960–1988 (hereafter Census Bureau Records), box 3, National Archives and Records Administration, Washington, DC.
41. Samora, *La Raza*.
42. Raquel Creit off to David Kaplan, May 17, 1974, Census Bureau Records, E.385, record group 29, box 3.
43. "Plans for March 1, 1974, Meeting of Spanish-American Persons; List of Persons to Whom the January 31, 1974, Letter of Invitation Was Sent," undated, Census Bureau Records, E.385, record group 29, box 3.
44. Minutes of the Census "Ad Hoc" Meeting with Persons of the Spanish Community, March 1, 1974, p. 1, Census Bureau Records, E.385, record group 29, box 3.
45. Ibid.
46. "Plans for March 1, 1974, Meeting."
47. Minutes of the Census "Ad Hoc" Meeting with Persons of the Spanish Community, March 1, 1974.
48. This committee was later renamed the Census Advisory Committee on the Spanish Origin Population.
49. Minutes of the Census "Ad Hoc" Meeting with Persons of the Spanish Community, March 1, 1974.

50. "Formation of 1980 Census Minority Advisory Groups," memorandum, August 19, 1974, Census Bureau Records, record group 29, box 3.

51. Minutes of the Census Advisory Committee on the Spanish Origin Population for the 1980 Census, December 8, 1978, p. 4, Choldin Collection, box 3, "Minutes, Census Advisory Committee on the Spanish Origin Population for the 1980 Census, 1977–80" folder.

52. Ibid., 6.

53. Minutes of the Census Advisory Committee on the Spanish Origin Population for the 1980 Census, June 3, 1977, p. 31, Choldin Collection, box 3, "Minutes, Census Advisory Committee on the Spanish Origin Population for the 1980 Census, 1977–80" folder.

54. Ibid.

55. See, for example, Hattam, *In the Shadow of Race.*

56. The idea that OMB influenced the bureau's decision to keep Hispanic ethnicity separate from race has also been echoed by journalists. See, for example, Darryl Fears, "The Roots of 'Hispanic': 1975 Committee of Bureaucrats Produced Designation," *Washington Post*, October 15, 2003, A21.

57. "Statistical Directive 15," *Federal Register* 43, no. 87 (1978): 19269–70.

58. See *Report of the Ad Hoc Committee on Racial and Ethnic Definitions*, Federal Interagency Committee on Education, April 1975, Census Bureau Records, record group 29, box 2.

59. Leobardo Estrada (former special assistant to the chief of the Population Division, 1975–77, and staff assistant to the deputy director, 1979–80, US Census Bureau), interview by G. Cristina Mora, March 12, 2009.

60. Estrada, interview.

61. Barraba, interview.

62. For an account that emphasizes the role of congressional action, see Luis Ricardo Fraga, John A. Garcia, Rodney E. Hero, Michael Jones-Correa, Valerie Martinez-Ebers, and Gary M. Segura, *Latino Lives in America: Making It Home* (Philadelphia: Temple University Press, 2009), 148. For an account that emphasizes the role of both Nixon and Congress, see Ruben Rumbuat, "The Making of a People," in *Hispanics and the Future of America*, ed. Marta Tienda and Faith Mitchell, 16–65 (Washington, DC: National Research Council, 2006).

63. For comments, see *Establish an Inter-Agency Committee on Mexican-American Affairs: Hearings before the Subcommittee on Executive Reorganization of the Committee on Government Operations*, United States Senate, 91st Cong. 481 (1969). For the NCLR's argument, see *Economic and Social Statistics for Spanish-Speaking Americans*, 93rd Cong. 156 (1974).

64. See Americans of Spanish Origins Social Statistics Act, 15 U.S.C. § 1516a (1976).

65. See Peter Skerry, *Mexican Americans: The Ambivalent Minority* (Cambridge, MA: Harvard University Press, 1995). While not taking a position on whether Mexicans are biologically white, others have stressed the way that

Mexican American leaders in the 1940s and 1950s argued that their communities were white. See John David Skrentny, *The Minority Rights Revolution* (Cambridge, MA: Harvard University Press, 2003); Ignacio Garcia, *White but Not Equal: Mexican Americans, Jury Discrimination, and the Supreme Court* (Tucson: University of Arizona Press, 2008); and Kaplowitz, *LULAC*.

66. "Deposition of Conrad Taeuber," 98. However, a year later Taeuber, reflecting on the 1970 census question, revised his story and noted that there were a number of Mexican American organizations that "were pushing different things." See Taeuber, oral history, 10.

67. Thomas Guglielmo, "Fighting for Caucasian Rights: Mexicans, Mexican Americans, and the Transnational Struggle for Civil Rights in World War II Texas," *Journal of American History* 92, no. 4 (2006): 1212–37.

68. See Neil Foley, *The White Scourge: Mexicans, Blacks, and Poor Whites in Texas Cotton Culture* (Berkeley: University of California Press, 1999).

69. See Samora, *La Raza*.

70. See Minutes of the Census Advisory Committee on the Spanish Origin Population for the 1980 Census, February 17–18, 1977, p. 24, Choldin Collection, box 3, "Minutes, Census Advisory Committee on the Spanish Origin Population for the 1980 Census, 1976–77" folder.

71. Ibid., 3.

72. Statement by Harry Puente-Duany, Minutes of the Census Advisory Committee on the Spanish Origin Population, June 3, 1977, p. 31, Choldin Collection, box 3, "Minutes, Census Advisory Committee on the Spanish Origin Population for the 1980 Census, 1977–80" folder.

73. See Minutes of the Census Advisory Committee on the Spanish Origin Population for the 1980 Census, February 17–18, 1977, 25.

74. Nampeo McKenney (former member of the Racial and Ethnic Statistics Division of the US Census Bureau), interview by G. Cristina Mora , May 16, 2012.

75. Ibid.

76. Unlike the census trials, the special censuses were conducted at the request and expense of local governments, which were often more interested in gaining data on total population figures than on the specific characteristics of inhabitants. Because of this, the bureau used special censuses as an opportunity to test different question formats.

77. Estrada, interview.

78. Ibid.

79. The bureau estimated that blacks would outnumber Hispanics at least through 2057. See Bill Boyarsky, "Hispanics Not Outnumbering Blacks, U.S. Says," *Los Angeles Times*, November 26, 1979, 1. For further insight as to the NAACP's apprehension about whether Hispanics would outnumber blacks, see letter to Vincent Barabba from Althea Simmons, NAACP, October 9, 1979, collection of Vincent Barabba; and letter to Althea Simmons from Vincent Barabba, November 8, 1979, collection of Vincent Barabba.

80. See Edward Fernandez, *Persons of Spanish Origin in the United States, March 1973*, US Census Bureau Current Population Reports, P-20, no. 250 (Washington, DC: Government Printing Office, 1973). For a discussion of the differences between the "Spanish Origin," "Spanish Language," and "Spanish Surname" categories, see Jacob Siegel and Jeffrey Passel, *Coverage of the Hispanic Population of the United States in the 1970 Census: A Methodological Analysis*, US Census Bureau Current Population Reports, P-23, no. 82 (Washington, DC: Government Printing Office, 1979).

81. E. Fernandez, *Persons of Spanish Origin in the United States*.

82. See Minutes of the Census Advisory Committee on the Spanish Origin Population for the 1980 Census, September 25–26, 1975, Choldin Collection, box 3, "Minutes, Census Advisory Committee on the Spanish Origin Population for the 1980 Census, 1976–77" folder.

83. Ibid.

84. Minutes of the Census "Ad Hoc" Meeting with Persons of the Spanish Community, March 1, 1974, 1.

85. See Minutes of the Census Advisory Committee on the Spanish Origin Population for the 1980 Census, September 25–26, 1975.

86. Ibid., 17.

87. Minutes of the Census Advisory Committee on the Spanish Origin Population for the 1980 Census, February 3, 1978, p. 27, Choldin Collection, box 3, "Minutes, Census Advisory Committee on the Spanish Origin Population for the 1980 Census, 1977–80" folder.

88. See, for example, exchange among Dr. Jose Hernandez, Edward Fernandez, and Luz Cuadrado, Minutes of the Census Advisory Committee on the Spanish Origin Population, September 25–26, 1975, 9–13.

89. Minutes of the Census Advisory Committee on the Spanish Origin Population for the 1980 Census, June 3, 1977, 11.

90. Ibid.

91. Minutes of the Census Advisory Committee on the Spanish Origin Population for the 1980 Census, February 17–18, 1977, 43.

92. Ibid., 28.

93. Minutes of the Joint Meeting of the Census Advisory Committees on the Black, Spanish Origin, and Asian and Pacific Americans Population for the 1980 Census, September 8, 1977, Choldin Collection, box 3, "Minutes, Census Advisory Committees on the Black, Spanish Origin, and Asian and Pacific Americans Population for the 1980 Census, 1977" folder; and Minutes of the Census Advisory Committee on the Spanish Origin Population for the 1980 Census, December 8, 1978.

94. Minutes of the Census Advisory Committee on the Spanish Origin Population for the 1980 Census, December 8, 1978.

95. Estrada, interview.

96. See "Final Report from the Task Force on Hispanos," from Stanley Pottinger to Section Chiefs, Civil Rights Division, undated [1973], J. Stanley Pottinger

Papers, 1968–81, file 120: Spanish Speaking Americans Task Force (hereafter Pottinger Papers), box 43, Ford Library. See also Memorandum to Stanley Pottinger from Jim Turner, October 23, 1973, Pottinger Papers, box 43.

97. See Memorandum from Stanley Pottinger to Anne Armstrong, "Presidential Memorandum on Federal Equal Opportunity for Hispanic Americans," June 19, 1974, Pottinger Papers, box 43.

98. "Why the Term Hispanic?," *Hispanic Magazine*, September 1996, 64.

99. Estrada, interview.

100. See David Gutierrez, *Walls and Mirrors: Mexican-Americans, Mexican Immigrants and the Politics of Ethnicity* (Berkeley: University of California Press, 1995).

101. See *Establish an Inter-Agency Committee on Mexican-American Affairs*, 91st Cong. 740 (1969).

102. See Antonia Pantoja, *Memoir of a Visionary: Antonia Pantoja* (Houston: Arte Público Press, 2002).

103. See Minutes of the Census Advisory Committee on the Spanish Origin Population for the 1980 Census, September 22, 1976, pp. 9–11, Choldin Collection, box 3, "Minutes, Census Advisory Committee on the Spanish Origin Population for the 1980 Census, 1976–77" folder.

104. Ibid. See also Minutes of the Census Advisory Committee on the Spanish Origin Populationfor the 1980 Census, February 19–20, 1976, p. 15, Choldin Collection, box 3, "Minutes, Census Advisory Committee on the Spanish Origin Population for the 1980 Census, 1976–77" folder.

105. Minutes of the Census Advisory Committee on the Spanish Origin Population for the 1980 Census, September 22, 1976, 12.

106. Estrada, interview.

107. Minutes of the Census Advisory Committee on the Spanish Origin Population for the 1980 Census, September 22, 1976, 12. See also Minutes of the Census Advisory Committee on the Spanish Origin Population for the 1980 Census, February 19–20, 1976, 14.

108. Balderrama and Rodriguez, *Decade of Betrayal*, describe the 1931 events as a series of raids, scare tactics, and public pressure coordinated by federal, state, and local governments.

109. See "Hispanos victimas de rencillas politicas en los censos," *El Puertorriqueno*, June 4, 1980, p. 4, Census Bureau Records, E.443, record group 20, Meeting Files of Vincent P. Barabba, 1978–81 (hereafter Barabba Files), box 4.

110. Minutes of the Census "Ad Hoc" Meeting with Persons of the Spanish Community, March 1, 1974.

111. See chap. 2 for more information on the Forum of National Hispanic Organizations.

112. See "National Hispanic Leadership Conference, Second Phase 'Executive Summary,'" NCLR Records, record group 2, series 2, box 46, folder 1.

113. "Vamos a Contar! We Are Going to Count in the 1980s!," address by Ambassador Abelardo Valdez, US chief of protocol, before the National Council

of La Raza, Albuquerque New Mexico, July 23, 1980, MALDEF Records, record group 6, box 50, folder 9. Through these political contacts, the bureau was also able to reach out to the Catholic Church. Pablo Sedillo was a board member of the FNHO and also the secretariat for Hispanic affairs of the US Catholic Bishops Conference. It was through Sedillo's office that the bureau attained the help of Catholic bishops. Additionally, the bureau sent letters to archdioceses that were located in areas with large Latino populations, asking them for help in publicizing the 1980 census. In turn, the archbishops of these organizations sent letters to individual priests, urging that they promote the census to their Latino constituents. See letter template, December 26, 1979, by Timothy Cardinal Manning, archbishop of Los Angeles, MALDEF Records, record group 5, box 374, folder 3.

114. Minutes of the Census Advisory Committee on the Spanish Origin Population, February 19–20, 1976, 15.

115. See America Rodriguez, *Making Latino News: Race, Language, Class* (Thousand Oaks, CA: Sage Publications, 1999); and Federico A. Subervi-Vélez, Charles Ramírez Berg, Patricia Constantakis-Valdés, Chon A. Noriega, Diane I. Ríos, and Kenton T. Wilkinson, "Mass Communication and Hispanics," in *The Handbook of Hispanic Cultures in the United States: Sociology*, ed. Félix Padilla, Nicolás Kanellos, and Claudio Esteva-Fabregat, 304–57 (Houston: Arte Público Press, 1994).

116. Felix Gutierrez and Jorge Reina-Schement, *Spanish Language Radio in the Southwestern United States* (Austin: Center for Mexican-American Studies, 1979); and Subervi-Vélez et al., "Mass Communication and Hispanics."

117. The National Association of Spanish Broadcasters (NASB) was founded in October 1979, and the National Association of Hispanic Publications (NAHP) emerged in 1982; see "NAHP," accessed April 26, 2009, http://www.nahp.org/About_NAHP/index.asp. See also *NASB News Letter*, vol. 1, no. 1, Census Bureau Records, E.443, record group 29, Barabba Files, box 1.

118. Rendon was a Chicano activist who had recently published the *Chicano Manifesto*. Armando Rendon, *Chicano Manifesto: The History and Aspirations of the Second Largest Minority in the United States* (Oakland, CA: Ollin and Associates Press, 1971).

119. Ed Gomez (founder, KABQ), interview by G. Cristina Mora, March 17, 2008.

120. Caroline Bush, "Note for Dan Baily," August 16, 1979, Census Bureau Records, E.443, record group 29, Barabba Files, box 1.

121. SIN was connected to the Spanish International Communications Corporation, forerunner of Univision Communications Corporation. See chap. 4.

122. See Antonio Guernica and Irene Kasperuk, *Reaching the Hispanic Market Effectively: The Media, the Market, the Methods* (New York: McGraw-Hill, 1982).

123. *Destino 80*, pamphlet, undated, Census Bureau Records, E.443, record group 29, Barabba Files, box 2. See also Memorandum from Robert Garcia to the Census Bureau, undated [1979?], Census Bureau Records, E.443, record group 29, Barabba Files, box 2.

124. Armando Rendon (founder of Los Cerezos Media, SIN affiliate, and former member of the Census Bureau's Office of Public Relations, 1979–88), interview by G. Cristina Mora, May 20, 2012.

125. Antonio Guernica, "The 1980 Census: Who Counts?," in *News/Noticias* (National Association of Spanish Broadcasters Newsletter), p. 1, Census Bureau Records, E.443, record group 29, Barabba Files, box 1.

126. For more information about the role of the 1980 census in the development of Spanish-language television, see chap. 4.

127. Data compiled from the Broadcasting directory series for 1965–75 (Washington, DC: Broadcasting Publications).

128. See Arlene Davila, *Latinos Inc.: The Marketing and Making of a People* (Berkeley: University of California Press, 2001).

129. Robert Kominski, *Educational Attainment in the United States: March 1987 and 1986*, US Census Bureau Current Population Reports, P-20, no. 428 (Washington, DC: Government Printing Office, 1988), 1.

130. Frederick Hollmann, *United States Population Estimates by Age, Sex, Race and Hispanic Origin, 1980–1988*, US Census Bureau Series P-25, no. 1045 (Washington, DC: Government Printing Office, 1988), 9.

131. Whereas a typical census report on, for example, income in the 1960s and early 1970s would have highlighted differences between black and white populations, or black, white, and "other" populations, by the 1980s "Hispanic" had become a standard comparison category. For a recap on many of the Census Bureau reports on Hispanics, see Frank D. Bean and Marta Tienda, *The Hispanic Population of the United States* (New York: Russell Sage Foundation, 1987).

132. See, for example, US Census Bureau, *The Hispanic Population of the United States: March 1988*, US Census Bureau Current Population Reports, P-20, no. 431 (Washington, DC: Government Printing Office, 1988).

133. See, for example, US Census Bureau, *Money, Income, and Poverty Status in the United States: October 1988*, US Census Bureau Current Population Reports, P-60, no. 166 (Washington, DC: Government Printing Office, 1989).

134. Ibid. This was important because the bureau used this information to calculate undercounts of racial, especially black, minorities. Yet, because individual states classified Latin Americans as "white," the bureau would not be able to use this comparison in future estimates of "Hispanic" undercounts.

135. See chap. 2.

CHAPTER FOUR

1. Scholars of Mexican media have argued that Azcárraga's success would not have been possible without the assistance of Mexican political leaders, but they disagree on just how political leaders perceived Azcárraga's activities. Joy Hayes, in *Radio Nation: Communication, Popular Culture and Nationalism*

in Mexico, 1930–1950 (Tucson: University of Arizona Press, 2000), suggests that the Mexican government was wary of Azcárraga's success and concerned about what his venture might mean for its ability to control the airwaves. Other scholars argue that this commercialized venture was actually favored by the state because it was a low-cost way for the government to help build a national broadcast infrastructure. See Fernando Mejia Barquera, *La industria de la radio y la television y la politica del estado mexicano*, vol. 1, *1920–1960* (Mexico City: Fundacion Manuel Buendia, 1989); and Andrew Paxman and Alex Saragoza, "Globalization and Latin Media Powers: The Case of Mexico's Televisa," in *Continental Order? Integrating North America for Cybercapitalism*, ed. Vincent Mosco and Dan Schiller, 64–85 (Lanham, MD: Rowman and Littlefield, 2001).

2. Claudia Fernandez and Andrew Paxman, *El tigre: Emilio Azcárraga y su imperio televisa* (Mexico City: Editorial Grijalbo, 2000).

3. Luis Antonio de Noriega and Frances Leach, *Broadcasting in Mexico* (London: Routledge & Kegan Paul, 1970); and Mejia Barquera, *La industria*.

4. James Schwoch, *The American Radio Industry and Its Latin American Activities, 1930–1939* (Urbana: University of Illinois Press, 1990).

5. Investment in Latin American media was not solely an economic enterprise taken up by US media corporations. The US government also helped Latin American media programming with the hope of influencing the character of international relations. Bruce N. Gregory notes that Presidents Calvin Coolidge and Franklin Roosevelt both entertained policies to create shortwave radio frequencies that could reach Latin American broadcast stations. Coolidge approved Executive Order 5067 and assigned frequencies for use by the navy for the specific purpose of broadcasting special pro-America radio programs produced by the Pan American Union. Later, Roosevelt approved a series of measures that allowed privately owned US broadcast stations associated with the Pan American Union to provide programming and shortwave services to Latin America. See Bruce N. Gregory, *The Broadcasting Service: An Administrative History*, United States Information Agency Special Monograph Series, no. 1 (Washington, DC: USA1A Historical Collection, 1970). See also Elizabeth Fox, *Latin American Broadcasting: From Tango to Telenovela* (Luton, Essex, UK: University of Luton Press, 1997).

6. Julio Moreno, *Yankee Don't Go Home: Mexican Nationalism, American Business Culture, and the Shaping of Modern Mexico, 1920–1930* (Chapel Hill: University of North Carolina Press, 2003). See also Paxman and Saragoza, "Globalization and Latin Media Powers."

7. Mejia Barquera, *La industria*; and Paxman and Saragoza, "Globalization and Latin Media Powers."

8. Paxman and Saragoza, "Globalization and Latin Media Powers."

9. "Hemispheric Hookup," *Time* magazine, September 8, 1941.

10. Mejia Barquera, *La industria*.

11. Fátima Fernández-Christlieb, *Los medios de difusión masiva en México* (Mexico City: Juan Pablos, 1982).

12. De Noriega and Leach, *Broadcasting in Mexico*; and Fernández-Christlieb, *Los medios de difusión masiva en México*.

13. Some suggest that Azcárraga's status was buoyed by his connections to top Mexican politicians. Fernández-Christlieb argues that top government officials turned a blind eye to Azcárraga's anticompetitive tactics and that as Telesistema grew, Azcárraga would come to repay these favors by employing some of these politicians, and their sons, in his corporation. Fernández-Christlieb, *Los medios de difusión masiva en México*.

14. Fernando Mejia Barquera, "50 anos de television comercial en Mexico, 1934–1984," in *Televisa el quinto poder*, ed. Raul Trejo Delabre, 19–39 (Mexico City: Claves Latino americanas, 1985), 29.

15. Maria del Carmen Olviares Arriagara, *Emilio Azcárraga Vidaurreta: Bosquejo biografico* (Mexico: Universidad Autonoma de Tamaulipas, 2002).

16. John Sinclair, *Latin American Television: A Global View* (Oxford: Oxford University Press, 1999).

17. De Noriega and Leach, *Broadcasting in Mexico*.

18. Federico A. Subervi-Vélez, Charles Ramírez Berg, Patricia Constantakis-Valdés, Chon A. Noriega, Diane I. Ríos, and Kenton T. Wilkinson, "Mass Communication and Hispanics," in *The Handbook of Hispanic Cultures in the United States: Sociology*, ed. Félix Padilla, Nicolás Kanellos, and Claudio Esteva-Fabregat, 304–57 (Houston: Arte Público Press, 1994).

19. Raúl Cortez was a prominent member and former president of San Antonio's League of United Latin American Citizens, which had important Mexican American businessmen on its roster. See Craig A. Kaplowitz, *LULAC, Mexican Americans, and National Policy* (College Station: Texas A&M University Press, 2005).

20. Subervi-Vélez et al., "Mass Communication and Hispanics."

21. Ibid.

22. Ibid.

23. See C. Fernandez and A. Paxman, *El tigre*. See also In the Matter of Spanish International Communications Corporation, FCC 86D-1, FCC LEXIS 4175 (1986).

24. Section 310(b) of the Communications Act "prohibits the issuance of broadcast licenses to aliens, to the representatives of aliens, or to corporations in which aliens control more than one-fifth of the stock." See Felix Gutierrez and Jorge Reina-Schement, *Spanish Language Radio in the Southwestern United States* (Austin: Center for Mexican-American Studies, 1979).

25. Nicolas A. Valenzuela, "Organizational Evolution of a Spanish Language Television Network: An Environmental Approach" (PhD diss., Stanford University, 1985).

26. Daniel Villanueva (former SICC/SIN executive and KMEX station manager,

1971–89), interview by G. Cristina Mora, December 12, 2007; and Sinclair, *Latin American Television*.

27. SICC was initially named the Spanish International Broadcast Corporation, but this name was changed in the early 1960s. Valenzuela, "Organizational Evolution."

28. Emilio Azcárraga owned 100 percent of the shares of SIN between 1961 and 1971; Anselmo was provided with a 25 percent ownership in 1971. Upon Emilio Azcárraga's death in 1972, 75 percent of SIN shares were inherited by a Mexican media company headed by his son, Emilio Azcárraga Milmo. Valenzuela, "Organizational Evolution."

29. Ibid.

30. Of course, each station also had its own ownership structure. Although the members of SICC's executive board were the main investors in the stations, the percentage of shares for each station license differed substantially. See Valenzuela, "Organizational Evolution."

31. KWEX and KMEX became the first stations to broadcast full-time on this alternative wave frequency. To receive SIN's UHF signal, television audiences had to purchase a converter box. Although this may have been an obstacle, a report in the *Los Angeles Times* stated that in 1962 sales of converter boxes, which were priced between ten and twenty-five dollars in the Los Angles market, spiked dramatically soon after KMEX announced that it would begin using UHF. See Martin Rossman, "New Station Aims at Spanish Speaking," *Los Angeles Times*, September 30, 1962, H1.

32. Valenzuela, "Organizational Evolution."

33. Subervi-Vélez et al., "Mass Communication and Hispanics."

34. Valenzuela, "Organizational Evolution."

35. Ibid.

36. Before then, SIN, like other major US networks, had to bring its programs in by bicycle from a central location. This created a programming lag time and impeded the ability to create synchronized real-time shows. The stations connected to Mexico were all in the Southwest; thus, its New York and Miami stations and affiliates were excluded from this initial satellite arrangement. See Subervi-Vélez et al., "Mass Communication and Hispanics"; and Valenzuela, "Organizational Evolution."

37. Scholars of Latino media note that the SICC's satellite system began operating before that of any other US television network, including NBC, ABC, or CBS. See Sinclair, *Latin American Television*; Valenzuela, "Organizational Evolution"; and Subervi-Vélez et al., *Handbook of Hispanic Culture*.

38. Subsidies, financed with loans from Azcárraga, helped Anselmo, Nicolás, and other SICC executives purchase the Bahia de San Francisco Television Company and the Seven Hills Television Company, which held station licenses in Northern California and other regions in the Southwest. See In the Matter of Spanish International Communications Corporation, FCC 87R-64, 1 FCC Rcd 844 (1986).

39. Valenzuela, "Organizational Evolution"; and Sinclair, *Latin American Television*.

40. Frank D. Bean and Marta Tienda, *The Hispanic Population of the United States* (New York: Russell Sage Foundation, 1987).

41. In interviews conducted with former SIN and SICC executives like Daniel Villanueva (KMEX station manager, 1971–89) and Joaquin Blaya (WLTV station manager, 1972–88, and Univision president, 1988–91), they generally noted that panethnic expansion was part of Azcárraga's and Anselmo's "vision" for Spanish-language television. Indeed, Joaquin Blaya stated that "Anselmo's desire was to create a new medium for all . . . Latinos in the United States." Joaquin Blaya, interview by G. Cristina Mora, January 2008.

42. Valenzuela, "Organizational Evolution."

43. Carlos Barba (general manager of WNJU, 1970–89, and Univision president, 1993–96), interview by G. Cristina Mora, December 2007; Saul Steinberg (founder of the Telemundo Group), interview by G. Cristina Mora, November 2007; and Emilio Nicolás Jr. (SICC/SIN/Univision executive, 1975–89), interview by G. Cristina Mora, March 9, 2011.

44. This would have been important given that Mexicans composed the majority of Hispanics in the United States. Bean and Tienda, *Hispanic Population of the United States*.

45. Rene Anselmo, quoted in Mercedes de Uriarte, "Battle for the Ear of the Latino," *Los Angeles Times*, December 14, 1980, F5.

46. Julian Samora, introduction to *La Raza: Forgotten Americans*, ed. Julian Samora, xi–xvii (South Bend, IN: Notre Dame University Press, 1966).

47. Ibid. See also Leo Grebler, Joan W. Moore, and Ralph C. Guzman, *The Mexican-American People: The Nation's Second Largest Minority* (New York: Free Press, 1970).

48. "Que Grande Es el Mercado Hispano? How Big Is the Spanish Market?," *Sponsor*, November 5, 1962, 35.

49. Eduardo Caballero (former SIN executive, 1967–72, and founder of Caballero Spanish Media), interview by G. Cristina Mora, November 14, 2007.

50. Nielsen and Arbitron tallied how many persons were watching channels, but they used English-language instruments. SIN and SICC executives argued that Arbitron and Nielsen were discriminating against their audiences and producing an undercount of SIN audiences. SICC president Rene Anselmo penned several op-ed pieces to media marketing journals arguing this point. See, for example, Rene Anselmo, "Minority Undercount Remains Severe Research Problem," *Advertising Age*, April 16, 1979.

51. "Spanish Stations Protest Ratings," *Los Angeles Times*, March 5, 1966, B3.

52. Caballero, interview.

53. Ibid.

54. Caballero said that Anselmo's decision to hire him was in part happenstance. At the time, Caballero was one of the only Spanish-language media executives with sales experience working in New York. Caballero thought

that because Anselmo knew no one else, he turned to Caballero as the only option. Caballero, interview.

55. Ibid.

56. The SIN sales team developed a different a strategy for garnering local advertising accounts. While the national strategy considered all Latino subgroups together as a Spanish-speaking panethnic population, local sales focused on ethnic distinctions. This was most notable in the way that Mexican corporations were encouraged to purchase airtime on regional and local stations in the Southwest, while Puerto Rican corporations—especially Goya—were courted for the New York and Miami stations. Caballero, interview.

57. Villanueva also noted that SICC stations were always being tested for market viability. Corporations were reluctant to take on faith alone the sales team's arguments that language was crucial for successful advertising. Oftentimes a company would purchase a small amount of airtime, at a heavily discounted rate, and test it by monitoring its products' success in key Hispanic districts. Villanueva notes that this happened so often because it was hard to convince companies about the viability of SIN and SICC's consumer audience. Villanueva, interview.

58. "SIN Pays," *Advertising Age*, April 6, 1981, S17 (emphasis added).

59. "Spanish Eyes Are on SIN 24 Hours a Day," *Advertising Age*, April 7, 1980, S21.

60. Antonio Guernica and Irene Kasperuk, *Reaching the Hispanic Market Effectively* (New York: McGraw-Hill, 1982).

61. See chap. 3.

62. Emilio Nicolás (SICC vice president, 1962–86), interview by G. Cristina Mora, March 9, 2011.

63. Caballero, interview. By then, Caballero had left SIN to work in Spanish-language radio marketing and had solidified his position as one of the country's foremost Latino media marketers. See Arlene Davila, *Latinos Inc.: The Marketing and Making of a People* (Berkeley: University of California Press, 2001).

64. Davila, *Latinos Inc.*; and America Rodriguez, "Commercial Ethnicity: Language, Class and Race in the Marketing of the Hispanic Audience," *Communication Review* 2, no. 3 (1997): 283–309.

65. In her interviews with Latino marketers, Davila also finds that they credit the Census Bureau for legitimizing the idea of a Hispanic, panethnic group. See Davila, *Latinos Inc.*

66. Fred Ferretti, "Soap Opera: Winner for Spanish TV Here," *New York Times*, September 5, 1969, 75.

67. Blaya, interview.

68. Villanueva, interview.

69. Rubén Salazar, "Best Kept Secret in L.A. TV," *Los Angeles Times*, May 8, 1970, G33.

70. The KMEX news team received the prestigious Peabody Award for its

comprehensive coverage of public services in Mexican American neighborhoods. See Maury Green, "Villanueva: From Dream to Reality," *Los Angeles
Times*, August 4, 1972, F18.

71. Jose Lozano, letter to the editor, December 28, 1980, *Los Angeles Times*, 103.

72. Villanueva, interview.

73. "SIN-West: A Historic Media Step for Chicanos," *Agenda* 2, no. 3 (1972),
p. 44, NCLR Records, record group 6, series 4, box 24, folder 4, Department
of Special Collections, Stanford University Libraries, Stanford, CA.

74. Barba, interview.

75. Ibid.

76. For Televisa, Puerto Rico was a prime export market. Much of the same programming that was purchased from Televisa for broadcast on SICC stations
was also likely being aired on Puerto Rican stations that purchased Televisa
feed. See C. Fernandez and A. Paxman, *El Tigre*.

77. Until at least the mid-1980s, WNJU and WXTV continued to vie for the top
rating and advertising slots; they would often alternate in the top positions
from year to year. See Udayan Gupta, "New York's WNJU Channel 47:
Spanish TV's Hottest Item," *Hispanic Business*, March 1983, 16–27.

78. Blaya, interview.

79. See Gonzalo R. Soruco, *Cubans and the Mass Media in Southern Florida*
(Gainesville: University Press of Florida, 1996).

80. Ibid.

81. Ramos writes that shortly after arriving in Miami to host *Mundo Latino* in
the early 1980s, he was criticized and labeled "non-objective" for simply
being Mexican. He recalls that during one public forum, a Cuban took the
mike and shouted, "Look Ramos, for me you are a Mexican before you are
a journalist and that's why I'm not going to believe anything you say." See
Jorge Ramos, *No Borders: A Journalist's Search for Home* (New York: Harper-
Collins, 2003).

82. Blaya, interview.

83. Villanueva, interview.

84. Ibid.

85. Blaya, interview.

86. Villanueva, interview.

87. *SIN Noticiero* was briefly produced in Washington, DC, before being moved
permanently to Miami in 1981. Gustavo Godoy (former director of *SIN
Noticiero*, 1981–87), interview by G. Cristina Mora, May 13, 2008.

88. See de Uriarte, "Battle for the Ear of the Latino"; and America Rodriguez,
Making Latino News: Race, Language, Class (Thousand Oaks, CA: Sage Publications, 1999).

89. Godoy, interview.

90. Godoy recalls that one of the more popular Spanglish words at the time
was *rentar*, which is an incorrect iteration of the English word *rent*; it was often used in Spanish-language sentences in lieu of the more correct Spanish

word *alquilar*. A typical Spanglish sentence would be "Voy a rentar el auto," instead of "Voy a alquilar el auto." Ibid.

91. Godoy, interview.

92. Nicolás, interview.

93. See Patricia Constantakis-Valdes, "Univision and Telemundo on the Campaign Trail: 1988," in *The Mass Media and Latino Politics: Studies of the U.S. Media Content, Campaign Strategies and Survey Research, 1984–2004*, ed. Federico A. Subervi-Vélez, 131–53 (New York: Routledge Press, 2008).

94. See "National Representation of TV Stations in National Spot Sales: Requests of Spanish International Network," FCC 78-628, 43 Fed. Reg. 45895 (1978).

95. Ibid.

96. Spanish International Communications Corporation, FCC 45 RR 2d 1303 (1979). The low-power translator stations relayed the programming from established SICC stations. The translator station in Denver, for example, relayed programming from KWEX; it had no local programming or studio facilities. It extended the range of the network but was more cost-effective than establishing a new station.

97. Valenzuela, "Organizational Evolution."

98. The NCLR also discussed its efforts to persuade the FCC to pay more attention to the lack of "Hispanic" content on television and the paucity of Latino media owners with the Forum of National Hispanic Organizations. See Minutes of the Board of Directors Meeting, August 25, 1978, Washington, DC, NCLR Records, record group 1, series 1, box 2, folder 8.

99. Ibid.

100. Ibid.

101. See John David Skrentny, *The Minority Rights Revolution* (Cambridge, MA: Harvard University Press, 2003).

102. Ibid. See also chap. 1.

103. See Howard Kleiman, "Content Diversity and the FCC's Minority and Gender Licensing Policies," *Journal of Broadcast and Electronic Media* 35, no. 4 (1991): 411–25.

104. Ibid.

105. Interview with Armando Rendon (founder of Los Cerezos Media, SIN affiliate, and former member of the Census Bureau's Office of Public Relations, 1979–88), interview by G. Cristina Mora, May 20, 2012.

106. Spanish International Communications Corporation, FCC 45 RR2d 1303 (1979) (emphasis added).

107. J. Gregory Sidak, *Foreign Investment in American Telecommunications* (Chicago: University of Chicago Press, 1997); and US Department of Commerce, *Globalization of the Mass Media* (Washington, DC: DIANE Publishing, 1994).

108. Specifically, see the opinion by Norman B. Blumenthal wherein he states that the commission had been aware, via station license renewal applica-

tions, of the complex relationship between Azcárraga and SICC station managers. Seven Hills Television Company (FCC 87R-5), 2 FCC Rcd. 6890 (1987). See also Spanish International Communications Corporation, 1 FCC Rcd. 93 (Rev. Bd.); and Spanish International Communications Corporation, 2 FCC Rcd. 3339.

109. See Spanish International Communications Corporation, 1 FCC Rcd. 93 (Rev. Bd.); and Spanish International Communications Corporation, 2 FCC Rcd. 3339.

110. Villanueva, interview.

111. In its petition, Trans-Tel noted that: (1) Anselmo and the other SICC executives had been employed under or had held contractual interests in Azcárraga's Telesistema prior to establishing SICC; (2) most of KMEX and KWEX's programming came from Azcárraga's Telesistema network; (3) Anselmo had a dual role as an executive of SICC and a sales representative of SIN, whose majority shareholder was Azcárraga; (4) Anselmo was still employed at Teleprogramas Acapulco, a subsidiary of Telesistema, while being employed by SIN/SICC; and (5) Azcárraga's personal lawyer, Julian Kaufman, was also general manager of SICC's San Francisco Bay Area station. Spanish International Television Co. Inc., 5 RR 2d 3, 5(1965); see also Seven Hills Television Company (FCC 87R-58), 2 FCC Rcd. 6867 (1987).

112. See Valenzuela, "Organizational Evolution."

113. Fouce Amusement Enterprises, Inc. v. Spanish International Communications Corp., no. CV 76-3451-MRP (C.D.Cal.) (1976); and *Memorandum Opinion and Order Designating Applications for Consolidated Hearing on Stated Issues*, 48 Fed. Reg. 28549 (1983). See also Valenzuela, "Organizational Evolution."

114. Spanish International Communications Corporation, hearing (FCC 83-263), 48 FR 28549 (1983).

115. In an interview with the *Los Angeles Times*, Ed Gomez expounded on this idea by stating that he had long been concerned about the "Mexican influence" in television, and that the "FCC had [allowed for] a monster to be created that . . . ultimately stifle[d] the development of TV programming by *Hispanic-Americans*." "FCC Probing Spanish Language Television Programming Service," *Los Angeles Times*, September 5, 1980, E1 (emphasis added). See also G. Cristina Mora, "Regulating Immigrant Media and Instituting Ethnic Boundaries: The FCC and Spanish Language Television, 1960–1990," *Latino Studies* 9, nos. 2–3 (2011): 242–62.

116. Eduardo Caballero, who had by that time left SIN to establish Spanish Language Radio, appeared before the FCC to argue that the special provisions for SIN and SICC were hindering, not helping, Mexican-American and, more generally, Latino media ownership. He stated that by helping the corporations, the FCC was allowing one "foreign" company to monopolize the Spanish-language market and undercut all other US Latino firms. See Seven Hills Television Company (FCC 87R-58), 2 FCC Rcd. 6867 (1987).

117. Spanish International Communications Corporation, initial decision (FCC 86D-1), 1 FCC Rcd. 92 (Rev. Bd. 1986). Judge John H. Conlin ruled that Rene Anselmo often locked SICC stations into financial contracts that proved more beneficial to SIN than to SICC. Conlin cited instances where Azcárraga—through Televisa—had enforced a minimum benchmark for what SICC stations could charge advertisers based on Azcárraga's own calculations. This, in addition to several similar instances, amounted in Conlin's perspective to de facto foreign control. See also Spanish International Communications Corporation, 2 FCC Rcd. 3962; and Seven Hills Television Company (FCC 87R-58), 2 FCC Rcd. 6867 (1987). An overview is provided in Mora, "Regulating Immigrant Media."

118. Spanish International Communications Corporation, initial decision (FCC 86D-1), 121.

119. Spanish International Communications Corporation (FCC 86R-64), FCC Rcd. vol. 1, no. 1, p. 94 (1986).

120. Saul Steinberg, interview by G. Cristina Mora, January 22, 2008.

121. See Mora, "Regulating Immigrant Media."

122. See Minutes of the Board of Directors Meeting, Miami, FL, October 11, 1986, NCLR Records, record group 1, series 1, box 8, folder 6. In a *Hispanic Business* article written around the time of the FCC decision, several Latino leaders, such as Henry Cisneros and representatives of the Mexican American Legal Defense and Education Fund, reiterated that Hallmark had heard their concerns about the need to fund US-based programs. See Steve Beale, "Hallmark Si, Hallmark No," *Hispanic Business*, December 1986, 50.

123. For an overview, see Mora, "Regulating Immigrant Media."

124. Villanueva, interview. Villanueva stated that Emilio Nicolás retained a small advisory role in Hallmark, but this was short-lived.

125. Steve Bergsman, "New and Improved," *Hispanic Business*, December 1988, 42–46.

126. See John Ferretti, "Blaya and Univision at the Turn of the Decade," *Hispanic Business*, December 1989, 15.

127. See, for example, Steve Bergsman, "Item: Networks Invest in Nielsen Ratings: Will Their Audiences Measure Up?," *Hispanic Business*, December 1989, 38–41.

128. Ibid.

129. Rick Mendosa, "Telemundo Wired Up for TV Wars," *Hispanic Business*, December 1992, 50.

130. Humberto Lopes, "Musical Chairs at TV Network," *Hispanic Business*, July 1992, 8–10.

131. The FCC approved this sale because the relationship between Perenchio and Azcárraga Milmo was not as entwined as the relationship between Anselmo and Azcárraga had been. Furthermore, the presence of Diego Cisneros assured that Azcárraga Milmo's ownership would be capped at

12.5 percent. Upon assuming control of the corporation, Perenchio retained much of the US-based programming scheduled by Blaya and Hallmark. With the new partnership between Univision and Azcárraga Milmo, Univision shows could be promoted through Televisa in Mexico. Indeed, Azcárraga Milmo's presence in Univision was welcomed by Perenchio because Azcárraga Milmo agreed to carry Univision shows in Mexico. One example was *El Show de Cristina*: with the help of the promotion provided by Azcárraga Milmo, it quickly became a top-rated show in Mexico and garnered international profits for SIN. A. Rodriguez, *Making Latino News*.

132. Davila, *Latinos Inc.*
133. See Jube Shiver, "Ad Industry Learns to Say It in Spanish," *Los Angeles Times*, June 7, 1987, 1 D1.
134. Ibid. See also Davila, *Latinos Inc.*
135. Shiver, "Ad Industry Learns to Say It in Spanish."
136. Data collected by the author from *Broadcasting* (Washington, DC: Broadcasting Publications, 1975–85). The number of radio stations went from 57 in 1975 to 158 in 1985.
137. Data collected by the author from *Standard Periodical Directory* (New York: Oxbridge Communications, 1975–85). The number of periodicals went from 83 to 105 between 1980 and 1984.
138. Data collected by the author from *Broadcasting* for 1980 and 1985. The number of full-time Spanish-language television stations increased from ten in 1980 to thirteen in 1985.
139. Steinberg, interview, January 22, 2008.
140. Ibid.
141. Barba, interview.
142. Steinberg, interview, January 22, 2008.
143. Ibid. See also Ana Lopez, "Our Welcomed Guests: Telenovelas in Latin America," in *To Be Continued . . . Soap Operas around the World*, ed. Robert Allen, 256–75 (New York: Routledge, 1995).
144. Claire Poole, "Viewers Looking for the U.S. Look," *Hispanic Business*, December 1987, 26–28; see 28.
145. Ibid.
146. Julia Kay Kilgore, "Take Two," *Hispanic Business*, December 1988, 52–58.
147. Ibid.
148. Mendosa, "Telemundo Wired Up," 38–52.
149. Steinberg, interview, January 22, 2008.
150. Ibid.
151. See Arlene Davila, "Mapping Latinidad: Language and Culture in the Spanish TV Battlefront," *Television and New Media* 1, no. 1 (2000): 75–94.
152. Scott McCartney, "Hispanic Voters: Both Parties Plot Strategies," *Victoria Advocate*, July 24, 1988, 3C; and "The Growing Clout of Hispanic Voters," *Philadelphia Inquirer*, June 5, 1988, A13.

153. Patricia Constantakis, "Spanish Language Television and the 1988 Presidential Elections: A Case Study of Dual Identity Ethnic Minority Media" (PhD diss., University of Texas, Austin, 1993), 141.

154. See "Bush Likely to Win," *Ocala Star-Banner,* November 1, 1992, 3D; Roger Hernandez, "Hispanic Voters Key in Florida Races," *Ocala Star-Banner,* November 1, 1992, 6E; and William Booth, "In Sign of Latino Clout, California Debate Is Broadcast Also in Spanish," *Washington Post,* May 24, 1998, A02.

155. James Bennet, "In Spin Wars after the Debate, Clinton Campaign Takes Lead," *New York Times,* October 8, 1996, A1; and Michael Totty, "Candidates Pay to Spread Their Message in Spanish," *Wall Street Journal,* October 28, 1998, I-T1.

156. See "Muchas Gracias," The Living Room Candidate website, accessed September 7, 2012, http://www.livingroomcandidate.org/commercials/2000/muchas-gracias.

157. Rodriguez, *Making Latino News;* Davila, *Latinos Inc.*

CONCLUSION

1. Emilio Nicolás (SICC vice president, 1962–86), interview by G. Cristina Mora, March 9, 2011.

2. "SIN Pays," *Advertising Age,* April 6, 1981, S17.

3. Peter Berger, *The Sacred Canopy: Elements of a Sociological Theory of Religion* (New York: Anchor Books, 1967).

4. See Mary Douglas, *Purity and Danger: An Analysis of the Concepts of Pollution and Taboo* (New York: Routledge Press, 1966); and Dror Etzion and Fabrizio Ferraro, "The Role of Analogy in the Institutionalization of Sustainability Reporting," *Organization Science* 21, no. 5 (2010): 1092–1110.

5. Armando Rendon, "WE . . ." (Suitland, MD: Bureau of the Census, April 1995), 4.

6. "Hispanic Corporate Partnerships: Some Observations and Examples," p. 4, speech delivered by Raul Yzaguirreto the First Corporate/Hispanic Partnership Summit, October 23, 1982, Sheraton Place, San Francisco, NCLR Records, record group 6, series 2, box 11, folder 38.

7. Benedict Anderson, *Imagined Communities: Reflections on the Origins and Spread of Nationalism* (London: Verso, 2006).

8. To be clear, this shift was likely due to a variety of factors, including the desire to mimic other states and pressure from federal agencies such as the National Center for Health Statistics. Activist lobbying efforts, then, were only one part of the shift. See National Center for Health Statistics, "US Vital Statistics System: Major Activities and Developments, 1950–1995," PHS 97-1003 (Hyattsville, MD: Department of Health and Human Services, 1997).

9. See "Briefing Outline," Office of Hispanic Affairs, May 15, 1975, Marrs Files, 1974–76, box 26, "Spanish Speaking People" folder, Ford Library.

10. José de la Isla, *The Rise of Hispanic Political Power* (Santa Maria, CA: Archer Books, 2003).
11. Ibid.
12. Interview with Emilio Nicolás Jr. (SICC/SIN/Univision executive, 1975–89), interview by G. Cristina Mora, March 9, 2011.
13. See chap. 1 in this book.
14. See Arlene Davila, *Latinos Inc.: The Marketing and Making of a People* (Berkeley: University of California Press, 2001); Marissa Abrajano, *Campaigning to the New American Electorate: Advertising to Latino Voters* (Palo Alto, CA: Stanford University Press, 2010); de la Isla, *Rise of Hispanic Political Power*.
15. Michael McQueen, "Republicans Persevere in Their Uphill Campaign to Woo and Win a Bigger Slice of the Hispanic Vote," *Wall Street Journal*, August 10, 1990, A12; and NCLR, "Holding Firm to Principles," NCLR website, accessed January 13, 2013, http://www.nclr.org/index.php /about_us/history/holding_firm_to_principles/.
16. Paul Richter, "Clinton Pitches His Health Care Plan to Latinos: Reform: President Speaks to La Raza at Miami Meeting," *Los Angeles Times*, July 19, 1994, A14; Michael Wines, "The Health Care Debate: Clinton, on the Stump, Opens a Final Health Care Push," *New York Times*, July 16, 1994, 1.9; and David Rogers, "Conservatives Seek Wider Tax Breaks Tied to Health Care," *Wall Street Journal*, July 19, 1994, A2.
17. See Joan Moore and Harry Pachon, *Hispanics in the United States* (Englewood Cliffs, NJ: Prentice-Hall, 1985); and Frank D. Bean and Marta Tienda, *The Hispanic Population of the United States* (New York: Russell Sage Foundation, 1987).
18. See Henry Ramos, Kennedy School of Government, to Raul Yzaguirre, April 16, 1984, NCLR Records, record group 2, series 2, box 11.3, folder 3, Department of Special Collections, Stanford University Libraries, Stanford University.
19. Michael Jones-Correa and David Leal, "Becoming 'Hispanic': Secondary Panethnic Identification among Latin American Origin Groups," *Hispanic Journal of Behavioral and Social Sciences* 18, no. 2 (1996): 214–54.
20. Alejandro Portes and Dag MacLeod, "What Shall I Call Myself? Hispanic Identity Formation in the Second Generation," *Ethnic and Racial Studies* 19 (1996): 523–47; and John Itzigsohn and Carlos Dore-Cabral, "Competing Identities? Race, Ethnicity and Panethnicity among Dominicans in the United States," *Sociological Forum* 15, no. 2 (2000): 225–47.
21. Felix Padilla, *Latino Ethnic Consciousness: The Case of Mexican Americans and Puerto Ricans in Chicago* (South Bend, IN: University of Notre Dame Press, 1985).
22. Earl Shorris, "Latinos: The Complexity of Identity," *NACLA: Report on the Americas* 26, no. 2 (1992): 19–26; and Sheila L. Croucher, *Imagining Miami: Ethnic Politics in a Postmodern World* (Charlottesville: University of Virginia Press, 1997).

23. Suzanne Oboler, *Ethnic Labels, Latino Lives: Identity and the Politics of (Re)Presentation in the United States* (Minneapolis: University of Minnesota Press, 1995).

24. See Juan Flores, "Latino Studies: New Contexts, New Concepts," *Harvard Educational Review* 67, no. 2 (1993): 208–21.

25. Herman Badillo (cofounder of PRLDEF [Puerto Rican Legal Defense and Education Fund], 1972), interview by G. Cristina Mora, March 25, 2010; Benjamin Marquez, *LULAC: The Evolution of a Mexican American Political Organization* (Austin: University of Texas Press, 1993); and Craig A. Kaplowitz, *LULAC, Mexican Americans, and National Policy* (College Station: Texas A&M University Press, 2005).

26. See MANA—A National Latina Organization website, accessed February 23, 2013, http://www.hermana.org/frequently-asked-questions-faqs.

27. See PRLDEF, Latino Justice website, accessed December 5, 2012, http://latinojustice.org/about/history_2000s/.

28. America Rodriguez, *Making Latino News: Race, Language, Class* (Thousand Oaks, CA: Sage Publications, 1999); see also Cristina Saralegui, *Cristina: Confidencias de Una Rubia* (New York: Warner Books, 1998).

29. The efforts of Univision were ultimately reinforced by transnational migration. Indeed, as US immigrants took trips back to their countries of origins, they explained their Hispanic identity to others. Thus, a Dominican immigrant to the Untied States could return to his hometown on yearly visits and speak about panethnicity, teaching his family there about a new identity. At the same time, however, the people in the Dominican Republic could tune into Univision programming and watch the Hispanic shows that were imported from the United States. See Wendy Roth, "Latino before the World: The Transnational Extension of Panethnicity," *Ethnic and Racial Studies*, 32, no. 6 (2009): 927–47; and Wendy Roth, *Race Migrations: Latinos and the Cultural Transformation of Race* (Palo Alto, CA: Stanford University Press, 2012).

30. Eduardo Caballero (former SIN executive,1967–72, founder of Caballero Spanish Media), interview by G. Cristina Mora, November 14, 2007. See also Joel Russell, "Media Deal of the Year," *Hispanic Business*, December 1995, 24–30.

31. Isabel M. Valdes, *Marketing to American Latinos: A Guide to the In-Culture Approach* (Ithaca, NY: Paramount Market Publishing, 2002); and Angharad Valdivia, *Latina/os and the Media* (New York: Polity Press, 2010).

32. John Garcia, *The Success of "Hispanic" Magazine: A Publishing Success Story* (New York: Walker, 1996).

33. For early critics of the notion of panethnicity, see David E. Hayes-Bautista, "Identifying Hispanic Populations: The Influence of Research Methodology on Public Policy," *American Journal of Public Health* 70, no. 4 (1980): 353–56; and Martha E. Gimenez, "Latino/Hispanic—Who Needs a Name? The Case against a Standardized Terminology," *International Journal of*

Health Services 19 (1989): 557–71. For the roles of indigenous and African communities, see David Gonzalez, "What's the Problem with Hispanic? Just Ask a Latino," *New York Times*, November 15,1992, A.6.

34. See Frank De Olmo, "Latino Si, Hispanic No," *Los Angeles Times*, October 24, 1985, C9. See also a retrospective piece on the issue, Darryl Fears, "Latinos or Hispanics? A Debate about Identity," *Washington Post*, August 25, 2003, A01.

35. Edward Murguia, "On Latino/Hispanic Ethnic Identity," *Latino Studies Journal* 2, no. 3 (1991): 8–18.

36. See Paul Taylor, Mark Hugo Lopez, Jessica Hamar Martinez, and Gabriel Valasco, *When Labels Don't Fit: Hispanics and Their Views of Identity* (Washington, DC: Pew Hispanic Research Center, 2012), 10.

37. Bean and Tienda, *Hispanic Population of the United States*.

38. Laird Bergad and Herbert Klein, *Hispanics in the United States: A Demographic, Social, and Economic History, 1980–2005* (Cambridge: Cambridge University Press, 2010).

39. Alejandro Portes and Alex Stepick, *City on the Edge: The Transformation of Miami* (Berkeley: University of California Press, 1994); and Guillermo Grenier and Alex Stepick, introduction to *Miami Now! Immigration, Ethnicity and Social Change*, ed. Guillermo Grenier and Alex Stepick, 1–18 (Gainesville: University Press of Florida, 1992).

40. See Roger Waldinger and Mehdi Bozorgmehr, *Ethnic Los Angeles* (New York: Russell Sage Foundation, 1996).

41. See Roger Waldinger, *Still the Promised City? New Immigrants and African Americans in Post-industrial New York* (Cambridge, MA: Harvard University Press, 1996).

42. There were small areas that had been panethnic since the late 1960s. Padilla, for example, describes sections of west Chicago as home to both Mexican American and Puerto Rican residents. Nonetheless, panethnic spaces became more pronounced with the increase in Central and South American as well as Dominican migration throughout the 1980s. See Padilla, *Latino Ethnic Consciousness*.

43. Milagros Ricourt and Ruby Danta, *Hispanas de Queens: Panethnicity in a New York City Neighborhood* (Ithaca, NY: Cornell University Press, 2002); and Michael Rosenfeld, "The Salience of Pan-national Hispanic and Asian Identities in U.S. Marriage Markets," *Demography* 38, no. 2 (2001): 161–75.

44. Much more research on interethnic marriage patterns is needed. We do not know, for example, what role location or time period might have played in who married whom. We might imagine, for example, that Mexican Americans in 1970s Chicago were more likely to marry interethnically (presumably because of the larger proportion of non-Mexican Hispanics living there at the time) than were their counterparts in Los Angeles. See Bergad and Klein, *Hispanics in the United States*, for an assessment of the broader, national trends in intermarriage.

45. Ricourt and Danta, *Hispanas de Queens*.

46. Ibid. See also Ana Maria Diaz-Stevens, "From Puerto Rican to Hispanic: The Politics of the Fiestas Patronales in New York," *Latino Studies Journal* 1, no. 1 (1990): 28–47.

47. Work on the rise of Asian American civic organizations suggests that variables on occupational segregation and competition are important indicators of panethnic organizing. See Dina Okamoto, "Institutional Panethnicity: Boundary Formation in Asian American Organizing," *Social Forces* 85, no. 1 (2006): 1–25.

48. Of course, much more research is needed to understand the parameters of Hispanic self-identification. There might be a self-selection process at work here, or it may be that these organizations help to foster more identification. Future studies that examine correlations between media consumption and panethnic identification, or organizational participation and identification, may help clarify these issues.

49. See NWX–US Department of Commerce, "Results of the 2010 Census Race and Hispanic Origin Alternative Questionnaire Experiment News Conference," George Washington University, August 8, 2012, 18.

50. See Edward Telles and Vilma Ortiz, *Generations of Exclusion: Mexican Americans, Assimilation, and Race* (New York: Russell Sage Foundation, 2008).

51. See Richard Alba and Tariqul Islam, "The Case of the Disappearing Mexican Americans: An Ethnic-Identity Mystery," *Population Research and Policy Review* 28, no. 2 (April 2009): 109–21; see also Peter Skerry, *Mexican Americans: The Ambivalent Minority* (Cambridge, MA: Harvard University Press, 1995).

52. See NWX–US Department of Commerce, "Results of the 2010 Census Race and Hispanic Origin Alternative Questionnaire Experiment."

53. This is not meant to discount, however, that a high percentage (upward of 30 percent and sometimes as high as 60 percent, depending on the form and the way that the question is phrased) do consider themselves to be racially white. Yet some of this might also have to do with expectations. Following historical precedent, many Latinos might choose the white racial option on census forms simply because they know that the bureau will often recategorize them as such. Respondents might not have this expectation, however, when filling out surveys or other noncensus forms that directly ask respondents whether Latinos are a distinct race. Nonetheless, more research is needed to clarify the issue further. See Luis R. Fraga, John A. Garcia, Rodney E. Hero, Michael Jones-Correa, Valerie Martinez-Ebers, and Gary M. Segura, *Latinos in the New Millennium: An Almanac of Opinion, Behavior and Policy Preferences* (New York: Cambridge University Press, 2012). See also Luis Ricardo Fraga, John A. Garcia, Rodney E. Hero, Michael Jones-Correa, Valerie Martinez-Ebers, and Gary M. Segura, *Latino Lives in America: Making It Home* (Philadelphia: Temple University Press, 2009); and Taylor et al., *When Labels Don't Fit*.

54. Leo Chavez, *The Latino Threat: Constructing Immigrants, Citizens, and the Nation* (Palo Alto, CA: Stanford University Press, 2008); and Nicholas DeGenova, "Introduction: Latino and Asian Racial Formations at the Frontiers of US Nationalism," in *Racial Transformations: Latinos and Asians Remaking the United States*, ed. Nicholas DeGenova, 1–22 (Durham, NC: Duke University Press, 2006).

55. Bergad and Klein, *Hispanics in the United States.*

56. See Nancy Denton and Douglas Massey, "Racial Identity among Caribbean Hispanics: The Effect of Double Minority Status on Residential Segregation," *American Sociological Review* 5, no. 5 (1989): 790–808; Tanya Hernandez, "Too Black to Be Latino/a: Blackness and Blacks as Foreigners in Latino Studies," *Latino Studies* 1, no. 1 (2003): 152–59; and Alison Newby and Julie Dowling, "Black and Hispanic: The Racial Identification of Afro-Cuban Immigrants in the Southwest," *Sociological Perspectives* 50, no. 3 (2007): 343–66.

57. Fraga et al., *Latinos in the New Millennium.*

Index